Neo-Victorianism, Empathy and Reading

Neo-Victorianism, Empathy and Reading

Muren Zhang

BLOOMSBURY ACADEMIC
LONDON • NEW YORK • OXFORD • NEW DELHI • SYDNEY

BLOOMSBURY ACADEMIC
Bloomsbury Publishing Plc
50 Bedford Square, London, WC1B 3DP, UK
1385 Broadway, New York, NY 10018, USA
29 Earlsfort Terrace, Dublin 2, Ireland

BLOOMSBURY, BLOOMSBURY ACADEMIC and the Diana logo are trademarks of
Bloomsbury Publishing Plc

First published in Great Britain 2022
This paperback edition published 2024

Copyright © Muren Zhang, 2022

Muren Zhang has asserted her right under the Copyright, Designs and Patents Act, 1988,
to be identified as Author of this work.

For legal purposes the Acknowledgements on p.viii constitute an
extension of this copyright page.

All rights reserved. No part of this publication may be reproduced or transmitted
in any form or by any means, electronic or mechanical, including photocopying,
recording, or any information storage or retrieval system, without prior permission
in writing from the publishers.

Bloomsbury Publishing Plc does not have any control over, or responsibility for, any
third-party websites referred to or in this book. All internet addresses given in this
book were correct at the time of going to press. The author and publisher regret any
inconvenience caused if addresses have changed or sites have ceased to exist, but
can accept no responsibility for any such changes.

A catalogue record for this book is available from the British Library.

A catalog record for this book is available from the Library of Congress.

ISBN: HB: 978-1-3501-3559-8
PB: 978-1-3502-9720-3
ePDF: 978-1-3501-3560-4
eBook: 978-1-3501-3561-1

Typeset by Newgen KnowledgeWorks Pvt. Ltd., Chennai, India

To find out more about our authors and books visit www.bloomsbury.com
and sign up for our newsletters.

To Lynne,
for her empathy

Contents

Acknowledgements	viii
Introduction	1
1 Suspicious reading	43
2 Reading (with) shame	71
3 Tragic man	105
4 Affective embodiment	139
Conclusion	171
Bibliography	177
Index	199

Acknowledgements

Thanks are due, first and foremost, to my parents. Without them, this book would never have seen the light of the day. I am particularly grateful to Lynne Pearce, who has read earlier drafts of the book for numerous times and offered plenty of invaluable advice. Lynne is a model for the kind of critic that I aspire to be. Thanks also to Claire Westall, whose empathetic support years ago changed the course of my life.

Special thanks to Michael Reagan, for his wit and friendship. To Frank Ling, for his extraordinary assistance with my research. To Han, whose company has made the breaks from revising the manuscript much more enjoyable.

Finally, I would like to thank Lucy Brown at Bloomsbury for proving to be such a supportive editor: your belief in this project is greatly appreciated.

I am very grateful for the permission to reprint previously published work in this book. Parts of the introduction, chapter one and the conclusion first appeared as 'Reading with(out) Suspicion: Atwood, Sedgwick and Critical Practice', in *Critique: Studies in Contemporary Fiction* (2021), copyright Taylor & Francis, available online: https://doi.org/10.1080/00111619.2021.2004988; chapter two is an expanded version of 'Awkward Encounters with Sarah Waters: Shame, Reading and Queer Subjectivity', *Contemporary Women's Writing* (2021), copyright Oxford Academic, available online: https://doi.org/10.1093/cww/vpab014; and chapter four includes almost all of '"Unofficial Englishmen": Landscape, Mobility and Identity in Julian Barnes's *Arthur & George* and Its TV Adaptation', *Critique: Studies in Contemporary Fiction* (2019), copyright Taylor & Francis, available online: https://doi.org/10.1080/00111619.2019.1582473.

Introduction

Double time

In his 2007 book *The Victorians in the Rearview Mirror*, Simon Joyce uses the rear-view mirror as a metaphor to illustrate the complicated temporality inherent in the twentieth century's – and in particular, the modernists' – engagement with the Victorian legacy in literature, politics, film and visual culture. Joyce takes his cue from Raymond Williams's discussion of how the genre of the literary pastoral repeatedly locates an idealized pastoral perfection in the past. Unlike the sense of backward referencing Williams identifies in *The Country and the City* (1973), Joyce suggests that the modernists' writings are defined by the impulse to move forward. Given the privileging of 'the here and now' in modernist representations of the Victorians, Joyce reverses Williams's model and argues that the twentieth century's engagement with the Victorians pushes 'the decisive point of transformation forward instead of back in time':

> The starting point for this study, then, is the observation that we never really encounter 'the Victorians' themselves but instead a mediated image like the one we get when we glance into our rearview mirrors while driving. The image usefully condenses the paradoxical sense of *looking forward to see what is behind us*, which is the opposite of what we do when we read history in order to figure out the future. It also suggests something of the inevitable distortion that accompanies any mirror image, whether we see it as resulting from the effects of political ideology, deliberate misreading, exaggeration, or the understandable simplification of a complex past. (2007: 4, emphasis added)

The image of the rear-view mirror brings out some key concerns in Joyce's examination of the relationship between the Victorian period and the twentieth century, including the role of temporality in the representation of the Victorians, and the ethics, politics and aesthetics of this kind of adaptation and appropriation. For Joyce, the modernists' approach to the Victorians is governed by a double time, referring to the juxtaposition of anticipation and retrospection. As his metaphorical use of the rear-view mirror illustrates, 'the here and now' we experience during the process of driving is characterized by activities of moving forwards and looking backwards, which posits the past and the present as the objects of future recollection. By highlighting the role of anticipation in engaging the past, Joyce's model suggests that the way we approach the past is informed by the present we may find ourselves in and the future we expect to arrive at. In this regard, we are not passive readers of – or witnesses to – the past. Rather, we are active participants in the (re)construction of the past. To a certain extent, this model reverses the cause-and-effect sequence of an event, in the sense that the projected future decides the way we engage with the past rather than the other way around, the latter of which is exemplified by the practice of 'read[ing] history in order to figure the future' (Joyce 2007: 4). Mark Currie explains this future-orientated approach to the past as consequent upon what he describes 'a highly developed media capitalist society' ([2007] 2012: 11). In his engagement with Jacques Derrida's theorization of 'archive fever', Currie points out that in today's media culture 'an event is recorded not because it happens, but it happens because it is recorded' (ibid.). By positioning the archive (as in Derrida's example) as 'an active producer' – rather than 'a passive record' – of the present, Currie demonstrates how the present is structured 'in anticipation of its recollection' in the process of archivization or narration ([2007] 2012: 12). Currie's formulation of narrative as a form of anticipation resembles the forward impulse Joyce identifies in his work on the twentieth century's engagement with their Victorian precursors.

Joyce's focus on the twentieth-century adaptations and appropriations of the Victorians – ranging from the work of the Bloomsbury Group to a variety of recent films (witness, e.g. a number of heritage films produced by Merchant Ivory in the 1980s and 1990s) – may be seen as a contribution to the study of the 'neo-Victorian': a term originally coined by Dana Shiller to describe the burgeoning of 'a subset of the historical novel' in contemporary literature, one that is 'characteristic of postmodernism and imbued with a historicity reminiscent of the nineteenth-century novel' (1997: 538). However, unlike

Joyce's preoccupation with the writings of the modernists, Shiller posits the neo-Victorian as part of literary postmodernism, which raises the important question of exactly when neo-Victorianism as a cultural phenomenon and/or literary genre came into existence (and it should be noted that Joyce did not use the term 'neo-Victorianism' itself in his work). Critics in the field have tried to situate the origin of neo-Victorianism in different historical periods. As Marie-Luise Kohlke and Christian Gutleben suggest, it could be 'after the death of Queen Victoria', or 'after the Second World War and the end of high Modernism', or 'in the 1960s' when Jean Rhys's *Wide Sargasso Sea* ([1966] 1968) and John Fowles's *The French Lieutenant's Woman* (1969) – two novels that are largely considered as the defining texts of the neo-Victorian genre – were published (Kohlke and Gutleben 2012: 3). This introduction does not intend to pin down the origin of neo-Victorianism as either a literary genre or a cultural phenomenon. It is more interested in examining how the study of neo-Victorianism develops, evolves and shapes itself in literary criticism in the past decade.

Notably, Joyce's work helps to map out one of the key issues that my research on neo-Victorianism explores: namely, the role of time – or more precisely, a *double time* – in contemporary engagements with the Victorians. As Joyce's illustration of the role the rear-view mirror plays in the act of driving suggests, this model of a double time is associated with the 'driver's' – or in this case, the reader's – active involvement in the construction of the (fictional) world. Taking my cue from Joyce, this book focuses on the text–reader relationship in neo-Victorian literature – and in particular, the role of empathy as part of that engagement – in examining the ways in which neo-Victorian narratives may be construed as both retrospective and future-orientated. It thus presents neo-Victorian fiction as a genre defined by its *contemporary* exploitation of, and experimentation with, 'narrative empathy', a concept I draw from Suzanne Keen's recent work on the relationship between novel reading and empathy and will return to in detail in the next section. It also follows J. Brooks Bouson's (1989) lead in presenting the act of reading as 'an empathic event'.[1] Comparing the role of the critic/reader to that of the psychoanalyst, Bouson suggests that

---

[1] Both 'empathetic' and 'empathic' are used as the adjective form of 'empathy'. In this book, I use 'empathetic' since it is derived from the more familiar pairing of 'sympathy' and 'sympathetic'.

'the empathic reader' is 'a participant-observer', who, in the acts of reading and interpreting, is both subject to 'the disruptive and disturbing responses' the characters and texts engender and 'aware of the negotiated roles he or she is invited to play when responding to fictional texts' (27). With a focus on the affective engagement between the text and the reader, Bouson's 'psycho-critical' model of reading serves as a useful complement to the development of reader-response theory in the twentieth century, which, Lynne Pearce points out, is marked by a 'lack of interest in the affective aspects of the reading process' (Bouson 1989: 27; Pearce 1997: 4). As Pearce further explains, although theorists such as Wolfgang Iser, Stanley Fish, Jonathan Culler and Roland Barthes have shown 'considerably more interest in the role and significance of the reader', their discussions of the reader tend to privilege the cognitive aspects of reading and are largely conducted 'in the context of interpretation and meaning-production' (1997: 5).

Whilst Bouson's formulation of an empathetic model of reading takes its cue from the American psychoanalyst Heinz Kohut's conceptualization of empathy, this book draws from a wide range of literary and cultural theorists, psychoanalytic critics and philosophers, such as Mark Currie, Eve Kosofsky Sedgwick, Suzanne Keen, Lauren Berlant, Silvan Tomkins, Heinz Kohut, Jean-Paul Sartre, Robert Vischer, Amy Coplan and Dan Zahavi. By bringing the recent cultural-theoretical research on empathy and affect together, this book examines the ways in which the act of reading neo-Victorian literature and culture involves a dynamic interplay between suspicious hermeneutics and affective engagement. This is done with the aim of producing more complex ways of thinking about the discussion of reader pleasure in the field of neo-Victorian studies and contributing to the study of empathy. The overarching concern, then, is how the exploration and representation of the complexity of fictional characters and landscapes featured in a selection of neo-Victorian texts relate to, and often reproduce, the *unsettling* empathetic engagement between the text and the reader.

This introduction, meanwhile, serves as a theoretical foundation for the whole book. It approaches the issue of temporality from the perspective of narrative consciousness and literary criticism, both of which feed into a future-orientated theory of narrative. As such, it challenges the predominant understanding of neo-Victorian fiction as a retrospective or nostalgic genre.

In what follows, I begin with a review of the development of neo-Victorian studies in recent decades, with a particular focus on the issue of time. Then I move to a discussion of the work of Currie and Sedgwick to demonstrate the sense of anticipation at the core of narrative consciousness in neo-Victorian fiction and its role in transformative criticism. Through a review of the study of empathy in the fields of philosophy, psychology and literary criticism, I link the issue of narrative temporality together with the affective and the political registers of reading in neo-Victorian literature. I conclude the introduction with a detailed chapter overview.

Dialogic encounters

As a kind of 'dialogic' genre, neo-Victorian fiction stages various kinds of 'spectral' communications between the Victorians and us. The following review of several recent studies suggests that the entangled relationship between the nineteenth century and the contemporary period is not merely a thematic concern – but also informs the narrative – of neo-Victorian fiction. Tatiana Kontou's *Spiritualism and Women's Writing: From the Fin de Siècle to the Neo-Victorian* (2009), for example, presents the authors of neo-Victorian fictions as 'spiritualist mediums' who '*ventriloquize* the dead' (1, 2, original emphasis). Through an interrogation of the gendered history of spiritualism, Kontou demonstrates the gendered nature of historical narrative and the political and ethical issues involved in our access to and engagement with the past. Helen Davies's *Gender and Ventriloquism in Victorian and Neo-Victorian Fiction: Passionate Puppets* (2012) also adopts the metaphor of ventriloquism in her discussion of the engagement between the Victorian and contemporary ages. By examining the power dynamic between the 'dummy' and the 'ventriloquist', Davies raises some ethical concerns about the contemporary authors' appropriation of the past, and in particular the ways in which they position the Victorian precursors as 'dummies' that are 'manipulated and voiced to suit contemporary concerns' (11). These ethical issues are explored by Davies in further detail in relation to the representation of the 'freaky' or disabled bodies in neo-Victorian literature and culture in *Neo-Victorian Freakery: The Cultural Afterlife of the Victorian Freak Show* (2015). In this book Davies takes up the lead of Kohlke and Gutleben in her recognition that 'neo-Victorian representations – traumatic or otherwise – are not always motivated by the "best of intentions"' (8). As Kohlke and Gutleben observe, 'fictional reimaginings of the nineteenth century can also be sensationalist, cynical, trivialising, coarse' (2010: 23). However, despite the aforementioned ethical concerns, Davies also touches on the significance of neo-Victorian literature and culture in opening up 'possibilities for understanding and empathy' (2015: 15). This book shares and further explores Davies's concern about the ethical agenda of neo-Victorianism in its examination of the different kinds of reading pleasures afforded by neo-Victorian literature.

In recognition of the uncanny recurrence of the Victorians in the contemporary literary imagination, Rosario Arias and Patricia Pulham (2009) as well as Mark Llewellyn (2008) have used tropes such as 'haunting' and 'spectrality' in their respective considerations of how the unsettling or unresolved Victorian issues about gender, sexuality, race and empire are (re)negotiated in neo-Victorian fiction. These tropes also highlight the link between the thematic content of the neo-Victorian novels (which often feature ghosts, mediums and other characters that mediate between the past and the present) and their metacritical political projects.[2]

Critics have also made various attempts to examine the poetics, aesthetics and politics of the dialogic engagement between the Victorian and the contemporary periods. Taking her cue from Dana Shiller, Louisa Hadley positions neo-Victorian fiction in relation to the genre of historical fiction in *Neo-Victorian Fiction and Historical Narrative: The Victorians and Us* (2010). Focusing on different forms of historical narratives (i.e. biography and detective fiction), Hadley examines 'the complex combination of [the Victorians'] historical proximity to and distance from the contemporary era' in neo-Victorian narratives (14). Kate Mitchell's *History and Cultural Memory in Neo-Victorian Fiction: Victorian Afterimages* (2010) also acknowledges the genre's value in exploring the accessibility and comprehensibility of historical knowledge.

---

[2] Other critical texts which deal specifically with this thematic preoccupation of the way in which the past and the present shadow one another include Mitchell's book (2010), which explores a range of narrative strategies that are used by novelists in putting the Victorian and the contemporary periods into dialogue (either explicitly or implicitly).

Ann Heilmann and Mark Llewellyn's *Neo-Victorianism: The Victorians in the Twenty-First Century, 1999–2009* (2010), by contrast, distinguishes the neo-Victorian genre from historical fiction set in the nineteenth century and links it specifically to Linda Hutcheon's notion of 'historiographic metafiction' (4). Their analysis and evaluation of the genre is thus preoccupied with the aesthetics and politics of postmodernism, as demonstrated by their definition of the field. Heilmann and Llewellyn use the term neo-Victorianism to refer to texts – be they literary, filmic or audio/visual – that are in some respect *'self-consciously engaged with the act of (re)interpretation, (re)discovery and (re)vision concerning the Victorians'* (4, original emphasis). Building on Heilmann and Llewellyn's work but taking a more precise focus, Kym Brindle extends the discussion of the postmodern self-consciousness and self-reflexiveness in neo-Victorian literature in *Epistolary Encounters in Neo-Victorian Fiction: Diaries and Letters* (2013). With a specific focus on epistolary devices, Brindle examines the ways in which the Victorian past is positioned as 'the locus of an intertextual, dialogic, historicised self-understanding' for the contemporary period (Letissier qtd in Brindle 2013: 13). Taking the role of epistolary forms in the text–reader dynamic into consideration, Brindle also develops the discussion of the dialogic relationship afforded by neo-Victorian literature from that between the Victorian and the contemporary to that between writers of neo-Victorian fictions and their readers.

All these critical explorations aim to answer the following two questions that are promoted by the burgeoning of neo-Victorianism in the past few decades: 'Why the Victorian(s)?' and 'Why now?' Critics such as Heilmann and Llewellyn, who identify themselves as Victorianists, attribute the contemporary interest in the Victorian past to its 'enduring influence' in 'contemporary culture, post-millennium' (3). By foregrounding the role of the Victorians in the construction of the postmodern present, Heilmann and Llewellyn's approach celebrates the Victorian legacy in contemporary literature, culture and politics, whilst also helping to construct a sense of historical continuity between the Victorian era and the contemporary period.[3]

---

[3] In his 2008 article 'What Is Neo-Victorian Studies?', Llewellyn positions neo-Victorian fiction as a derivation of Victorian literature: 'What the neo-Victorian represents, then, is a different way into the Victorians – for students and faculty alike. This is not contemporary literature as a substitute for the nineteenth century but as a mediator into the experience of reading the "real" thing' (168).

Some earlier critics, including John Kucich and Dianne F. Sadoff, have also underlined the role of the nineteenth century in the theorization of postmodernism. In their introduction to their co-edited collection of essays *Victorian Afterlife: Postmodern Culture Rewrites the Nineteenth Century* (2000), Kucich and Sadoff remark that the Victorian period is characterized by 'major critical texts that claim to have found in the nineteenth century the origins of contemporary consumerism (Baudrillard), sexual science (Foucault), gay culture (Sedgwick et al.), and gender identity (Gilbert and Gubar, Showalter, Armstrong)' (xiii–xiv). In this context, the nineteenth century serves as what Elizabeth Ho describes as 'a narcissistic mirror' for the postmodern present to 'reflect its own origins', or a fertile soil for postmodernism's identificatory needs ([2012] 2013: 7). In some respects, Heilmann and Llewellyn share Kucich and Sadoff's concern about the identity 'crisis' of postmodernism. For example, they consider the issue of adaptation as the generic characteristic of neo-Victorian text and position the Victorian as 'the *Urtext*' for the contemporary to engage with (65). Furthermore, their readings of selected neo-Victorian novels in *Neo-Victorianism* are informed by the work of theorists such as Baudrillard (chapter 6) and Foucault (chapter 1), and tropes that are linked with identity issues, such as 'ancestral houses' in chapter 1, 'glass' in chapter 4 and 'mirrors' in chapter 5.

Admittedly, Heilmann and Llewellyn's approach to the study of neo-Victorian literature and culture demonstrates the ways in which neo-Victorian texts invoke particular versions of the Victorian(s), the aesthetic and ethical implications of such adaptation and appropriation. With a focus on the dynamic between the past and the present, their work illustrates how the contemporary period attaches significance to the past and the present in the mode of continuous retrospection. Its preoccupation with the retrospective mode of narrative is, nevertheless, limited since narrative can hardly be retrospective without also being anticipatory, a point I will explain in the next section. It is therefore important to examine how the present is structured by both retrospection and anticipation.

Llewellyn's consideration of neo-Victorian fiction as a kind of 'mediator' makes it clear that for him the neo-Victorian genre is a secondary replicate of the 'authentic' Victorians. This contention problematically 'robs the neo-Victorian novel of its status as an independent – and contemporary – literary artefact' (Carroll 2010: 179).

Another feature of Heilmann and Llewellyn's stance on neo-Victorian fiction is their premise on the 'knowing reader', who is able to acknowledge the points of Victorian references in neo-Victorian texts.[4] The political implications of this line of argument are something that Marie-Luise Kohlke has taken issue with and challenged by showing why extensive historical knowledge and other kinds of 'cultural capital' are *not* necessary for the enjoyment of these texts. As Kohlke asserts, 'The success of neo-Victorian revisitations with variation [...] is not necessarily dependent on any clear-cut recognition of *what* exactly is being replicated or *how* it is being varied. It stems as readily from the manipulation of readers' generalised, frequently stereotyped, and ritually comforting preconceptions of the "Victorian" and the "Victorians"' (2014: 25, original emphasis). By suggesting that the pleasure of reading neo-Victorian fiction is not limited to a self-confirming critical knowingness or omniscience, Kohlke proposes a different approach to the study of neo-Victorian literature: one that focuses on the needs, desires and anxieties of the present featured in neo-Victorian literature rather than the 'living' presence of the Victorian past in contemporary discourse. Unlike Heilmann and Llewellyn's historical approach, Kohlke is more concerned with how the contemporary society addresses itself by responding to the 'other' which takes the form of the 'generalised' and 'frequently stereotyped' Victorian(s). As Kohlke proposes, 'neo-Victorian literature may be better understood in terms of a liminal "zone"': a concept she takes up from Jay Clayton in presenting the nineteenth-century's afterlife as what Clayton calls a 'contingent field of relevance' (29). For Kohlke, neo-Victorian literature 'intersect[s]' but is also 'discrepant with historical fiction as a whole' (ibid.). This book shares Kohlke's understanding of the neo-Victorian genre and approaches the concept of neo-Victorianism from the broadest perspective by considering any 'text' – be it literary, filmic or cultural – that engages with the nineteenth century as a kind of neo-Victorian practice in order to explore the various pleasures it affords.

Even more important for the thesis I am pursuing here is the fact that Kohlke also highlights the role of neo-Victorian representations of the

---

[4] In their joint work *Neo-Victorianism*, Heilmann and Llewellyn acknowledge that the distinction they made between 'the "ordinary" reader' and 'the more "knowledgeable" critical reader' is controversial (17–18).

Victorian(s) in the construction of the future. Through the issue of trauma, Kohlke presents neo-Victorian fiction as a transformative space in which the contemporary world imaginatively confronts and works through past traumas, therefore linking the imperative to rewrite the past in neo-Victorian texts with the impulse to reconfigure the future. Indeed, there are a good number of physically disabled, traumatized and psychologically disturbed characters in neo-Victorian fiction, as can be seen in novels such as Margaret Atwood's *Alias Grace* (1996), Sarah Waters's *Affinity* (1999) and *Fingersmith* (2002), Darin Strauss's *Chang and Eng: A Novel* (2000), Michael Cox's *The Meaning of Night* (2006) and Julian Barnes's *Arthur & George* (2005). These past traumas are evoked and worked through in neo-Victorian fiction in the interests of the present and the future. In the words of Kohlke and Gutleben, neo-Victorian literature signifies 'a belated abreaction or "working through" of nineteenth-century traumas, as well as those of our own times, albeit more obliquely' (2010: 3). During this process, historical traumas serve as 'interactive foils or mirrors of present-day traumas' and are essential in projecting and figuring the future (13). Kohlke and Gutleben's psychoanalysis of the manifestation of 'afterwardness' in contemporary culture points to the performativity of the past: the past, they suggest, is capable of doing things too. Conceptualizing the past as 'performative' is to recognize the past as a field that 'can be reencountered in ways that might transform present affective and political orientations' (Pedwell 2014: 66). The imaginative exploration of alternative past(s) in neo-Victorian fiction, then, gestures towards the possibility that both the present and the future could be different.

Elizabeth Ho's 2012 book, *Neo-Victorianism and the Memory of Empire*, treads similar ground in her postcolonial approach to neo-Victorian literature and culture. Ho considers the neo-Victorian phenomenon as 'part of a global politics rather than a "pathology" of memory' in the context of post-imperial Britain ([2012] 2013: 26). She also challenges this Anglocentric understanding of neo-Victorianism by moving to an exploration of 'a sea change in postmillennial neo-Victorian fiction', a term Ho uses quite literally to conceptualize novels which are based on sea voyages such as Matthew Kneale's *English Passengers* (2000) and Amitav Ghosh's *Sea of Poppies* (2008) (25). In this manner, Ho identifies a shift in neo-Victorian fiction which 'free[s] the genre from the referent of Britain' and positions the neo-Victorian project as one that is concerned with 'an unbounded globality' (26). Like Kohlke, Ho is also interested in the transformative potential of neo-Victorian narratives. Furthermore, Ho's postcolonial and psychoanalytical approach to the neo-Victorian genre reveals collective desires for 'reparation, political and economic compensation, the righting of injustice, the demand for witness and apology' behind contemporary adaptations and appropriations of the Victorians (17). The reparative potentials Ho delineates here point to the significance of neo-Victorian literature and culture in navigating what Cora Kaplan calls 'the *political future* in which we, as readers and citizens, do have a voice and a role to play' (2007: 162, emphasis added). This approach brings the role of readers into consideration and gives prominence to their responsibilities for the construction of a different future, a point that will be further explored in relation to Sedgwick's conceptualization of 'reparative reading' in the next section.

In this book, I present neo-Victorian fiction as a genre that stages the problem of reading/interpreting the past through its self-conscious and self-reflexive textuality and its engagement with the wider affective, ethical and political issues that are associated with narrative temporality. With a focus on the modes and effects of storytelling and reading, I consider the ways in which neo-Victorian fiction involves the reader in the (construction of the) textual world affectively. This critical interest in the examination of the dynamic between textual positioning and readerly participation is derived from Wolfgang Iser's influential conceptualization of reading as a kind of 'realization' that is 'accomplished by the reader' (1972: 279).[5] Focusing on the 'convergence' of the text and the reader, Iser's phenomenological sketch of the activity of reading highlights both the role of the reader – being the 'actualizer' – in the production of the meaning of literary texts and the transformative capacities of reading in relation to the reader's knowledge and practice in the actual

---

[5] It is important to note that my study of readerly empathy – following Iser – is primarily concerned with how literary texts position their readers, although there is a growing body of empirical studies that are interested in examining the actual readers' responses to narrative strategies in the field of cognitive psychology. Empirical study could also be limited since the laboratory setting impacts the reader/participants' responses to varying degrees. Critics including Amy Coplan (2004), Greg Currie (2016), Eva Maria Koopman and Frank Hakemulder (2015) have provided useful reviews of recent empirical researches on the impact of fiction reading on the reader's empathetic tendencies.

world, which lays the foundation for my argument of the ethical and political significance of reading (ibid.). I also explore the way the text 'disrupts' the reader's affective attachment and investment through an interrogation of the portrayal of an often painful and unsettling – as opposed to celebratory and comforting – version of the past. In light of Lauren Berlant's work on the politics of affect, I propose that this kind of disruption challenges the reader's 'habituated processing of affective responses to' what they encounter in both textual and non-textual worlds and prompts them to see the present in a *'historical'* manner (2008: 5, original emphasis). By considering the concept of empathy in relation to the affective landscape of neo-Victorian texts, this book therefore shifts the study of neo-Victorian literature from a postmodern critique of the discursive nature of historical knowledge to an ethical and political interrogation of the reader–text relationship. This breathes new life into the debates surrounding the texts, and in so doing illustrates how these texts enfold the past within the present, constraining or enabling action for the future.

Narrative temporality

This book discusses the transformative potential of neo-Victorian fiction by means of Mark Currie's identification of the sense of anticipation at the core of narrative consciousness in his book *About Time: Narrative, Fiction and the Philosophy of Time* ([2007] 2012). Currie's narratological and philosophical study of time in narrative fiction provides a useful framework for an examination of neo-Victorian temporality and helps to explain that the issue of narrative temporality is not limited to novels that thematize time explicitly, such as steampunk (a mixture of science fiction and (neo-)Victorian aesthetics).[6]

Taking the act of writing and storytelling into consideration, Currie points out that narrative is structured around a kind of 'double time', referring to

---

[6] As Cynthia J. Miler and Julie Anne Taddeo note, the term 'steampunk' was originally coined in the 1980s to describe 'a group of nineteenth-century-inspired technofantasies', referring to novels such as K. W. Jeter's *Morlock Night* (1979), *Infernal Devices* (1987), James P. Blaylock's *Homonculus* (1986) and Tim Powers's *The Anubis Gates* (1983) (2013: xv). These novels, in the words of Ken Dvorak, reimagine both the Victorian past and the future through 'a neo-Victorian lens' (2013: ix).

the temporal structure of both retrospection and anticipation (89). Through his engagement with the concept of time prompted by Derrida's theorization of archive fever, Currie challenges the dominant understanding of narrative as being 'retrospective', an idea derived from the observation that writers or tellers normally 'loo[k] back on events and relat[e] them in the past tense' (29). Derrida's own observations on the Janus-faced nature of any archiving project are worth quoting here:

> The archive, as printing, writing, prosthesis, or hypomnesic technique in general is not only the place for stocking and for conserving an archivable content *of the past* which would exist in any case, such as, without the archive, one still believes it was or will have been. No, the technical structure of the *archiving* archive also determines the structure of the *archivable* content even in its very coming into existence and in its relationship to the future. The archivization produces as much as it records the event. This is also our political experience of the so-called news media. (1996: 16–17, original emphasis)

As mentioned at the beginning of this introduction, Derrida's depiction of our experience of a media culture reveals, for Currie, an important truth; that is, 'an event is recorded not because it happens, but it happens because it is recorded' (11). This reversed cause-and-effect sequence of an event does not suggest that the future actually happens before the past. Rather, it highlights the fact that our narration of the present is structured by 'a future orientation', or 'a mode of anticipation' (ibid.). This point is vividly illustrated by the example Currie gives on video recording: 'The act of recording installs in the present an anticipated future from which the present will be re-experienced as representation of the past, or an infinite sequence of future presents from which the moment can be recollected' (41). Currie's example demonstrates that the way we record the world now is informed by an anticipatory thought about the function of the video in the future. The act of capturing some specific moments in the present through a lens makes it possible for the audience to revisit these moments as part of the past in the future. A similar idea can be found in Roland Barthes's proposition that 'the nature of the photography is not to represent but to memorialize' ([1978] 2002: 194). In this context, the present is structured as 'the object of a future memory' (Currie [2007] 2012: 40). This temporal logic also informs the act of storytelling. Like the recording function of the archive, storytelling plays a double role in shaping our memory of the past and envisaging the future:

> If, in order to look back at what has happened, we tell a story, we must also know that the present is a story yet to be told. The present is the object of a future memory, and we live it as such, in anticipation of the story we will tell later, envisaging the present as past. The present might be lived in anticipation of some future present from which it is narrated, but this may also entail the anticipation of events between the present present and the future present from which it is narrated which will also be part of that story. (5–6)

For Currie, narrative is shaped by the present we are in – that we look back, retrospectively, from here and now to see what happened before – as well as the future we expect to arrive at, in the sense that we know the stories we are telling now will be 'past' narratives in the future. Put simply, in storytelling anticipation and retrospection bear upon each other. Currie's foregrounding of the double time in narrative not only challenges the retrospective model of narrative (which, to Currie, includes Hutcheon's formulation of historiographic metafiction), but also shifts the critical attention to the ways 'in which we attach significance to present moments' in 'the mode of continuous anticipation' (6).

This temporal structure is also inherent in the act of reading. Here Currie moves to the work of Peter Brooks who similarly traces the role of tense in the reading process. As Brooks, writing in *Reading for the Plot: Designing and Invention in Narrative* (1984), observes:

> If the past is to be read as present, it is a curious present that we know to be past in relation to a future we know to be already in place, already in wait for us to reach it. Perhaps we would do best to speak of the *anticipation of retrospection* as our chief tool in making sense of narrative, the master trope of its strange logic. (23, original emphasis)

Reading is often perceived as a process of presentification, or 'what Ricoeur calls the presentifying of the past' (Currie [2007] 2012: 5). The passage from Brooks, nevertheless, challenges and complicates Ricoeur's argument by suggesting that during the reading process, readers are encouraged to see the present in relation to the future (specified as the ending of the fictional narrative). The act of reading therefore involves 'a complex movement' that 'unfold[s] through time' as opposed to 'a straightforward linear movement' (Eagleton [1983] 1996: 67). It is full of 'perspectives, preintentions, recollections' (Iser 1972: 284). Considering the literary text as an organic unity, Iser claims that 'every sentence contains a preview of the next and forms a kind of viewfinder for what is to come; and this in turn changes the "preview" and so becomes a "viewfinder" for what has been read' (ibid.). From this point of view, the act of reading causes the reader to experience the past, the present and the future as a continuity. Here it is also worth noting that the future of written narrative is marked by an 'already-there-ness', in the sense that the ending of a narrative fiction is already there, waiting: this is what John Randolph Lucas describes as 'the reel of a film' (1989: 8). Thus the notion of futurity at the core of narrative consciousness is at odds with our lived experience, which is instead characterized by the provisionality and indeterminacy of what is to come. However, although the sense of futurity evoked by reading fiction and lived experience is different in nature, the act of reading develops the reader's ability to explore the present in relation to the future, thus preparing them for 'the continuous anticipation that takes place in non-fictional life' (Currie [2007] 2012: 6). By highlighting the similarities between our experience of time and the temporal logic of narrative, Currie demonstrates the significance of reading fiction for the actual life, a point that is essential to my following discussion of the political and ethical implications of reading neo-Victorian literature.

For the study of neo-Victorian fiction – a genre which seems, on the surface, to be predominantly retrospective – Currie's writing on narrative temporality proves useful for an exploration of the dynamic between the past, the present and the future in neo-Victorian narratives. As I will explain in detail in the chapter outline that follows, this book draws upon Currie's narratological study in its examination of the ways in which writers experiment with the temporal structure of different narrative genres (such as crime fiction and Bildungsroman) in involving the reader in the consumption of, and also critical reflection on, the reimagined past. In what follows, I therefore attempt to link Currie's discussion of double time with issues of ethics and reader responsibility in connection with the work of Sedgwick, which is also, as we shall see, pertinent to a future-orientated approach to neo-Victorian literature.

Reading with(out) suspicion

Writing from the perspective of gender and queer studies, Sedgwick investigates 'the converging analytics of affect and time' in critical enterprise through a pair of concepts she invents: 'paranoid reading' and 'reparative reading' (Wiegman 2014: 9).[7] Both practices are informed by a projection of the future, although their attitudes towards that future vary (a point I will explain in more detail in the next section). Sedgwick uses the term paranoid reading to refer to critical practices that are premised on the 'protocols of unveiling' (2003: 143).[8] Placing 'suspicion' as its central methodology, Sedgwick's theorization of paranoid reading is inspired by 'the hermeneutics of suspicion', a term coined by Paul Ricoeur in his discussion of the similar traits between the works of Marx, Nietzsche and Freud:

> For Marx, Nietzsche, and Freud, the fundamental category of consciousness is the relation hidden-shown or, if you prefer, simulated-manifested. [...] What all three attempted, in different ways, was to make their 'conscious' methods of deciphering coincide with the 'unconscious' *work* of ciphering which they attributed to the will to power, to social being, to the unconscious psychism. *Guile will be met by double guile.*

---

[7] Sedgwick developed her ideas of paranoid and reparative reading practices in a series of essays she published between 1996 and 2003. These two terms firstly appeared in a four-page introduction to the 1996 special issue of the journal *Studies in the Novel* under the title 'Queerer than Fiction'. In 1997, Sedgwick extended her discussion into a thirty-seven page long essay and published it as an introduction to the collection of essays *Novel Gazing: Queer Readings in Fiction* under the provocative title 'Paranoid Reading and Reparative Reading; or, You're So Paranoid, You Probably Think This Introduction Is about You' (1997). Later, this essay has been slightly revised and published in her 2003 collection *Touching Feeling: Affect, Pedagogy, Performativity*.

[8] Notably, Sedgwick is not the first critic to adopt the psychiatric term of 'paranoia' in describing a mode of reading that is defined by suspicion. In her 1992 article, Linda Fisher develops William Bywater's argument that postmodernism freezes us 'with intellectual paranoia' by suggesting that postmodernism is 'continuous in many ways with a longer hermeneutic tradition of critique and suspicion' (Bywater 1990: 79; Fisher 1992: 107). Its 'paranoid fear of absolutism' and 'essentialism', to Fisher, explains postmodernism's denial of 'the possibility of discursivity' (112, 113). Although there is no cross-referencing between Fisher and Sedgwick, it is not difficult to spot the similarities here: both share a concern about the 'incapacitating' and 'disabling' effect of the paranoid or hyper-suspicious mindset (Fisher 1992: 112). Taking up the lead of Freud and Lacan, Bran Nicol approaches the concept of paranoia from a slightly different perspective and construes it as 'a crisis in interpretation' (1999: 45). In recognition of its subtle desire to 'see connections' between everything, Nicol suggests that paranoia is the 'product of the epistemic shift' from modernism to postmodernism, the latter of which is described as 'a continual process of trying to find meaning in the face of the knowledge that meaning is always relative and contingent' (46).

Thus the distinguishing characteristic of Marx, Freud, and Nietzsche is the general hypothesis concerning both the process of false consciousness and the method of deciphering. The two go together, since the man of suspicion carries out in reverse the work of falsification of the man of guile. (1970: 33–4, original emphasis)

Ricoeur observes that the work of Marx, Nietzsche and Freud is premised on the belief that the 'true' meaning of the text is hidden and will be discovered through critical interpretation only.[9] This presumption of the 'hidden truth' also involves a spatial perception of the textual world, which is essential in the political explication of literary works. As Toril Moi explains, 'a specific picture of texts (as things with surfaces and depths) and reading (as critique, which brings the hidden to light) gets entangled in a political project: to undo an oppressive status quo, to raise our political consciousness' (2017: 177). However, the existence of 'true' meaning itself is what critics attribute to the text; hence Ricoeur invokes the idea of 'double guile' in his description of this mode of critical practice. The presumptuous faith in and daunting uncertainty about the 'truth' also prompt the critic to read in a constantly guarded manner in order to reveal the 'true' meaning of the text. Hermeneutics of suspicion therefore constitutes a 'defensive' practice, one that is grounded in and also contributes to a confrontational text–reader relationship. As Sedgwick's choice of vocabulary – using the language of 'paranoia' – suggests, this type of reading is characterized by 'analytical detachment', 'critical vigilance' and 'guarded suspicion' (Felski 2008: 2).[10] Although Sedgwick stresses that her use of the word paranoia is metaphorical rather than pathological, the kind of reader she portrays carries a hypervigilant and hypersensitive temperament. Sedgwick observes that insofar as their 'first imperative' is *There must be no bad surprise*, the paranoid reader is trapped in the loop of constant negotiation between fear of humiliation and the feeling of humiliation (2003: 130, original emphasis). It

---

[9] Susan Sontag has made a similar critique of the methodology of Marx and Freud in her discussion of the interpretation of art in her seminal essay 'Against Interpretation' ([1966] 2009). To her, this 'aggressive and impious' mode of critical practice 'excavates' and 'destroys' artwork (6).
[10] Sedgwick's choice of vocabulary also resonates with the development of queer studies, which has 'a distinctive history of intimacy with the paranoid imperative' (Sedgwick 2003: 126). In his analysis of Dr Schreber's autographical narrative, Freud (1958) considers Schreber's paranoid delusions as the outburst of his unconscious or repressed homosexual desires.

is in this sense that Heather Love describes paranoid readers as 'both aggressive and wounded' (2010a: 237). The aversion to surprise also determines the anticipatory mechanism of paranoia, thus rendering suspicious interpretation a 'frightening' and nearly infinite practice. D. A. Miller's assessment that they 'can never be paranoid enough' suggests that the paranoid reader would – in the words of Leo Bersani – 'inevitably be suspicious of the interpretations [they] inspire' (Miller 1988: 164; Bersani 1990: 188). The problem with this tendency is that under the reader's constant and vigilant pursuit of critical omnipotence, there will be no space for any alternative approaches. Sedgwick warns us that reading in a paranoid manner is like growing 'a crystal in a hypersaturated solution, blotting out any sense of the possibility of alternative ways of understanding *or* things to understand' (2003: 131, original emphasis).

On this point it is, nevertheless, important to acknowledge that Sedgwick is not disavowing the importance of paranoid reading in and of itself. Rather, she is concerned with its hegemonic status in literary criticism.[11] Her purpose is to highlight the fact that paranoid inquiry is just 'one kind of cognitive/affective theoretical practice among other, alternative kinds' (2003: 126). To her, 'Paranoia knows some things well and others poorly' (130). A similar point can be found in Susan Sontag's elaboration on the different implications of critical interpretation in different contexts. As 'a means of revising, of transvaluing, of escaping the dead past', interpretation serves as 'a liberating act' (Sontag [1966] 2009: 7). However, there are certain scenarios in which interpretation becomes 'reactionary, impertinent, cowardly, stifling' (ibid.).

The shared concern between Sedgwick and Sontag on the ethical and political controversies associated with suspicious hermeneutics is essential to my assessment of neo-Victorian fiction, a genre that both *thematizes* and *promotes* the question of reading/interpretation and its affective as well as ethical dimensions. As Heilmann and Llewellyn contend, neo-Victorian literature is engaged with 'a wide range of (re)interpretations of the nineteenth century' (3). Considering neo-Victorian appropriation as 'a destabilizing hermeneutic act', Eckart Voigts-Virchow further claims that 'neo-Victorian

---

[11] Inspired by Sedgwick's challenge of the methodological centrality of suspicion in criticism, Felski charges critique of highlighting 'the sphere of agon (conflict and domination) at the expense of eros (love and connection)', extending her target at the whole profession in her 2015 book *The Limits of Critique* (17).

writers theorize difference' and their focus is to find out how 'our experiential or biological situatedness make[s] us different from Victorian subjects' (2009: 108–9). Given its transformation imperative, neo-Victorian fiction is arguably preoccupied with the contemporary reader's desire to engage with the conventional narrative of the Victorian period and the very Victorians themselves *with suspicion*.[12] Neo-Victorian literature plays with this kind of 'paranoid' critical impulse or agenda in both its thematics and narratology. By rewriting the Victorians through the prism of the present, neo-Victorian fiction may be seen as fulfilling the contemporary reader's expository desire to demystify and expose systemic oppressions in the past. For example, we see same-sex desire in Victorian England where 'the concept of lesbianism supposedly did not exist' (Dennis 2008: 41) in Sarah Waters's neo-Victorian trio – *Tipping the Velvet* (1998), *Affinity* (1999) and *Fingersmith* (2002) – and the ideologically interpellated figures such as criminals, immigrants and prostitutes in novels include Margaret Atwood's *Alias Grace* (1996), Michel Faber's *The Crimson Petal and the White* (2002), Julian Barnes's *Arthur & George* (2005), and Jane Harris's *The Observations* ([2006] 2007) to name but a few. This particular focus on – to invoke Steven Marcus's 1966 book – the 'other' Victorians reveals the role of suspicion in the development of neo-Victorianism, which sees itself as 'overturning or unearthing the conventions of "standard" or heritage Victorianism' (Pike 2010: 254). Indeed, as a wider movement involving literature, film, arts and culture in general, neo-Victorianism can be considered as 'a deliberate misreading, reconstruction or staged return of the nineteenth century in and for the present' (Ho [2012] 2013: 5).

The problem of this kind of paranoid inquiry, as Sedgwick points out, is that 'visibility itself constitutes much of the violence' (2003: 140). As the leading textual example of *Neo-Victorianism, Empathy, and Reading*, Atwood's *Alias Grace* self-consciously explores the paranoid impulse behind the reader's expository desire to access the hidden past and its related ethical issues. By

---

[12] Indeed, not all neo-Victorian novels present suspicious reading of the nineteenth-century past. Through the example of Tom Phillips's *A Humunent* (a constantly evolving text), Christine Ferguson argues that there exists a 'non-hermeneutic tradition of neo-Victorian writing' (2013: 22), which 'uses a Victorian source text to create [...] an atypical way of reading', one that 'insists on an engagement with the past that is grounded primarily on the emotive presence of physical materials and aesthetic forms' (31).

presenting how other fictional characters consume the experience of the protagonist Grace – the convicted murderess of the notorious 1843 murders of Thomas Kinnear and his housekeeper Nancy Montgomery in Canada – in a prurient manner, Atwood exposes the reader's complicity in Grace's experience of exploitation and in so doing, encourages them to drop their suspicion and attend to the needs of the vulnerable other. By promoting an affective and ethical encounter between the textual other and the reader, *Alias Grace* exemplifies the way neo-Victorian fiction invites readers to participate in the non-fictional world. Here I follow J. Hillis Miller in advocating that 'the ethical moment in reading leads to an act' (1987: 4).

In response to the ethical issues promoted by the paranoid agenda, Sedgwick also proposes an alternative model of critical practice called 'reparative reading', a term she develops from the work of the psychoanalyst Melanie Klein. To read reparatively, Sedgwick elaborates via queer criticism, is to read without any 'proscribed object choice, aim, site or identification'; to read for 'important news about herself, without knowing what form that news will take'; to read with 'only the patchiest familiarity with its codes; without, even, more than hungrily hypothesizing to what questions this news may proffer an answer' (1997: 2–3). This critical position surrenders the anxious determination for the domination or appropriation of the textual object and seeks, instead, a more affective and sustainable text–reader engagement. As a speculative, superstitious and methodologically adventurous critical practice, reparative reading thus promises to bring the reader something surprising, but not necessarily positive (3). Sedgwick's description here echoes Maurice Blanchot's portrayal of the 'modest' reader who is submerged by – and thus able to appreciate – the inexhaustible potential and freedom of the text:

> He does not think that he fashions the work. Even if the work overwhelms him, and all the more so if it becomes his sole concern, he feels that he does not exhaust it, that it remains altogether outside his most intimate approach. He does not penetrate it; it is free of him, and this freedom makes for the profundity of his relation to the work. ([1982] 1989: 201)

What Sedgwick and Blanchot share is the belief that the reader's less imperious and affective response to the demand of the text has the potential to transform the reader themselves, or, to use Blanchot's figurative language, 'disposses[s]' the reader of the self (227). This 'self-less' text–reader relationship is interspersed by the joy of finding truths accidentally and understanding mistakes more positively. Reading in this manner offers the reader some space to realize that 'mistakes can be good rather than bad surprises' (Sedgwick 2003: 147).

Sedgwick's less tendentious perception of surprise proves useful for critics who are eager to (re)claim the value of interpretive humanities at a time when the transformative hope of earlier generations of critics – and of ideological critique in particular – has become exhausted.[13] Robyn Wiegman remarks that 'the equation between knowledge and political transformation' is no longer tenable (2014: 7), bringing to the fore the inefficiency of exposure or knowledge in ushering changes in the world. Matt Prout alternatively suggests that reading is not 'tied exclusively to an emancipatory politics' (2020: 608). The call for reparative reading, then, involves a desire for the reconfiguration of the critical practice. Striving for a text–reader relationship that is featured by 'affection, gratitude, solidarity, and love' – as opposed to 'correction, rejection, and anger' (Wiegman 2014: 7) – reparative reading is construed as a 'therapeutic' critical act that 'addresses the immediate needs of the subject and its practices rather than the system' (Anderson 2017: 326). It has also inspired explorations of alternative ways of reading including 'surface reading' (see Best and Marcus 2009), 'descriptive reading' (see Love 2020b) and so on.[14] This critical interest in how to read *differently* is shared by neo-Victorianism, a literary genre that foregrounds the interpretive process

---

[13] Wiegman explains that the paranoid obsession with exposure is derived from 'left critical conceptions of power as repressive, mystifying, and occluding' (6). In a time when the transformative capacities of knowledge/critique are no longer tenable, Sedgwick's formulation of reparative reading offers an excitingly inspiring way to read and think otherwise, as evidenced by the recent 'reparative turn' in literary criticism. The journal of *Representations*, for example, published a special issue named 'The Way We Read Now' in 2009 to further promote the discussion of how to 'attend to the surfaces of texts rather than plumb their depths' (Best and Marcus 2009: 1–2). Feminist and queer critics such as Heather Love (2007) and Elizabeth Freeman (2010) have also taken up the lead of Sedgwick in their respective and reparation-oriented study of backward feeling and queer time.

[14] David Kurnick argues that these discussions do not offer 'new ways to interpret texts but new ways to feel about ourselves when we do' and considers them as 'expressions of disciplinary anxiety' (2020: 351, 352). In her discussion of 'the turn to affect' in the field of cultural studies, Clare Hemmings likewise suggests that critics such as Brian Massumi and Eve Sedgwick are 'advocating a new academic attitude rather than a new method', the former of which is specified as 'an attitude or faith in something other than the social and cultural, a faith in the wonders that might emerge if we were not so attached to pragmatic negativity' (2005: 563). Indeed, current explorations of different modes of critical enterprise are featured by a particular focus on the affective dimension of reading. However, it is arguable that affect itself informs the way critics approach the literary text.

and self-consciously engages with the efficiencies of – and controversies associated with – suspicious reading.

For Wiegman, Sedgwick's model of reparative reading also serves to 'compensate for [the] increasingly damaged authority' of critics; they now become someone who is no longer narcissistically defensive and is able to respond to the future with 'affirmative richness' and hope (Wiegman 2014: 7, 11). The fact that hope is 'often a fracturing, even a traumatic thing to experience' suggests that reparative reading does not guarantee any less of a traumatic reading experience than the paranoid one (Sedgwick 2003: 146).[15] However, reparative readers are more willing and prepared to take risks. They are 'porous' subjects who are no longer fixated on the mastery of the text and are keen on exploring ways to, in the words of Ellis Hanson, 'build or rebuild some more sustaining relation to the objects' in our 'damaged and dangerous' world (2012: 547). The notion of hope installed in a reparative reading resembles Derrida's 'utopian hope', which, as Andrew Gibson explains, 'would not be teleological, and would not proceed on the assumption of a determinate logic binding what is to come to "our present"' (1999: 4). Rather, it is linked with an indeterminate future which we – as readers and critics – can have a voice on. To read reparatively, then, could facilitate not only the critic's self-transformation but also the construction of a more nurturing community.

Before moving to a further discussion of the link between reparation and empathy, I would like to spend a bit more time discussing the relationship between paranoid and reparative readings. The dynamic between these two styles of interpretation is essential for our understanding of the complicated temporal structure of neo-Victorian fiction, which, as my early engagement with Simon Joyce suggests, is about how the genre gestures towards the future by looking backwards.

As previously mentioned, paranoia and reparation are informed by different attitudes towards the future. Having said so, it does not mean that these two impulses act against each other. In fact, they are 'changing and heterogeneous relational stances' (Sedgwick 2003: 128). Through her engagement of Melanie

---

[15] Ernst Bloch explains the dialectical relation between hope and its failure as follows: 'It too can be, and will be, disappointed; indeed, it must be so, as a matter of honor, or else it would not be hope' (qtd in Chambers-Letson, Nyong'o and Pellegrini [2009] 2019: xiv). Hope's failure is 'not its negation but its condition of possibility' (ibid.).

Klein's theorization of the paranoid/schizoid position, Jackie Stacey investigates the dynamic between paranoia and reparation in detail. Focusing on the infant's ambivalent relation to its mother (in particular, her breast), Stacey considers how this informs an oscillating relationship between paranoia and reparation. She notes that 'the infant loves the good object that feeds and satisfies it but it hates the bad object that inevitably frustrates its needs', during the experience of which the figure of the breast/mother is split into a good and bad object (Stacey 2014: 44). In Kleinian object-relations theory, this good/bad division will result in the infant's 'fear and suspicion' of the breast (a phrase Klein registers as the paranoid/schizoid position), which is challenged or 'superseded' by the later discovery that 'the breast it hates and loves are the same breast' (the Kleinian depressive position) (ibid.). The 'constant *interaction* of love and hate' (in the words of Klein) towards the same object the infant experiences leads Stacey to the conclusion that reparation is not a process 'born solely of love' (43). Rather, it is in an oscillatory relationship with paranoia since they are in fact from the same source.[16]

The oscillating relationship between paranoia and reparation provides a useful model for an examination of how neo-Victorian fiction, a genre that seems to be preoccupied with a paranoid impulse to demystify the past, could prompt the reader to read reparatively. By staging a nostalgic, if paranoid, longing for an 'immersion' into the (alternative) past, neo-Victorian literature plays with the reader's generic reading expectations and desires. It also urges readers to reflect upon their reading motivations and desires by confronting them with often painful and unsettling versions of the past. In prompting the reader to reflect on their routine habits of perception, the neo-Victorian genre helps to develop the reader's self-knowledge and their understanding of intersubjective relations to reparative ends. This is arguably where the political and ethical power of neo-Victorian narrative lies. Here I understand the political in the sense Jeffrey Karnicky uses: 'politics is psychology as it plays out in groups larger than two' (Williams qtd in Karnicky 2007: 69). Focusing on the way in which neo-Victorian literature invites the reader to feel with, believe in,

---

[16] Diana Fuss makes a similar point in her rereading of Freud's analysis of Schreber. To her, the case of Schreber not only exemplifies suspicious reading, but also demonstrates 'one man's restorative and reparative efforts to live in the world again' (2017: 354).

and make judgements through its literary representation of the Victorian(s), this book demonstrates the significance of neo-Victorian literature to the study of narrative ethics.[17] It chooses to explore the complicated ethical agenda of neo-Victorianism from the perspective of empathy, a concept that plays with issues of subjectivity and intersubjectivity in a profound manner, as my following review of the study of empathy will demonstrate.

Genealogy of empathy

Comparing the reparative reader to the 'more loving one' (Auden [1960] 2007), Hilary Hinds summarizes the key features of reparative reading as follows: 'Intimate with or proximate to the object of study; open to and welcoming of the surprises that the text may spring on the reader; generous to the particularities of the text's character and processes, and to its manifest identifications of its agendas and purposes; and accepting of the text's limitations and weaknesses' (2017: para. 10). Although Hinds does not use the word empathy itself, the 'generous' and 'accepting' critical practice she delineates here is, in essence, an empathetic one. Drawing on a range of critical theories of empathy, I demonstrate the role empathy plays in (re)shaping intersubjective relationships and the reparative potential of empathetic reading.

As a growing inter- and cross-disciplinary field of investigation, empathy has received a good deal of attention from several academic disciplines in recent years, including neuroscience, social psychology, philosophy and literary studies. Although empathy and its historical 'precursor' sympathy have played an important role in the Western intellectual tradition, empathy itself is a diffused concept whose definition is under constant negotiation and

---

[17] Narrative ethics has been a recurrent debate in literary criticism in recent years. Unlike Wayne Booth and Martha Nussbaum, who are loyal 'guardians' of the liberal humanist values, critics such as Andrew Gibson (1999) and Rebecca N. Mitchell (2011) have applied Levinasian ethics – and in particular, his notion of 'radical alterity' – in their respective readings of (post)modern novels and Victorian fiction. To both Gibson and Mitchell, the ethical power of narrative lies in its emphasis on the singularity of the other's experience. Neo-Victorian fiction can be seen as playing with both models of narrative ethics through its use of various realist and postmodern narrative devices and its engagement with different literary genres.

interrogation. This becomes a problem for the study of empathy since it is 'difficult to keep track of which process or mental state the term is being used to refer to in any given discussion' (Coplan [2011] 2014: 4). Sharing Amy Coplan's concern, this book traces the development of the concept of empathy and its role in different fields of philosophy, psychology and aesthetics, including eighteenth-century Scottish moral philosophy on sentimental value (David Hume and Adam Smith), late-nineteenth- and early-twentieth-century aesthetics (Robert Vischer, Theodor Lipps and Vernon Lee), phenomenology (Edmund Husserl, Edith Stein and Dan Zahavi) and psychoanalysis (Heinz Kohut). This is done with the aim of providing a broader context for this book's examination of how neo-Victorianism engages with, and also contributes to, the study of empathy. Given its inherent dialogicality and preoccupation with issues such as intersubjectivity and subjectivity, neo-Victorian literature is presented as a useful platform for the exploration of the mechanism of empathy, its implications for morality and ethics in the reading process and the related political controversies.

Empathy as a word only entered English in the early-twentieth century as a coined translation of the German word *Einfühlung* by the English psychologist Edward B. Titchener (1909).[18] By then Titchener has already translated a number of German psychological terms for English-speaking students. In explaining his choice of vocabulary Titchener suggests that he wants to translate the German terms by way of their 'Latin-Greek origin', since this is a general practice in the field of natural sciences such as physics and chemistry (1895: 79). Derived from the Greek word *empatheia*, empathy carries the meaning of 'strong "pathos" and "feeling"' and is used by psychologists to refer to the self's perception of the other's mental status (Lanzoni 2018: 51). The German word *Einfühlung*, however, did not start as a psychological term. Coined by the German Romantic philosopher Robert Vischer in his 1873 doctoral thesis *On the Optical Sense of Form: A Contribution to Aesthetics* (*Über das Optische Formgefühl: Ein Beitrag zur Aesthetik*), *Einfühlung* is initially used to describe the encounter between the observing subject and the phenomenal object during aesthetic activities, a point I will discuss in detail in relation

---

[18] Although the term 'empathy' first appeared in psychological textbooks in 1909, it became the generally accepted translation in 1913 (Lanzoni 2018: 9).

to neo-Victorian aesthetics in Chapter 4. Vischer's focus on the embodied experience between humans and nature in his use of *Einfühlung* is adopted and further developed by another German philosopher, Theodor Lipps, who, proposes that the concept of *Einfühlung* must also become 'a fundamental concept of psychology' and 'the fundamental concept of sociology' (qtd in Pigman 1995: 242).[19] Linking aesthetic empathy with cognitive psychology, Lipps suggests *Einfühlung* is essential for the formation of self-consciousness. According to his observation, in viewing objects 'I necessarily permeate them with … striving, activity, and power. Grasped by reason, they bear within them, insofar as they are "my" objects, this piece of myself' (qtd in Koss 2006: 143–4). Focusing on 'my' input, Lipps perceives *Einfühlung* as an experience of 'self-perception' (Allesch 2017: 231). He asserts that it is 'me or my ego that is the cause of aesthetic pleasure; namely exactly the same ego which I am aware as pleased or delighted "in view of" or "confronted with" the object' (qtd in Allesch 2017: 231). Rae Greiner explains that Lipps posits *Einfühlung* as 'the engine of self-consciousness', which 'depends on my ability to humanize objects, including the object that is myself' (2011: 417). Although Lipps's self-orientated formulation of *Einfühlung* is criticized by later theorists as being egoistic, it in fact anticipates recent psychological discovery, that empathy is 'a prerequisite for the development of emotions and the notion of a self' (Assmann and Detmers 2016: 2).

Lipps's *Spatial Aesthetics and Optical Illusions* (1897) relates the idea of *Einfühlung* to the British author Vernon Lee, who is credited with advocating the term in British aestheticism.[20] Comparing the psycho-aesthetic concept of *Einfühlung* to sympathy, Lee and her co-author Clementina Anstruther-Thomson write:

---

[19] The different attitudes Vischer and Lipps hold towards *Einfühlung* have led to some confusion and skepticism about the concept itself. For Husserl, as Dan Zahavi notes, it remains 'unclear whether the term is meant to designate the projection of one's own self into a foreign body, or rather the actual encounter with a foreign embodied self' (2014: 114).

[20] Benjamin Morgan (2012) provides a detailed review of the development of Lee's views and writings on aesthetics. Morgan notes that the essay she co-writes with Clementina Anstruther-Thomson, 'Beauty and Ugliness' (1897), is inspired by Walter Pater, who, in his *The Renaissance* ([1873] 1980), posed a series of questions about the human body's physiological responses to art. However, at that time, Lee was not aware of the theories of Lipps (Morgan 2012: 37). Lee's subsequent encounter with German psychology made her aware that Lipps's conceptualization of *Einfühlung* could better explain some of her and Anstruther-Thomson's embodied experience to art. Her essay collection *Beauty and Ugliness* (1912) records Lee's reflection on this topic (37–8). Morgan also points out

This phenomenon of aesthetic *Einfuhlung* [...] is therefore analogous to that of moral sympathy. Just as when we 'put ourselves in the place' or, more vulgarly, 'in the skin' of a fellow-creature, we are, in fact, attributing to him the feelings we should have in similar circumstances; so, in looking at the Doric column [...] we are attributing to the lines and surfaces, to the spatial forms, those dynamic experiences which we should have were we to put our bodies into similar conditions. (1912: 20)

Lipps's writing on *Einfühlung* provides Lee with a useful concept to restore art's moral value. However, Lee's advocation of morality is irrelevant to 'Victorian puritanism' (Burdett 2011a: para. 3). Dissatisfied with 'the moral impasses' that features 'fin-de-siècle politics and culture' (Burdett 2011a: para. 5), Lee inherits 'notions of beauty and goodness' from eighteenth-century Romanticists in associating sensory bodies with 'moral forms of right feeling' (Burdett 2011b: 259–60). Through the mechanism of *Einfühlung*, Lee and Anstruther-Thomson explore the effects of art from perspectives other than representation: 'This special activity is the interpretation of form according to the facts of our own inner experience, the attribution to form of modes of being, moving, and feeling similar to our own; and this projection of our own life into what we see is pleasant or unpleasant because it facilitates or hampers our own vitality' (1912: 17). Together with Anstruther-Thomson, Lee also explores how the aesthetic and psychological experience of *Einfühlung* transforms or destabilizes identity in an autobiographical manner.[21]

Another important point to note is that Lee's notion of 'sympathy' is similar to modern understanding of 'empathy', the meaning of which, in turn, is derived from the writings of eighteenth-century philosophers David Hume and Adam Smith. The entangled relationship between these two terms, however, does not suggest that the modern use of empathy serves to renew Humean sympathy in contemporary discourse. Rather, as Rae Greiner points out, it 'seeks to answer different questions or to answer old ones in new ways', referring to empathy's

---

that it is Lee's later publication – *The Beautiful* (1913) – that helps to disseminate 'the concept of empathy in Anglo-American aesthetics' (42).

[21] In their co-authored article 'Beauty and Ugliness' (1897), Lee and Anstruther-Thomson record and reflect on their physiological reactions to the art works they have observed during various trips they made across continental Europe during the 1890s. The romance between these two adds a queer and erotic dimension to their aesthetic experience. Daniel Maltz's remark that 'to tell a story of psychological aesthetics is to tell a love story' points to the intensive emotional entanglements *Einfühlung* involves (1999: 212).

aesthetic origin and its role in classical debates about how we perceive the other's feelings and minds, respectively (2012: n.p.). Taking the nuanced differences into consideration, modern theories of empathy can be divided into two categories: one tends to consider it as 'an ephemeral and contingent affective state' that can be provoked by a range of emotive circumstances and 'is hardly more than a somatic reflex' (Assmann and Detmers 2016: 5); the other sees empathy as a mechanism that needs conscious endeavour. For the first model of empathy, neuroscientists' recent research on 'mirror neurons' provides scientific evidence.[22] Defined as 'premotor neurons that fire both when an action is executed and when it is observed being performed by someone else' (Gallese 2009: 520), the discovery of mirror neurons suggests that human minds are 'installed' with the ability to imitate another's emotional state; empathy is therefore construed as a 'hardwired' mechanism that lays the foundation for an advanced sense of morality in human beings.[23] Behavioural scientist Marco Iacoboni claims mirror neurons 'are the foundations of empathy and the possibility of morality, a morality that is deeply rooted in our biology' (2008: 4–5). In spite of the scientific dispute about the existence of mirror neurons in the human brain and its role in action observation and execution, the biological perception of empathy – and in particular, the focus on the mechanism of mirroring in the transmissibility of emotions – resembles Hume's speculation of human minds as 'mirrors to one another', by which Hume meant that human beings can 'reflect each other's emotion' and these emotions 'may often be reverberated' (1978: 365). Hume also described the

[22] The lab of the Italian neuroscientist Giacomo Rizzolatti 'discovered' the 'mirror neurons' in 1993 in a series of experiments they conducted on pigtail macaque monkeys. According to their findings, there is 'a distinctive class of neurons' in their brain that 'discharge both when the monkey executes a motor act and when it observes another individual (a human being or another monkey) performing the same or a similar motor act' (Rizzolatti and Destro 2008: para. 1). Scientists therefore use the term 'mirror neurons' in a figurative way to explain the function of these neurons. Later, the mirror neuron system is used by a group of scientists to explain the mechanism of empathy (see Rizzolatti and Craighero 2004; Decety and Lamm 2006). Gregory Hickok interrogates the main theories of mirror neurons in detail in his 2014 book.

[23] The discovery of mirror neurons has also led to the massive publication of books on the popular science of empathy. A simple relevant search on the shopping website Amazon shows over ten thousand relevant items. Carolyn Pedwell explains this phenomenon as closely related to 'both mainstream neo-Darwinian discourses of "emotional intelligence"' and 'neoliberal requirements for affective dexterity and management in the capitalist market place', a point that demonstrates the interconnectedness between science, culture and ideology (2014: 40).

mirroring capacity of human beings in a quite animated manner: 'As in strings equally wound up, the motion of one communicates itself to the rest; so all the affections readily pass from one person to another, and beget correspondent movements in every human creature' (576).

The other group considers empathy as a mechanism that can be voluntarily accessed and trained through the imagination. It 'comprises a complex, artful but also effortful practice that enrolls feelings, intellect, and imagination' (Lanzoni 2018: 280). The key features of this notion of empathy have already been discussed by Adam Smith under the term sympathy. In *The Theory of Moral Sentiments*' ([1976] 1982), Smith proposed an imagination-based model of sympathy and made imagination a central plank of his moral theory: 'By the imagination we place ourselves in his situation, we conceive ourselves enduing all the same torments, we enter as it were into his body, and become in some measure the same person with him, and thence form some idea of his sensations, and even feel something, which, though weaker in degree, is not altogether unlike them' (9). Smith's emphasis on the role of imagination presents sympathy as a *conscious* act of perspective-taking that is coupled with 'intellectual and imaginative power' as well as 'will' (Greiner 2009: 294), a model that is taken and developed by the contemporary philosopher Amy Coplan (as we will see in Chapter 1 in relation to the ethical controversies associated with suspicious reading in neo-Victorian fiction). It also positions the sympathizer as a human subject who has the cognitive and affective faculties to perceive, comprehend and vicariously experience the other's mental state, therefore bringing out an issue about the power dynamic between the sympathizer and the sympathized. This is arguably where Smith's conception of sympathy differs from that of Hume. As Brigid Lowe explains, 'Smith seeks to replace Hume's celebration of sympathy as a fundamental principle of radically intersubjective communication, as the spontaneous and passionate subjective dispersal that is the raw material of society, with a model of sympathy as distance, spectatorship, impartiality, control and subjective consolidation' (2007: 9–10). Lowe's account maps out the inherent asymmetry in sympathy: the one who sympathizes is positioned in a privileged place which allows him/her to make judgements about the one who is being sympathized. The issue about the dynamic that exists between the two subjects in the mechanism of sympathy – or empathy (as in my book) – is essential for my following discussion of the ethics and politics of reading, and will be interrogated through different conceptualizations of empathy in the chapters that follow.

Considered as a touchstone for morality, sympathy is also widely explored and advocated by the Victorians as a response to 'the increasingly urban, disconnected, and morally uncertain world of full-blown capitalism' (Greiner 2012: n.p.). Victorian social-problem novelists, such as Charles Dickens, Elizabeth Gaskell and George Eliot, 'articulate a project for the cultivation of the sympathetic imagination' in their writings (Keen [2007] 2010: 38). This is often done through the realist representation of serious social issues including poverty, child labour, violence against women and so on. By encouraging readers to take up the position of the sympathizer, Victorian fiction demonstrates the ways in which Smith's model of sympathy operates in the reading of fiction. Ian Duncan explains that Smith's writings on sympathetic transaction 'constitute the modern subject as a reader' (1998: 42). The spectator-like sympathizer does not find sympathy per se 'in' the (textual) other or their own psychology; rather, it is activated in a 'dialogical' manner (47).[24] Considering sympathy as 'a process rather than a feeling', Greiner proposes that sympathy is 'built into the structure of (and not merely thematized by) realism' (2011: 418). The same can be said of neo-Victorian fiction, a genre that is, as previously argued, essentially dialogic. Here it is also worth noting that this book is not only concerned with contemporary writers' exploration of the theme of empathy in their imaginative reconstruction of the nineteenth century, but also the empathetic engagement between literary texts and their readers.

In her field-defining work, Suzanne Keen takes up *both* Hume's model of the embodied process of sharing and Smith's conscious imaginative perspective-taking in her conceptualization of 'narrative empathy' as 'the sharing of feeling and perspective-taking induced by reading, viewing, hearing, or imagining narratives of another's situation and condition' (2013: para. 1). Although Keen's understanding of narrative empathy is built upon the work of Hume and Smith on sympathy, she is aware of how these two terms – sympathy and empathy – differ from each other in contemporary

---

[24] Focusing on the Victorian middle-class's social status as 'spectator', Kirsty Martin makes an interesting link between issues of 'visuality and representation' and sympathy in Victorian fiction (2013: 8).

philosophical and psychological debates. As she explains, empathy is 'the spontaneous, responsive sharing of an appropriate feeling', while sympathy is 'the more complex, differentiated feeling for another' (Keen [2007] 2010: 4). In today's Western culture, empathy is typically understood as a mechanism by which we 'feel with', while sympathy is to 'feel for'; hence *I feel your pain* is an empathetic gesture while *I feel pity for your pain* is being sympathetic (5; original emphasis). The current understanding of sympathy has drifted away from the eighteenth-century perspective. The term is no longer used to refer to affective communications between subjects; instead, it now entails an emotional and moral judgement. Meanwhile, the earlier meaning of sympathy has been incorporated into the contemporary perception of empathy.

In light of Keen's research on narrative empathy, this book examines the ways in which the neo-Victorian text involves the reader in an empathetic engagement with the textual other. It aims to answer the following two questions: Is empathy necessarily ethical? In which ways does reading – or the empathetic engagement with the textual other – prompt the reader to imagine and possibly become involved in the projection and construction of a different future? Using neo-Victorianism as a platform for the exploration of the relationship between empathy and ethics, this book also takes up the link Mark Currie builds between the acts of reading and living (as discussed above) in its engagement with the recent debate about the role empathy plays in the current political landscape. In what follows, I move to a discussion of the rhetoric of empathy in politics and historiography, drawing upon the work of Lauren Berlant, Meghan Marie Hammond, Sue J. Kim, Paul Bloom and Dominic LaCapra in order to better contextualize the examination of the political and ethical implications of empathy.

Transformative promises

Contemporary politics seems to have inherited the eighteenth-century Scottish moral philosophy on sentimental value in its hailing of empathy as a key catalyst for social justice and community construction. Speaking at the 2020 Democratic National Convention (which is still ongoing as I am writing this book), the former first lady of the United States Michelle Obama blasts Donald

Trump as an incompetent president who shows an 'utter lack of empathy' (Obama 2020: n.p.). This blistering criticism of Trump is nothing new. Since his inauguration in 2017, Trump's controversial presidency has sparked plenty of psychoanalytical discussions of his narcissistic and hyperbolic self-display and his apparent lack of interest in cultivating social integration. Empathy is a term that has been used repeatedly in these evaluations. In addressing the challenging issues which America is now confronted with (such as the Covid-19 pandemic, an inadequate healthcare system and racial discrimination), Michelle Obama's attack on Trump's lack of empathy is premised on the belief that empathy itself is a powerful actor in efficient governmentality and social justice. Indeed, the Obama couple have long advocated the moral and political value of empathy. To them, current American society is characterized by what Barack Obama called 'empathy deficit' in his 2006 commencement address to graduates of Northwestern University, with the connotation that people's unwillingness to feel with – or to imagine the sufferings of – *others* results in the various manifestations of social divisions and political conflicts that we witness in twenty-first-century America (Obama 2006: n.p.). In the words of Anthony Clohesy, the 'empathic experience of difference' is perceived as a powerful response to contemporary crises of cultural and political polarization (2013: 2).

Yet is Trump as unempathetic as many of his critics suggest? The fact that Trump's supporters stand by him regardless of his personal scandals and incompetent governmentality tells a different story: Trump seems to have a magnificent power to evoke admiration from a certain group of people and their identification with him may be thought of as a kind of solid empathy (which challenges the usual conception of empathy as an ephemeral and volatile response/feeling). Indeed, writing for *The Guardian* in 2017, psychiatrist Richard A. Friedman labels Trump as 'a master of empathy' who strengthens his supporters' loyalty by 'stok[ing] their fear' (n.p.). Fritz Breithaupt makes a slightly different argument in *The Dark Sides of Empathy* (2019) by suggesting that Trump uses 'the scheme of one-against-all' (specified as Trump's self-positioning as 'the victim of a media conspiracy' and the one 'standing up against false elites, intellectuals, other countries, foreign influences') to present himself as 'the great victim who deserves support, pity, and empathy' (105–6).[25]

---

[25] Writing against the background of the financial crisis in 2008, Tammy Amiel Houser argues that the public turn to Trump could be considered as their rejection of 'the neoliberal embrace of

In spite of their different understandings of the strategies Trump uses in cultivating empathy from his supporters, both writers acknowledge Trump's ability to build and sustain emotional connections with people of certain backgrounds, which leads to a troubling question about the political value of empathy: is empathy as efficient in promoting social unity as many of us are willing to believe? As a particular form of intersubjective communication, empathy gestures towards not only inclusiveness – specified as feeling with others who are different from us – but also exclusiveness.[26] Michelle Obama's emphasis on the role empathy plays in the formation of *American* character in the aforementioned speech is a useful reference: the use of the adjective 'American' clearly delineates the national boundary of the empathy she champions here, which also links the virtue of empathy to 'the promotion of American cultural and moral exceptionalism' (Pedwell 2012b: 288). Whether the previous first lady of America is willing to acknowledge it or not, the kind of empathy she advocates does share some similarity with the one we witness in the Trump phenomenon: both occur within an in-group, although the groups involved are different in many aspects.

Empathy has become not only a prevailing culture in contemporary politics, but also a virtue that is essential for community life. The suicide-prevention charity, the Samaritans, is one of those institutions that claim to put empathy and trust into practice in offering 'support to people and communities in times of need' (The Samaritans n.p.). It describes itself as dedicated to the promotion of 'moments of connection between people' and sees empathy as a key factor in building those kinds of connections. The way the Samaritans works – through the act of listening – points to the unique nature of empathetic communication, that it is a matter of 'personal agency' and 'individual emotion' (Garber

---

empathy', specified as the uncontested link between empathy and social justice that prevails public and political discourses (2019: 26).

[26] This point also relates to debates in phenomenology more generally about whether any expression of intentionality is problematic inasmuch as it depends upon the privileging of one set of relationships at the expense of other. In the field of geography studies, e.g., post-phenomenologists take the lead of Levinas and become especially critical or uneasy about any expressions of 'belonging' to a landscape or location because it is predicated on the exclusion of others. However, as Paul Harrison points out, 'the very concept of the nonrelational threatens to undermine the status of commitment and mutual understanding and to offer little in their place but despair and solitude' (2007: 598). As I go on to explain, the call for empathy in political rhetoric involves the desire for relationality, which is part of the ontology of human beings and plays an essential role in the formation of any identifiable community (although this tendency can also be mobilized, politically, to dangerous ends).

2004: 24). By returning us to the private world, empathy nevertheless risks the danger of neglecting the structural and systematic causes of personal crises. For Lauren Berlant, this is the core issue of sentimental politics:

> When sentimentality meets politics, it uses personal stories to tell of structural effects, but in so doing it risks thwarting its very attempt to perform rhetorically a scene of pain that must be soothed politically. Because the ideology of true feeling cannot admit the nonuniversality of pain, its cases become all jumbled together and the ethical imperative toward social transformation is replaced by a civic-minded but passive ideal of empathy. The political as a place of acts oriented toward publicness becomes replaced by a world of private thoughts, leanings, and gestures. (1998: 641)

Berlant's concern about the political value of the sentimental narrative is valid: charities like the Samaritans arguably relocate the issue of 'social interdependence' from the structural to 'a visible, lived-in community' (2004: 3). The rhetoric of empathy in politics is problematic precisely because of the transformative possibilities – or 'cruel optimism' as Berlant alternatively calls it in her 2011 book – it promises. The kind of 'national sentimentality' empathy channels promises solidarity 'across fields of social difference' (Berlant 2000: 34) so as to 'eradicate systemic social pain' (35). Empathetic politics is, nevertheless, 'animated by neoliberal and neoimperial logics' (Pedwell 2014: xiv). Berlant explains that sentimental politics constitutes 'the ethics of privilege', referring to the moral obligation political virtues such as compassion and affective identification involve (2004: 1). The sentimental narrative works best 'when relatively privileged citizens are exposed to the suffering of their intimate Others', and in these scenarios, 'to be virtuous requires feeling the pain of flawed or denied citizenship as their own pain' (Berlant 2000: 35). The power hierarchy inherent in the discourse of sentimental narrative reveals the perilous and problematic aspect of affective politics, that it involves 'a liberal fantasy of knowing the Other without actually understanding histories of structural oppression and violence' (Hammond and Kim 2014: 9). Clare Hemmings also notes that 'the *enjoyment* of authority and judgment [...] remains with the one who empathises' (2012: 154, original emphasis).

Berlant's concern about the ethical and political value of sentimental narrative is shared by a number of critics. Taking a more precise focus,

Paul Bloom launches a trenchant critique of the perception of empathy as 'a powerful force for goodness and moral change' in his discussion of contemporary politics of sentimentality in *Against Empathy: The Case for Rational Compassion* (2016: 2). In recognition of its 'spotlight' nature, Bloom suggests that empathy navigates the general public's attention to 'certain people in the here and now' (9), leading to the dangerous possibility that 'one individual can [be felt to] matter more than a hundred', a point that echoes but is also discrepant from Berlant's discussion about the contradiction between the personal and the public spheres in sentimental politics (89). Bloom's uneasiness about the political mobilization of affective identification has particular relevance for the highly developed media society we live in. Indeed, in a time when the internet is inundated with sentimental discourses of pain and suffering, it seems plausible that we may become either emotionally numb or unable to go beyond our fleeting and arguably surface emotional transactions with the other. It is therefore easy to be suspicious about the extent to which empathy can push forward 'proper' social changes. However, the premise of Bloom's objection to empathy – that empathy itself facilitates social justice – constitutes a 'teleological' understanding of the term (Pedwell 2014: 35). Carolyn Pedwell further elaborates that the perception of empathy as a kind of 'affective remedy implicitly supposes a natural telos or end-point, at which tensions have been eased and antagonisms rectified' (ibid.). Featuring both affective and cognitive relations between subjects, empathy is better understood as a mechanism – or what Rae Greiner calls a 'process' – a point that has been dealt with in the previous section. The focus of this book, then, is not to teach readers any moral lesson about empathy (as will be seen, this is a complex and hotly contested debate that has a long way to run). Rather, it is interested in exploring how neo-Victorian fiction *stages* various kinds of text–reader relationship and the role empathy plays in that dynamic engagement. In light of Sedgwick's model of reparative reading, my approach to neo-Victorian fiction also reveals its double consciousness of time, without any intention to assert that the projected future in neo-Victorian narrative is necessarily better.

My selection of neo-Victorian novels engages with these ethical and political controversies of empathy self-consciously. Focusing on characters that are either vulnerable to empathetic exploitation or difficult (if not impossible) to empathize with, this book is primarily interested in the unsettling experience of empathy afforded by neo-Victorian fiction. In his work on Holocaust narrative, historian Dominick LaCapra (1999) proposes the useful concept of 'empathetic unsettlement', referring to the ethnographer or witness's critical self-consciousness about the alterity of the other during their affective engagement with traumatized others. LaCapra explains that empathetic unsettlement 'involves a kind of virtual experience through which one puts oneself in the other's position while recognizing the difference of that position and hence not taking the other's place' (722). The feeling of unsettlement is situated in the empathizer 'who not only recognizes (rather than erases) difference but also recognizes how empathetic practices participate in defining (or contextualizing) others' (Shuman 2011: 168). Different from boundaryless identification, empathy constitutes not only the self's perception – but also plays an important role in the formation – of the target subject's otherness. The capacity for empathy, writes Briethaupt, 'speaks to the structure of the person as a whole', a point that emphasizes the importance of self-other differentiation in identity construction (43). As a kind of 'reflexive approach' (Ward 2012: 3), the concept of empathetic unsettlement is useful for my exploration of how neo-Victorian narratives of the suffering of others prompt the reader to reflect on their own readerly desires and their potential complicity in the other's experience of exploitation, a reading process that also challenges the reader's 'normative ways of thinking and being' (Koopman 2010: 240) and practices their ability to imagine different kinds of intersubjective relationships in both textual and non-textual worlds. The experience of unsettling empathy therefore points to the possibility of a reparative engagement with the (textual) other. As the following chapter outline further demonstrates, the feeling of unsettlement is often evoked through the use of disruption in narrative, which may take the form of hermeneutic uncertainty (Chapter 1), retrospective narrative and narratological intrusion (Chapter 2), textual refusal against readerly expectation (Chapter 3) and lack of emotional connection (Chapter 4).

Chapter overview

This book is structured by four different approaches to the study of empathy in neo-Victorian literature and culture: the model of cognitive perspective-taking, the phenomenological conception of empathy, the psychological approach to empathy and the aesthetic conceptualization of *Einfühlung* (the German etymological origin of the English term empathy). These models of empathy are chosen due to their relevance for the particular reading pleasures afforded by neo-Victorian fiction that I explore in the following chapters, including erotic voyeurism and suspicious reading in Chapter 1, shameful or shameless consumption in Chapter 2, reparative empathy in Chapter 3 and affective embodiment in Chapter 4. In each chapter, I apply one model of empathy in examining the way chosen neo-Victorian novels satisfy and/or frustrate readerly desires and expectations so as to contribute to the discussion of the reading pleasures of neo-Victorian literature, which, as argued in the previous section, is often limited to a self-confirming critical knowingness or omniscience. In light of Sedgwick's critique of paranoid reading, I propose that this kind of 'readerly narcissism' makes it difficult for the reader to imagine a different future. With a focus on the way neo-Victorian fiction disrupts the reader's identificatory and immersive reading process, this book also highlights the significance of unsettling empathy in the reader's projection and construction of alternative futures in both fictional and real worlds.

Chapter 1 argues that, through the use of hermeneutic uncertainty, neo-Victorian fiction involves the reader in an unsettling empathetic engagement with the past, which prompts them to envisage, and ultimately work towards, alternative futures both in terms of textual outcomes and how they relate to 'unknowable' situations in the material world. Through a close reading of two neo-Victorian texts that are concerned with mystery-solving – Jane Harris's *The Observations* and Margaret Atwood's *Alias Grace* – I demonstrate the dynamic that exists between suspicious reading and empathy in neo-Victorian literature. In particular, I focus on the ways in which these texts play with the narratological conventions of crime fiction in probing the question of whether the reader's empathetic engagement with the text facilitates or frustrates the textual pleasures associated with mystery, suspense and problem-solving. To this end, I engage with Amy Coplan's cognitive approach to empathy – and in particular, her differentiation between 'self-orientated perspective-taking' and 'other-orientated perspective-taking'. This helps us to sketch out some of the complex ethical issues associated with the reading processes: notably, the often paranoid impulse to demystify the unsettling experience of engaging with the vulnerable characters that have become such a staple of neo-Victorian fiction. In terms of my textual rationale, Atwood's *Alias Grace* is a fitting point of departure for an ethical approach to neo-Victorian literature on account of the way in which it both thematizes and promotes the ethical issues associated with suspicious reading.

Chapter 2 shifts our attention from the cryptic narrative properties of neo-Victorian texts and the mystery-solving (un)pleasures these create for the reader, to the reader's affective relationship with the characters. It examines how the explicit focus on the extremely uncomfortable feeling of shame in two neo-Victorian texts – Sarah Waters's *Tipping the Velvet* and *Affinity* – disrupts the reader's immersive consumption of the Victorian underworld and involves them in the character's shame. Putting the phenomenological conception of empathy and Silvan Tomkins's affect theory into dialogue, I argue that shame and empathy are opposite manifestations of the same intersubjective relationship. In so doing I shift away from the established 'symptomatic reading' of shame as signs of repressed or 'deviant' sexuality and move to a reparative exploration of the political productivity of shame, and in particular, its role in the transformation of subjectivity and intersubjectivity. With a focus on the use of retrospective narrative and narratorial intrusion in both novels, I demonstrate how the mechanism of shame is built into the narrative structure of Waters's writings and its implication for the reader's affective empathy. Meanwhile, the reason I chose Waters's texts for this exploration is because their exploration of queer sexuality and lesbian desire provokes, as well as appeals to, the reader's 'shameless' reading expectations of – and desires for – an understanding of lesbian sexuality.

By contrast, Chapter 3 moves to a discussion of the reader's more intellectual inability to empathize with certain fictional characters, narrators and implied authors and for reasons other than embarrassment or shame. With reference to Michael Cox's debut novel *The Meaning of Night*, the chapter proposes that this *failure of empathy* may be linked to issues of contingency and solipsism (as defined in Jean-Paul Sartre's account of existentialism in his 1938 philosophical novel *Nausea*) in the neo-Victorian text in question. Through a close reading of Sartre's novel and the American psychoanalyst Heinz Kohut's work on narcissism and empathy, I construe the inclusion of an 'interlocutory other' in Cox's novel as symptomatic of the text's desire for an empathetic response to its morally reprehensible character, even if this is a response that we, as readers, are reluctant to give. Also, with reference to Sartre, I explain this reluctance in terms of the character's 'bad faith' (i.e. his exercise of violence at the expense of the innocent other) and propose that the 'nausea' experienced by the character on account of his existential insecurity is quickly transferred to the reader. Cox's text presented itself as an obvious choice for this discussion on account of its thematic engagement with contingency (the central protagonist, Edward Glyver, reflects upon his dilemma in language very similar to Sartre's Roquentin) and the fact that it challenges the reader's empathy for Edward by identifying him as a murderer on the very first page. In this chapter, I also draw upon Graeme Macrae Burnet's *His Bloody Project* (2015) – a recent neo-Victorian text which also seems to explain violence against others in existential rather than psychological terms – in presenting some of the more complex ways in which a reader's ethical and moral stance is tested. While it is one thing to engage reparatively with a text which features characters who are the victims of injustice, it is quite another to extend the same openness and generosity to texts whose characters' reprehensible actions cannot be easily accounted for in terms of their psychology or social oppression.

Leaving the discussion of the reader's empathetic engagement with fictional characters per se, in the fourth and final chapter I instead move to an exploration of the dynamic that exists between space, place and empathy in neo-Victorian literature and culture. Here, I trace the idea of empathy back to its origin in nineteenth-century German aesthetics. By drawing upon Harry Francis Mallgrave and Eleftherios Ikonomou's work on the writing of Robert Vischer (who, as we have seen, coined the term *Einfühlung* in 1873), I demonstrate the role that corporeal movement plays in involving the viewing subject affectively in both the art work and landscape. In order to better illustrate Vischer's idea, I begin this chapter with a discussion of the architectural replicas of English townscapes in Shanghai, China. I suggest that although these replicas are not exclusively neo-Victorian in practice (being 'mash-ups' of many different historical periods), the dynamic they promote between the visitor and the landscape is similar to the one that exists between the (international) consumers and the simulated landscape of late-nineteenth- and early-twentieth-century England in neo-Victorian filmic and TV adaptations.

However, the kind of immersive pleasure afforded by these filmic texts is arguably disrupted by a good deal of neo-Victorian fiction. With reference to Margaret Atwood's *Alias Grace* and Julian Barnes's *Arthur & George*, this chapter demonstrates the ways in which neo-Victorian literature frustrates the contemporary reader's desire to 'enter' or 'empathize with' the simulated landscape of the past for different purposes. In the case of *Alias Grace*, the chapter examines the ways in which Grace's empathetic engagement with her surroundings is presented as part of her psychological disorder; Grace is, as it were, a subject who is 'too close' to the material spaces she inhabits. This is then contrasted with Barnes's characterization of the protagonist George, a mixed-race (Scottish/Indian) solicitor, who is presented as a habitual walker and regular train commuter, and is also distinguished by his peculiar inability to relate to the landscape through which he passes. Whereas Grace, then, is 'too close' to what she sees, George is too 'distant'. This comparative reading also demonstrates the political and ethical controversies associated with empathy, which have been at the heart of the book as a whole. While in Atwood's text, Grace's 'over-identification' with the non-human 'other' questions the practice of empathy in terms which are similar to Vischer's, Barnes's portrayal of George's alienation in terms of both place and nationhood reminds us how debilitating it can be not to have this emotional connection with your surroundings. Although a good deal has now been written about *Arthur and George* in a neo-Victorian and postcolonial context, my focus on George's 'outsider' status as an effect of his 'failure of empathy' lends a new dimension to the discussion by shifting our focus from the human to the non-human. This also relates to the chapter's focus on the ways in which readers and viewers can sometimes struggle to immerse themselves in the 'landscapes' of texts unless they have pre-existing schemas or stereotypes available to help them.

By bringing recent cultural and theoretical research on narrative temporality, empathy and affect together, this book presents neo-Victorian literature as a genre defined by its experimentation with empathetic narrative. With a focus on the modes and effects of storytelling and reading, I examine the ways in which neo-Victorian fiction facilitates and/or challenges the empathetic engagement between the text and the reader. This kind of text–reader relationship, I argue, involves the reader in the (construction of the) textual world affectively. Also, through an interrogation of the portrayal of the often painful and unsettling version of the past in the text, I propose that neo-Victorian literature not only prompts the reader to critically reflect upon their reading expectations and strategies, as well as their wider ethical responsibilities, but also encourages them to envisage a potentially different future for both the character(s) in the text and human behaviour in general.

1

Suspicious reading

Initially delivered as the Bronfman Lecture at the University of Ottawa in 1996, and later published as an article in 1997, Margaret Atwood's 'In Search of *Alias Grace*: On Writing Canadian Historical Fiction' traces her writing of the novel. There she uses the example of Nathaniel Hawthorne's *The Scarlet Letter* (1850) in demonstrating the importance of revisiting the past in addressing contemporary anxieties and crises:

> However, it was out of this questioning and assessing climate – where did we come from, how did we get from there to here, where are we going, who are we now – that Nathaniel Hawthorne wrote *The Scarlet Letter*, a historical novel set in seventeenth-century New England. […] *The Scarlet Letter* is not, of course, seventeenth century in any way the Puritans would have recognized. […] Instead, it's a novel that uses a seventeenth-century New England Colonial setting for the purposes of a newly forged nineteenth-century American Republic. And I think that's part of the interest for writers and readers of Canadian historical fiction now: by taking a long hard look backwards, we place ourselves. (1998: 1512)

The difference Atwood draws between the actual seventeenth-century New England and Hawthorne's imaginative reconstruction of it brings to the fore the double consciousness of time that features in literary works such as *The Scarlet Letter*, which, as argued in the introduction, involves the double movement of looking backwards in order to move forwards. It challenges the perception of historical discourse as a straightforward linear process and emphasizes, instead, the embeddedness between the past, the present and the future in both acts of writing and reading. Atwood's own novel, *Alias Grace*, engages with the idea of 'double time' in its representation of a double story (which, as Mark Currie notes from Tzvetan Todorov, is characteristic of detective fiction): one about crime, the narration of which goes backwards; and one about investigation, the experience of which goes forwards in time ([2007] 2012: 36). It details the process of how the fictional doctor, Simon Jordan, tries to recover Grace's notionally repressed memory about her involvement in the murders of her employer Thomas Kinnear and his housekeeper Nancy Montgomery. In its imaginative reconstruction of the notorious 1843 murders in Canada, *Alias Grace* thematizes the hermeneutics of exposure, rendering itself a useful example for this chapter's exploration of neo-Victorian fiction's engagement with suspicious reading and readerly empathy as well as its transformative promises.

The double-story structure of *Alias Grace* can be seen in a number of neo-Victorian novels that will be examined in this book, including Jane Harris's *The Observations* in this chapter, Sarah Waters's *Tipping the Velvet* and *Affinity* in Chapter 2, as well as Michael Cox's *The Meaning of Night* in Chapter 3, although, as we will also see, the forms of double story these novels take are all slightly different and will be discussed from different critical perspectives. For this chapter, I choose to work on two novels that revolve around a riddle concerning the central protagonist – *The Observations* and *Alias Grace* – in order to demonstrate the oscillating relationship between paranoid and reparative dynamics in neo-Victorian narratives. Both novels start with what Eve Sedgwick calls the 'paranoid' inquiry into the hidden 'truth' of the past. Both, in the meanwhile, are concerned with our empathetic engagement with the vulnerable textual other and its reparative potential.

In what follows, I consider the different reading pleasures of contemporary literary reconstruction of the Victorians (e.g. voyeuristic, expository, empathetic) by looking at two texts – Claire Tomalin's *The Invisible Woman: The Story of Nelly Ternan and Charles Dickens* ([1990] 1991), a biography of Dickens's mistress and Harris's *The Observations*. Although *The Invisible Woman* is not a neo-Victorian fiction, its preoccupation with the 'non-normative' figure of the nineteenth century has become a staple of the neo-Victorian genre (Carroll 2010: 194). I then examine the self-conscious and self-reflexive dimensions of *The Observations* so as to demonstrate how neo-Victorian fiction explicitly links empathy to the hermeneutic pleasures of reading and raises certain ethical concerns about the text–reader relationship. These ethical issues are answered in part by *Alias Grace* where the *choices* available to the reader are much more obvious. Linking together Sedgwick's formulation of paranoid and reparative practices with Amy Coplan's ([2011] 2014) differentiation between empathy as 'self-orientated perspective-taking' and 'other-orientated perspective-taking', I examine the way in which the 'intradiegetic' examples in *Alias Grace* 'mirror' different readerly responses to the story of Grace Marks.[1] I shall be concerned with how the reader's empathetic engagement with the text facilitates or frustrates their textual pleasures associated with mystery, suspense and problem-solving, as well as the related complex ethical problems. In light of Currie's formulation of a future-orientated model of reading, I argue that *Alias Grace* encourages contemporary readers to drop their quest for the 'truth' about the past and to empathize with the textual other by taking other-orientated perspective-taking, an act which inaugurates an ethical possibility and involves a concern about the future.

'Guilty pleasures'

With a recurrent focus on Victorian 'otherness' (specified as the figure of the criminal, maid, actress, etc.), neo-Victorian literature constitutes a repository of voyeuristic and cryptic pleasure for the contemporary reader. The beginning of *The Invisible Woman*, a biography of Dickens's mistress Nelly Ternan from 1857 until his death in 1870, perfectly captures such reading pleasure, which is also afforded by a great many neo-Victorian novels:

> This is the story of someone who – almost – wasn't there; who vanished into thin air. Her name, dates, family and experiences very nearly disappeared from the record for good. What's more, she connived at her own obliteration; during her lifetime her children were quite ignorant of her history. Why and how this happened is the theme; and how – by a hair's breadth – she was reclaimed from oblivion despite strenuous efforts to keep her there. ([1990] 1991: 3)

---

[1] I follow Shlomith Rimmon-Kenan in using the term 'intradiegetic' to refer to what exists 'within the first narrative' ([1983] 2002: 107). 'Extradiegetic', on the contrary, is concerned with what is ' "above" the first narrative' (ibid.).

Tomalin's biographical account of this 'invisible' woman clearly induces the reader's curiosity, rendering their reading of the text a transhistorical journey with the promise of some remarkable discovery. The focus on how the text operates against the 'strenuous efforts' that have, in the past, been made to keep the history of the 'real' Nelly Ternan invisible reinforces the liberal fantasies about the ownership of 'knowledge'. By telling readers that the text they are reading will enable them to 'gaze' at an 'invisible' woman and her secret romance with the canonical English writer Dickens, the text positions readers as the privileged voyeurs of a hermeneutic puzzle. This reading practice is mirrored by the way Tomalin plays with the elusiveness of Ternan's identity: 'She was "N", otherwise Nelly, Miss Ellen, the Patient, the Princess, E. L. T., the Dear Girl, the Darling, the magic circle of one, the little riddle, Miss T., Miss Fernan, Miss Terman, Miss Teman, Miss Turnham and probably Mrs Tringham' (10). The list Tomalin makes about Ternan's various identity markers indicates the intellectual enlightenment and emotional fulfilment expository reading generates. Meanwhile, the ultimate indeterminacy of Ternan's actual life experience promises that the pleasure of demystification and revelation will not be easily exhausted. Focusing on Ternan's experience as a professional actress and the dubious association the Victorians made between actress and prostitute in particular, Tomalin's text also exemplifies the role 'uncovering' plays in addressing structural oppression and social injustice. As a way of engaging with the 'invisible' past, the hermeneutics of exposure has a clear moral and political agenda. By 'fashion[ing] causal connections', Rita Felski argues, it 'assign[s] responsibility, and often attribute[s] guilt' (2011: 222).

Although *The Invisible Woman* is a historical biography rather than a neo-Victorian novel, the link it makes between voyeurism and the hermeneutic pleasures of reading can be found in other neo-Victorian novels. Harris's *The Observations*, for example, plays with the reader's desire for both voyeuristic consumption and mystery-solving through its use of a provocative intradiegetic narrator. Set in and around the world of a dilapidated country house outside Edinburgh in 1863, the story is narrated by one of the many marginal figures of Victorian fiction, a fifteen-year-old Irish prostitute, Bessy Buckley. Composed of a collection of diaries and first-person reports addressed to specific audiences and/or the extradiegetic reader, *The Observations* revolves around how Bessy, who chances upon a job as a maid to Arabella Reid, the twenty-year-old mistress of Castle Haivers, gradually falls under the spell of her eccentric mistress. The story finishes with the admittance of Arabella to a mental asylum, an ending that evokes contemporary examinations of the discursive construction of female madness in Victorian England (see Gilbert and Gubar 1979; Showalter [1985] 1987).[2] Similar to the opening paragraphs of *The Invisible Woman*, *The Observations* actively engages the reader in the hermeneutic process by presenting the reading experience as a journey, complete with the promise of solving a riddle: 'my missus often said to me, "Now then Bessy, don't be calling me missus." She said this especially when the minister was coming for his tea. My missus wanted me to call her "marm" but I always forgot' (vii). Beginning with an out-of-context dialogue regarding the form of address between Bessy and her mistress, Harris's text makes both curiosity and suspense a feature of the reading process, setting up a hermeneutic quest to 'solve' the nature of the relationship between these two characters. The final message from Bessy at the end of this extract connects Bessy with the reader, who, at this stage in the novel may be given to believe that s/he is her intradiegetic addressee of the text: 'but wait on. I am getting ahead of myself. Let me begin nearer the beginning' (vii). By revealing Bessy's awareness of and care for her interlocutor, this message clearly indicates that Bessy and her dialogist will travel together on the journey that lies ahead, thus causing the reader to drop their guard and get involved in 'solving the mystery'. In addition, the fact that the novel begins with a material journey – from Glasgow to Edinburgh – reinforces the sense that the reader will travel with Bessy on the narrative journey that follows.

This process of expository reading is complicated by the text's belated introduction to Bessy's *intra*diegetic addressees: the 'gentlemen readers' who first appear on page 63 of the novel: 'I have been assured that this document is only for the PRIVATE perusal of one or two gentlemen' (original emphasis). Bessy's mention of her gentlemen readers instantly clarifies who the 'real' interlocutors of the text are and repositions the reader as a voyeur rather than a fellow conspirator. This shift of textual positioning is arguably designed to provoke and reinforce the reader's voyeuristic and erotic pleasures. By

---

[2] For discussion about neo-Victorian perspectives on mental illness, see Sarah E. Maier and Brenda Ayres (eds), 2020.

emphasizing the secrecy of Bessy's narrative ('[Dr Lawrence] has shown me the locked cupboard where the manuscript is to be kept' (520)), the text raises further questions about the status of Bessy's account: for example, who has permitted the reader access to her writing? Who is mediating her writing for the gentlemen readers *to us*? The textual illusion that Bessy's manuscript must have been prepared for publication by a third party other than Bessy herself caters for the reader's voyeuristic interests. Further, if the readers pause for a moment, they will realize that all these layers of narration are the invention of the 'real-life' author, Jane Harris. The image of the secret, locked-away manuscript, in this context, makes all the readers somehow complicit in the revelation. This implied complicity presents the act of reading as a means of erotic manipulation. Although Bessy – the narrator – repeatedly warns her narratee(s) that 'these extracts should *not* be reproduced by *anybody* in *any way shape or form whatsoever* without prior application to me' (107, original emphasis), we know that anyone who has access to the key would have access to her secret – and we hope that this will include ourselves as readers. As Lynne Pearce argues, whenever readers prepare to read a text they become 'liable to' – or look forward to – 'enchantment' (1997: 86). Thus, this literal key reported upon in the text becomes a symbolic one: a code, as it were, for the readers to 'crack'. Also, the associated meaning of the lock – a latent desire for being opened and occupied – presents the image of the locked-up manuscript as a tantalizing, if cryptic, pleasure which permeates the text as a whole. It therefore produces two layers of pseudo-erotic pleasure for the reader; first, by simulation of a tactile encounter with the text, the reader is arguably 'inserting' themselves into its body when they open it. The relation a reader has to a book, writes Karin Littau, is precisely one between 'two bodies': 'one made of paper and ink, the other flesh and blood' (2006: 2). And, from there, the reader is able to peep into, read, spy upon and perhaps inhabit the physical body of Bessy during their reading of her story.

By positioning readers as voyeurs of Bessy's story, Harris's text aligns its extradiegetic readers with Bessy's gentlemen readers: they are united through the shared desire for the self-indulgent pleasure of consuming the other's hidden past. The complicity between the extradiegetic readers and the intradiegetic addressees is further established through the hint that Bessy's manuscript has been leaked by her gentlemen readers and that they, themselves, are the 'editors' of the text that is now presented to us. By highlighting the fact that Dr Lawrence has the key to the drawer where the secret manuscript is locked, Bessy's account creates a textual illusion that Dr Lawrence is the 'leaker'. Her insistence on the secrecy of her writing and her trust in Dr Lawrence's promise of using her writing for medical research only serve to make the reader uncomfortably complicit in the text's production and consumption; arguably we are corrupted by sharing with the gentlemen readers a desire to consume and expose Bessy's story without her permission.

The text's ethical imperative becomes evident when the 'other' role played by the gentleman figure in Bessy's life is revealed: that is, their use of her as a prostitute. Despite Bessy's unwillingness to recall these events ('Indeed it makes me feel queasy to remember some of the terrible things that followed and I dread writing about it'), Dr Lawrence insists that Bessy should 'relay the story "warts and all"' (152, 520). In response to this 'authorial' request, Bessy recalls her first sexual encounter, which is, in effect, a violent rape:

> He stroked my head and sighed. 'Yes, dear. And you are doing it very well. Just keep still and – let me –' He made some minor adjustment to my undergarments. 'That's better. Are you all right?'
>
> I nodded, hoping that he could not see that my eyes had filled with tears. It was quite clear to me what was going to happen.
>
> 'Now then,' he says. 'All being well and as advertised, this should cause you a small amount of discomfort.'
>
> When it came to it, I could not bear the thought of his dirty great jack anywhere near me and so I imagined in its place nothing more sinister than an umbrella (indeed it might as well have been an umbrella for the pain it caused me), a gentlemans umbrella, silky and unfurled. (237)

By using a quite pornographic and titillating image – 'an umbrella' – and a cue word for readerly participation – 'imagine' – the text corrupts its readers, associating them uncomfortably with Bessy's gentlemen readers once again. Bessy's subsequent account of her traumatic experience as a child prostitute seems to suggest that the pressure she is put under to tell her story could be viewed as a second rape: 'I was a virgin on five more occasions that week, each time with a different man' (237). The extent to which Bessy has been exploited by Dr Lawrence and his associates becomes clear when it is later revealed that her story is supposedly incidental to their main object of investigation: Arabella's 'Observations' – a treatise that adopts tools of phrenology and ethnography (i.e. observation, mapping, diagramming and charting) in the study of '*the nature, habits and training of the domestic class*' of the nineteenth century (90, original emphasis). If, as Bessy says, Dr Lawrence 'only wishes to examine the case of missus, in the hope of being more help to her', it is questionable why Bessy's own early sexual experiences matter (520). Bessy's later account of how she tries to publish Arabella's *The Observations* gives us a hint. A Mr G from a certain publishing house begs to know 'the true identity of "the mysterious Arabella R"', whom he assumes to be 'a man, *pretending* to be a woman' (518, original emphasis). Mr G's speculation brings to the fore the vicarious pleasure the gentlemen readers expect from the idiosyncratic accounts of the particularities of the domestic class, which also speaks to the experience of the extradiegetic reader. By exposing the many layers of readerly intrigue surrounding the intertwined stories of Bessy and her mistress in this way, the text raises certain ethical concerns about the reader's desire and expectation: are the readers, too, reading the text simply in order to gaze at Bessy's 'body'? The text may thus be seen as making a metacritical comment on the way we, as readers, are implicated in a scopophilic project.

The Observations further 'mocks' prurient readerly desire by revealing the 'fictional' nature of Bessy's account at the end of the story:

> Now that I am finished, Doctor Lawrence wants to know what I think of what I have wrote. All I can say is that it will be strange to be no longer doing it. I may have to think of another story to write to fill up those few hours between completing work and laying my head upon the pillow. (520–1)

Bessy's choice of vocabulary – 'another story' – hints at the fact that all she has been reporting is only what people want to hear, but not necessarily the 'truth'. Such message is made explicit much earlier when Arabella asks Bessy to tell 'the truth' about her past: ' "Now then, Bessy," she says. "Tell the truth and shame the Devil." My mother was forever telling me I wouldn't know the truth if it flew up my skirt and said "How do you do" ' (16–17). Bessy's exaggerated unreliability as a narrator, nevertheless, prompts the reader to critically reflect upon their prurient and voyeuristic consumption of the vulnerable other. The 'unfavorable' character traits of Bessy, such as her incredibility and slyness, are arguably the only means through which she could resist the gentlemen readers' attempt to exploit her life for 'squalid' pleasures (520). Here suspicion and mistrust provoke readerly empathy in a rather unexpected manner. James Phelan uses the term 'bonding unreliability' to describe 'unreliable narration that reduces the distance between the narrator and the authorial audience' (2007: 223–4). Phelan's discussion of 'the rhetorical effect' of unreliability provides some interesting insight into a reconsideration of the relationship between suspicious reading and reparative practice: 'in bonding unreliability, the discrepancies between the narrator's reports, interpretations, or evaluations and the inferences of the authorial audience have the paradoxical result of reducing the interpretive, affective, or ethical distance between the narrator and the authorial audience' (225). Positioning narratorial unreliability as a self-protective strategy, Bessy's self-conscious account in *The Observations* exemplifies under which circumstance suspicion and mistrust work to evoke the reader's empathetic responses.

The 'double' message Bessy leaves us at the end of the story further illustrates how her appeal for the reader's empathetic engagement with her plight emerges from these layers of suspicion and intrigue: 'so there you go. Farewell. *Au revoir*. Or, as they say where I come from, safe home' (521). Bessy's use of both 'Farewell' and '*Au revoir*' in her farewell message seems to address two different categories of readers. The fact that the French phrase '*Au revoir*' anticipates a future reunion gestures towards the beginning of a different literary journey, a journey that she probably does not want to travel with her intradiegetic gentlemen readers, but *us*. Here the implied sense of future orientation, when seen in the light of Currie's work on narrative temporality, has the potential to transform the meaning of preceding events in Bessy's account. In this context, we may suggest that Harris's *The Observations* tells – or at least promises – a kind of 'double' story: a retrospective one underpinned by a voyeuristic desire to consume the suffering of a vulnerable female subject; and, second, a future-orientated one which looks forward to travelling with Bessy as her friend and ally. Indeed, when we look at the text again, we come to realize that Bessy has advertised the 'doubleness' of her story through her repeated use of the irreducible fraction '½' throughout her account, which results from dividing one by two. The use of the plural – observations – in the title also 'hints at the possibility of subverting the gaze' of the prurient reader (Heilmann and

Llewellyn 2010: 111). Recognition of this sense of duality at the cryptic heart of the texts calls upon the self-conscious reader to shift their positioning and review what they have read from the position of an empathizer rather than a voyeur. Through the ingenious use of textual details, Harris may also be seen as encouraging readers to 'scrutinize' Bessy's account with extreme care and as such exhibits different roles exposure and demystification play in different projects. Suspicious reading, then, becomes a tacit game between Bessy and us, and lays the foundation for reparative practice.

Bessy's manipulative narrative in *The Observations* not only exposes our voyeuristic complicity as readers but also raises questions about what it takes to resist a voyeuristic reader positioning. These ethical issues are, in part, answered by *Alias Grace* where the choices available to the reader are much more clearly signposted. By telling us a story that is ultimately impossible to verify, *Alias Grace* reveals how both the law and hermeneutics flounder in the face of lack of evidence. In what follows, I read Atwood's text alongside the theoretical writings of Sedgwick on paranoia and reparation and Coplan on empathy in order to demonstrate how *Alias Grace* provokes, plays with, but then challenges the 'irresistible' pleasure of hermeneutic practice. In so doing, I take up Jackie Shead's lead in arguing that Atwood's *Alias Grace* provides the reader with the means to 'interrogate and adjust' their reading of not only the literary text but also the real world (2015: 37). Atwood's writing also provides a more nuanced and complicated reflection on the relation between different reader positionings than the one we see in *The Observations*.

Reading with suspicion

As one of the 'typical neo-Victorian narratives based on true crime' (Kohlke 2008/9: iii), *Alias Grace* reconstructs the life experience of Grace Marks, the convicted perpetrator of the notorious 1843 murders of Thomas Kinnear and Nancy Montgomery in Canada. Given its combination of historical facts and fictional inventions, the novel has long been considered a leading example of 'historiographic metafiction', a term Linda Hutcheon coins in referring to postmodern novels that are preoccupied with 'both epistemological and ontological questions' about historical narrative (1988: 50). Through an engagement with 'the act of narration' (Lovelady 1999: 35), critics including Stephanie Lovelady, Magali Cornier Michael (2001), Jennifer Murray (2003) and Fiona Tolan (2007) have examined the ways in which *Alias Grace* undermines the 'universal notion of "truth"' (Michael 2001: 421), and its implications for the construction of Grace's indeterminate identity. Focusing on the ways in which the characters within the text attempt to make sense of the story of Grace instead, I consider *Alias Grace* as a text that encourages its readers to reflect upon their readerly desires.

The text self-consciously links suspicious reading with readerly empathy through its portrayal of Dr Jordan's investigation of Grace's psyche and its use of first-person narration, a narrative technique that is often deemed as facilitating the cognitive and affective engagement between the narrator and the reader (Keen [2007] 2010: xi). Beginning the story with Grace's status as a convicted murderess and the quest to prove or deny her involvement in the crime, *Alias Grace* combines a cue towards empathetic reading with a simultaneous incentive to solve the mystery, which functions as what Roland Barthes calls the 'hermeneutic code' for the whole text (see Barthes [1974] 2002). As Grace puts it, 'If there has been a crime, they want to know who did it' (91).

The first conversation between Dr Jordan (Simon) and Grace provides the reader with a good example of the role suspicion plays in seeking the hypothetically repressed meaning. Narrated from Grace's perspective, Simon's questioning technique, and in particular, his insistence on 'hidden' meanings behind common objects such as an apple, is featured by 'a suspicious sensibility' (Felski 2015: 43):

> He smiles his lopsided smile. What does Apple make you think of? he says.
>
> I beg your pardon, Sir, I say. I do not understand you.
>
> It must be a riddle. I think of Mary Whitney, and the apple peelings we threw over our shoulders that night, to see who we would marry. But I will not tell him that.
>
> I think you understand well enough, he says.
>
> My sampler, I say.
>
> Now it is his turn to know nothing. Your what? he says.
>
> My sampler that I stitched as a child, I say. A is for Apple, B is for Bee.

> Oh yes, he says. But what else?
>
> I give my stupid look. Apple pie, I say.
>
> Ah, he says. Something you eat.
>
> Well I should hope you would, Sir, I say. That's what an apple pie is for.
>
> And is there any kind of apple you should not eat? he says.
>
> A rotten one, I suppose, I say.
>
> He's playing a guessing game, like Dr. Bannerling at the Asylum. There is always a right answer, which is right because it is the one they want, and you can tell by their faces whether you have guessed what it is. […]
>
> The apple of the Tree of Knowledge, is what he means. Good and evil. (40)

The questions Simon raises about the meaning of the apple exemplify how the presumption about hidden meanings and the method of deciphering go together. During their conversation, Simon not only imagines Grace to be as familiar with the biblical and moral meaning of the apple as he is, but eventually makes her become so through his 'cherry-picking' interpretation skills. Grace's initial response that apple means the 'sampler' she stitches as a child is quickly discarded by Simon. The other link she makes between apple and apple pie is closer to the 'right' answer Simon expects, so he responds by asking further whether there is 'any kind of apple you should not eat'. By guiding Grace to respond in a particular way and selectively picking up the information he needs, Simon's interrogation of Grace demonstrates the way 'paranoia' – as 'a highly organized way of interpreting information' – works (Tomkins 2008: 519). During any paranoid critical practice, Tomkins notes, 'what is possibly relevant can be quickly abstracted and magnified, and the rest discarded' (ibid.). Indeed, Simon's performance during his first conversation with Grace demonstrates how his proto-psychoanalytical interpretation is underpinned by a 'depth model of truth' and a vigilant mechanism which puts the analyst's needs before that of the (textual) others (Best and Marcus 2009: 10).

Grace's performative compliance in this extract is a good example of how contagious paranoia could be. She formulates her responses in a way that deliberately frustrates Simon's desire for the 'right answer', which, Grace explains with irony, 'is right because it is the one they want' (40). The display of Grace's knowingness, together with her weariness with being subject to such questioning ('I have had enough of them to last me for a long while' (ibid.)), accentuate the 'reflexive and mimetic' aspects of paranoia: that paranoia understands, and could only be understood, by imitation (Sedgwick 2003: 131). Paranoia's insistence on both positions also provides a significant model of readerly engagement. Grace's inner monologues in the previous extract cast doubt on her reliability as a narrator, which would appear to deliberately encourage the reader to approach her account with suspicion. The use of an unreliable narrator, Doug Battersby contends, is the 'most suspicious of narrative techniques' (2021: 68). These questions would appear to deliberately encourage the reader to approach Grace's account with doubt. The text's portrayal of Grace's wild hallucinations and dreams has the same effect on the reader, a point I will discuss in Chapter 4. In Atwood's fictive rendition, Grace is a self-conscious 'storyteller' who shares 'selective' information with her 'audience' (probably referring not only to Simon but also to us) (1998: 1515). In this regard, reading *Alias Grace* is to be involved in a protracted 'guessing game' (Atwood 1996: 40). This paranoid imperative is made openly visible in both the thematic and the narrative structure of the text. Using the name of quilt patterns as the subtitle for each chapter, the text functions as an attempt to sew together all these shattered fragments of the past. At the metafictional level, the quilting trope can also be seen as epitomizing the text–reader relationship. The fact that quilting – as a form of 'women's work' – is full of 'hidden messages' may be seen to encourage readers to 'look for hints of hidden messages' during their reading process (Ingersoll 2001: 388).[3] It also functions to 'weav[e] together ... multiple stories and multiple voices' in the novel, leading to the reader's unsatisfactory and inexhaustible pursuit of truth (Macpherson 2010: 69). In so doing, *Alias Grace* involves its readers in the hermeneutic process of decoding, during which suspicion plays a central role.

The text's refusal to provide a definite answer on whether Grace is innocent or guilty renders her case 'a puzzle [the reader] could not guess' (Atwood 1996: 202). By playing with the ambiguity about Grace's involvement in the murders, *Alias Grace* lays all the traps and incentives towards suspicious

---

[3] Critics have discussed Atwood's metaphorical use of quilting in this text from perspectives as various as gender, historical narration, metafictionality, postmodern knowledge and truth. For relevant examples, see essays collected in *Margaret Atwood: The Shape-Shifter* (1998); Rogerson (1998).

reading. This mode of practice, Rita Felski explains, offers a number of 'substantive pleasures', including 'the satisfaction of detecting figures and designs below the text's surface, fashioning new plots out of old, joining together the disparate and seemingly unconnected, acts of forging, patterning, and linking' (2011: 228). *Alias Grace* engages with the irresistible pleasure of suspicious reading through Grace's monologue about her bewildering personality, which also reveals the challenge of trying *not to* weave the known facts into a plausible narrative:

> I think of all the things that have been written about me – that I am an inhuman female demon, that I am an innocent victim of a blackguard forced against my will and in danger of my own life, that I was too ignorant to know how to act and that to hang me would be judicial murder, that I am fond of animals, that I am very handsome with a brilliant complexion, that I have blue eyes, that I have green eyes, that I have auburn and also brown hair, that I am tall and also not above the average height, that I am well and decently dressed, that I robbed a dead woman to appear so, that I am brisk and smart about my work, that I am of a sullen disposition with a quarrelsome temper, that I have the appearance of a person rather above my humble station, that I am a good girl with a pliable nature and no harm is told of me, that I am cunning and devious, that I am soft in the head and little better than an idiot. And I wonder, how can I be all of these different things at once? (23)

Similar to the list Tomalin makes about Ternan's indeterminate identity at the beginning of *The Invisible Woman* (as discussed in the previous section), Grace's self-scrutiny in front of the mirror also illustrates how the paranoid imperative to demystify the hidden 'truth' about her involvement in the murders could trap the reader, too, in a compulsive cycle of repetition. After a series of expository attempts, the reader may reach the exhilarating yet unsettling conclusion that it is simply impossible to exhaust all of their suspicious energies. In her reading of the novel, Kym Brindle arrives at a similar conclusion, arguing that 'without narrative confirmation or denial for readers, Grace could be any of the definitions reflected in the mirror, or indeed none of them' (2013: 102). The repeated use of the conjunction 'and' in Grace's account is a vivid example about how the act of trying to expose all plausible aspects of Grace's personality could lead to contradictory discoveries. In this manner, *Alias Grace* also contests the effectiveness of such 'paranoid' inquiry in the reconstruction of historical 'truth'. It becomes epistemologically challenging to approach a historical subject whose story has been mediated in too many fragmented and layered ways.

A similar point can be inferred from Simon's reflection on his proto-psychoanalytic sessions with Grace, through which the text further exhibits how suspicious reading greatly satisfies as well as frustrates the reader:

> He must be careful, he tells himself. He must draw back. Looked at objectively, what's been going on between them, despite her evident anxiety over the murders and her surface compliance, has been a contest of wills. She hasn't refused to talk – far from it. She's told him a great deal; but she's told him only what she's chosen to tell. What he wants is what she refuses to tell; what she chooses perhaps not even to know. Knowledge of guilt, or else of innocence: either could be concealed. But he'll pry it out of her yet. (322)

This portrait of Simon telling himself how careful he must be – as though it were a life and death matter – reminds us how intense, and desperate, paranoid reading can be. As a character 'who blends the characteristics of alienist, detective, and literary exegete', Simon's particular interest in the concealed parts of Grace's experience further manifests the irresistible allure of suspicion (O'Neill 2013: 655). Now their interaction becomes a well-matched and absorbing 'contest of wills' which Simon initiates with Grace, such that he starts wondering whether Grace has been 'studying from the same text he himself has been using, the better to convince him' (322). The figurative language Simon uses in describing his relationship with Grace – that 'he's got the hook in her mouth' to pull Grace 'out of the abyss, up to the light. Out of the deep blue sea' – strikingly illustrates how Simon mobilizes his imagination and creativity in order to draw out Grace's dark secrets and to outsmart her (ibid.). Here, critical interpretation is no longer 'an arid analytical exercise, but an inspired blend of intuition and imagination' (Felski 2011: 228).

The trap of suspicious reading is that you can never have enough of it. As their conversations proceed, Simon gradually finds himself incapable of 'keep[ing] track of the pieces' that Grace remembers and relates; he admits that his wrestling with Grace in trying to dig out all the information that is 'buried deep within her' is 'drawing his energy out of him' (291). Comparing himself to a spiritualist medium, Simon's self-reflection also reveals the role 'empathetic imagination' plays in suspicious reading: he realizes that he is 'using his own mental forces to materialize the figures in her story' in solving the mystery about Grace (ibid.). Simon's distrust of Grace's accounts and subsequent suspicion of his own professionalism further suggests how he 'inevitably [becomes] suspicious of the interpretations [he] inspire[s]' (Bersani 1990: 188). As Sedgwick explains, given their aversion to surprise, paranoid readers could only survive through the incentive of fear: '*you can never be paranoid enough*' (2003: 127, original emphasis). Indeed, Simon's desire for 'certainty' traps him in a cycle of self-doubt: 'perhaps it's his methods that have been at fault'; 'perhaps he's been too tentative, too accommodating; perhaps something more drastic may be in order' (322). The repeated use of the word 'perhaps' nicely captures the strong sense of vigilance or 'humiliation-fear' paranoia generates (Sedgwick 2003: 133). In this way, the text may also be seen as making a metacritical comment on the paranoid strategy. Trying to obtain a comprehensive knowledge of Grace's mind and build her behaviours into a consistent and coherent narrative does not help Simon to understand Grace in a more nuanced way, since his interpretation is 'reductive, aggressive and grounded in oppressive power-relations' (Amiel-Houser and Mendelson-Maoz 2014: 210). Simon's experience suggests that 'paranoia knows some things well and others poorly' (Sedgwick 2003: 130).

By incorporating various medical, poetical, journalistic and legal texts about Grace's experience into the pages of the novel, all of which centre on the question of Grace's innocence or guilt, it is clear that *Alias Grace* promotes a hermeneutics of suspicion among its readers. However, the text's self-conscious engagement with the paranoid impulse ultimately seems to question this kind of interpretive strategy. Through the use of intradiegetic examples, the text challenges the reader's attempt to reveal the 'truth' from an ethical perspective by linking together ideas of involuntary exposure and sexual violence. The metaphors Simon uses to describe his relationship with Grace are featured by acts of 'penetration' (King 2005: 74). He imagines himself 'open[ing] her up like an oyster' (133) and describes his approach towards Grace's mind 'as if it is a locked box, to which [he] must find the right key' (132), both of which play with the violent and erotic potentials of suspicious reading.

However, before we lay any moral judgement on the prurient fantasies of Simon, it is essential for readers to reflect on our own hermeneutic reading of

Grace's story: are we complicit in the same act of violence against Grace when we, too, desire and expect to get 'the pure, entire, and unblemished truth' about whether she is guilty or innocent of the crime, something that 'she refuses to tell' (322)? Through the example of Simon's trip to Mr Kinnear's house – the murder site – Atwood urges her readers to reflect upon the ethical and political implications of the hermeneutics of exposure. Before Simon makes a tour around Mr Kinnear's house, he questions himself about 'what can be gained from looking [at the house]' apart from 'a vulgar frisson, and the indulgence of morbid interest' (384). However, for Simon, as for ourselves as readers, the pleasure of self-indulgence is not easy to resist. Although Simon is aware that actual experiences 'are always a disappointment', 'he knocks at the front door, then knocks again' (ibid.). The text's particular focus on the cellar, the place where the bodies of Mr Kinnear and Nancy Montgomery are found, reveals that Simon's tour is essentially a 'discreditable peepshow' (386). Compared to other parts of the house, which have been quickly dealt with by the unidentified intradiegetic narrator ('He is shown the dining room, the library, the winter kitchen; the summer kitchen, the stable and loft' (385)), the description of the cellar is more meticulous. It is stereotypically gloomy and depressing, as evidenced by the narrator's choice of vocabulary – 'dim', 'cobwebbed', 'dank' (ibid.). Simon's inner struggle between his interest in, and discomfort with, the cellar demonstrates how the pleasure of voyeurism overrides ethical concerns. Although he is worrying about 'what sort of a voyeur [he has] become', and he 'wants to be gone', he then 'heads straight for the Presbyterian church', behind which Mr Kinnear and Nancy are buried (386). In Simon's case, voyeurism relates not only to 'a perverse [sexual] fantasy', referring to his desire 'to marry a suspected murderess (Grace)' (389), but also a paranoid obsession in that he wants to visit the grave of Mary Whitney in order to 'make sure that she really exists' (387). Simon's behaviour here 'mirrors' the reader's complex erotic and expository desires. It also leads to a further concern about where this paranoid impulse – the compulsion to repeat – will lead the reader. Following Simon's thorough research of Grace's past, he comes to realize that 'nothing has been proved. But nothing has been disproved, either' (388).

With regard to the predicament that Simon finds himself in, which is arguably shared by the text's extradiegetic readers, *Alias Grace* may be seen as offering an alternative to the paranoid inquiry through its central trope: the act of quilting. In spite of the fact that quilting could be understood as a metaphor for the hermeneutic practice, it may also refer to a reparative one, since quilting is 'an art that pulls together pieces of the past into a cover promising a warm future' (van Herk 1998: 110). Taking up Aritha van Herk's future-orientated interpretation of the central metaphor of the novel, I propose that *Alias Grace* tells a 'second' story: one that shifts away from the investigation of the 'truth value' of historical reconstruction and is more concerned with the reader's responsibility for the vulnerable other. As Atwood remarks in the 1996 Bronfman Lecture, it is important to acknowledge that 'although there undoubtedly was a truth – somebody did kill Nancy Montgomery – truth is sometimes unknowable, at least by us' (1998: 1515). A similar point is made in the novel by the character Kenneth Mackenzie, Grace's attorney, in his address to Simon: 'The stories she told ought never to be subjected to the harsh categories of Truth and Falsehood. They belong in another realm altogether. Perhaps Grace Marks has merely been telling you what she needs to tell, in order to accomplish the desired end' (377). By abandoning a 'knowing, anxious paranoid determination' towards the textual object, the reader could enjoy a constructive and reparative relationship with it, which will enable them to respond to the future with hope (Sedgwick 2003: 146). In this context, the reading of *Alias Grace* inaugurates a potentially different, if not necessarily better, future.

Reparations

It is clear that Grace's 'confessional' narration of her earlier traumatic experience invites the reader's empathetic engagement, inducing them to abandon their quest to establish her innocence or guilt. Indeed, as Burkhard Niederhoff remarks, 'Grace comes across as a compassionate, reliable and sensible woman, the last person on earth we would suspect of committing the murders she has been charged with' (2006/7: 77). However, her textual positioning as an unreliable narrator and her 'real life' conviction as a murderess keep challenging the reader's empathetic tendencies. By playing with the dynamic between paranoid and reparative styles of reading, *Alias Grace* foregrounds a wide range of possible interpretations. If we consider the text as a 'trial' of

Grace (Blanc 2006: 102), as illustrated by the way in which it sets itself up as a hermeneutic quest for the 'truth', then the ultimate futility of such an approach quickly becomes clear: having examined hundreds of pages of evidence (along with the intradiegetic characters), we are still no closer to knowing whether she was innocent or guilty. By the same token, this opens up possibilities for 'reading' Grace – and the text – reparatively; that is, as Atwood puts it, the importance of 'listening' first (1998: 1515).

The invitation to 'listen' empathetically to – or with – Grace begins with the observation that she 'would like to be found' and 'to be seen', as well as the first-person account of her life experience (379). Throughout her narrative, Grace mentions different scenes of drowning she has experienced in her life in ways that affectively involve the reader.[4] In recalling the dispatching of the mother's body to the Atlantic Ocean (who tragically dies of seasickness during their voyage from Ireland to Canada), Grace expresses her uncanny anxiety and deep sense of shame through a symbolic interpretation of the broken teapot, a souvenir that is given to her mother by her Aunt Pauline before their departure.[5] Grace suggests that the demise of the teapot is caused by her mother's spirit, which is now 'trapped in the bottom of the ship because [they] could not open a window' (122). She also imagines her mother's body as 'a moth in a bottle' that sails back and forth within an enclosed space (ibid.). The agony caused by this state of perpetual suspension and placelessness is graphically evoked in Grace's description: 'I hadn't thought about where she was going until this moment, and there was something dreadful about it, to picture her floating down in a white sheet among all the staring fish. It was worse than being put into the earth, because if a person is in the earth at least you know where they are' (121). Through the use of the cue phrase 'to picture',

---

[4] Atwood's text uses water imagery in a heavily symbolic manner to conjure up the nature of Grace's oppression. In *Alias Grace*, drowning is also a recurrent motif in Grace's own psyche and imagination. When Grace's friend Mary dies of an abortion, she seems to be out of mind and insists that 'Grace was lost, and had gone into the lake' (180). The use of waterlogged images – tears and the lake – exemplifies the way Atwood engages with Gaston Bachelard's discussion of the symbolic link between women, liquids and death. In his discussion of the 'Ophelia Complex', Bachelard considers 'drowning' as 'the truly feminine death in the dramas of literature and life' (Showalter 1985: 80). For discussion about the ways in which neo-Victorian fiction engages with contemporary feminism, see Kathleen Renk, 2020.

[5] Focusing on the image of drowning, Ian Baucom examines the tragic and 'shameful' history of Irish immigrants who lost their lives on their voyage to the Atlantic after the Great Famine in the nineteenth century. Baucom's fascinating reading of the writings of contemporary Irish poet Paul Muldoon outlines the role drowning plays in confronting that traumatic past (see Baucom 2000).

Grace's vivid account of the nightmare voyage calls for the reader's unreserved empathetic engagement. Indeed, this is a good illustration of how the text self-consciously plays with the empathetic reading position. After recalling the traumatic scene, Grace addresses her intradiegetic interlocutor, Simon, in the following way: 'Perhaps you would like to open the window', revealing her awareness of how stifling and claustrophobic her narrative is (116). From a metacritical point of view, this is clearly also an address to the reader. As well as posing uncomfortable questions about the reader's responsibilities to textual others like Grace, it raises issues about how we deal with the suffering of the vulnerable subjects in the non-fictional world of the present and the future. The text can thus be seen as cultivating the reader's empathy to a reparative end.

However, the act of picturing or listening to the other's suffering could also be motivated by coarse, sensationalist and perverse desires. Through the example of James Walsh, Grace's husband, Atwood's text exposes the role empathetic identification plays in the erotic consumption and further exploitation of the oppressed other.[6] James's particular interest in Grace's sexual harassment experiences, that he 'listens to all of that like a child listening to a fairy tale', reveals the perversity of the 'empathy' that has invaded this relationship (456). After listening to 'a few stories of torment and misery', James is 'almost in ecstasies' (457) and would ask Grace repetitively whether she will forgive him since he considers himself as 'the author of all' (456). James's obsessive fascination with, and troubling claims to authorship of, stories of Grace's exploitation demonstrate how self-serving empathy deprives the empathized other of their agency and serves as a catalyst for erotic fulfilment. It also raises questions about what we, as readers, are doing when we attempt to uncover all details of Grace's earlier life. Grace's account of her past is the means by which James arrives at a comprehensive possession of her. And at the end of the novel, this is literally true: Grace marries James after being granted a pardon, and since then 'all trace of her vanishes' (465). James's reaction to Grace's story

---

[6] This is arguably one of the main differences between empathy and sympathy. Martha Nussbaum uses an example that is similar to what we see in *Alias Grace* in arguing that empathy does not necessarily lead to altruistic responses. She writes that 'a malevolent person who imagines the situation of the other and takes pleasure in her distress may be empathetic, but surely not be judged sympathetic. Sympathy, like compassion, includes a judgment that the other person's distress is bad' (Nussbaum [2001] 2003: 302).

graphically illustrates how he takes self-indulgent pleasure from the exposure of Grace's dark history, explicitly linking violence and sexual harassment with problematic reading strategies.

Alias Grace self-consciously engages with contemporary debates about the perils of empathetic practices, that they seem to serve the interest of the empathizer rather than the empathized, and have both 'the potential to help *and* harm' (Hammond and Kim 2014: 11, original emphasis). This is indeed the case in the unnerving relationship between James and Grace. Yet the palimpsestuous nature of Atwood's text provides the reader with different reading choices. As previously argued, Grace's life story challenges her image as 'a celebrated murderess' (25). It also, as Marie Thérèse Blanc suggests, 'constitutes a *counternarrative* to the novel's collected narratives of her arraignment for murder, of her trial, of her post-trial confession, and of her conviction and incarceration' (2006: 106, original emphasis). The fact that Grace emerges from her own narrative as a complex and multifaceted character arguably invites what Amy Coplan ([2011] 2014) terms 'other-orientated perspective-taking', which, as I explain in detail in the following paragraph, calls for the reader's full attention to Grace's situation and their recognition of the social and political circumstances which make her who and what she is. To this end, the reader needs to let go their hermeneutic quest for the 'truth' and approaches Grace's narrative in a less invasive and suspicious manner.

Coplan develops Adam Smith's model of sympathy as imagination-driven in her proposition of empathy as a kind of 'perspective-taking', by which she means the 'imaginative process through which one constructs another person's subjective experience by simulating the experience of being in the other's situation' (9). Focusing on the dynamic between the empathizer and the empathized, Coplan suggests that there are at least two appreciably different forms of perspective-taking. For her, *self-orientated perspective-taking* is a 'default mode of mentalizing', referring to the imaginative process of how we 'imagine *ourselves* in the other's circumstances' so as to 'understand and predict others' mental states' (10, original emphasis). This model of perspective-taking, nevertheless, is 'subject to egocentric bias' since we 'attempt to imagine how the other is feeling or what she is thinking' with a belief in the 'greater similarity between self and other' (10). Also, it might lead to what psychologists call 'false consensus effects' since self-orientated perspective-taking can assume similarities that do not exist or fail to attend sufficiently to crucial areas of difference (11). Coplan therefore proposes that only *other-orientated perspective-taking* is the genuine form of empathy. Defined as the representation of 'the other's situation from the other person's point of view', other-orientated perspective-taking focuses on the other and moves us beyond our own experiences (10). Having said so, it does not mean that other-orientated perspective-taking is absolutely immune to various forms of potential bias, which may be linked with one's familiarity and identification with the other. Still, as Coplan highlights, it helps to diminish 'egocentric biases' that are implicated in self-orientated perspective-taking (ibid.). Coplan's focus on self-other differentiation also echoes Dominic LaCapra's discussion of the reflective experience brought by empathetic unsettlement (a point that is explained in detail in the introduction). Similar to LaCapra, Coplan maintains that in empathy 'we relate to the other as an other but share in the other's experience in a way that bridges but does not eliminate the gap between our experiences' (16). This self-other distinction makes it clear that we are not 'introject[ing] the other's desires, feelings and thoughts' or 'substituting them for [our] own' in our empathetic encounter with the other (15). As such empathetic engagement will not lead to any 'personal distress, false consensus effects, and prediction errors' (17).

The above discussion makes it clear that Coplan's conceptualization of empathy is nevertheless quite restrictive, rendering empathy a highly 'motivated and controlled process' (14). Indeed, as Coplan stresses, empathy requires a certain level of 'mental flexibility' and 'regulatory mechanisms' that can help 'to modulate our level of affective arousal and suppress our own perspective' (13). In Coplan's model, empathy does not guarantee any cognitive comprehension of the other.[7] Instead, it provides us with what she calls 'experiential understanding', which does not necessarily – although it may – 'figure into the explanations, predictions, and even the actions of the observer' (17). As Coplan explains: 'to say that empathy is "experiential"

---

[7] A similar argument may be seen in Karsten R. Stueber's *Rediscovering Empathy* (2006), where Stueber examines empathy in the context of contemporary philosophy of mind and the debate about the nature of our mindreading abilities. Stueber likewise acknowledges that although empathy could help us understand the other, there are certain limitations on its ability to make sense of the other.

is to say (1) that it is itself an experience for the observer; (2) that it is a representation of, among other things, the experience of a target; and (3) that it involves representations that are not representations of causes and effects' (ibid.). Coplan's account makes it clear that empathy does not foster 'scientific explanations' of the other, which, to her, are often 'mechanistic, functional, dynamical, teleological, or genetic' (ibid.). The point that empathy should be seen as 'one source of data among many' suggests empathy could help us understand 'another person from the "inside"' in a certain way, but not comprehensively (18). In this context, we may consider Coplan's formulation of empathy as a useful alternative to the hermeneutics of suspicion, a point that is essential for the discussion of the different reading positions available to the reader in this chapter.

With a focus on the other, it is also arguable that Coplan's formulation of empathy inaugurates an ethical possibility, one that takes the form of 'empathic caring' and refers to the way in which the self 'attend[s] to the specific needs of particular others and attempt[s] to understand situations from the other's point of view' (Coplan and Goldie [2011] 2014: xxvii).[8] In *Alias Grace*, Atwood's imaginative reconstruction of Grace's relationship with Jeremiah (later Dr DuPont, the 'neuro-hypnotist' who arguably stages the hypnotism with Grace) may be seen as introducing what an other-orientated perspective-taking of a vulnerable other looks like. Jeremiah is arguably the only character in the story who cares for Grace in a disinterested way and, interestingly, tries to rescue her from the vantage point of knowing or guessing the future. Jeremiah's position as a peddler – that is, he is a 'giver' – makes him different from all the other people in Grace's life, since 'no one comes to see [Grace] unless they want something'

---

[8] The link between empathy and care is made by Nel Noddings in her influential yet contentious book *Caring: A Feminine Approach to Ethics and Moral Education* (1984). Noddings approaches different models of empathy from a gendered perspective. For her, the projection model of empathy is 'a peculiarly rational, western, masculine way of looking at "feeling with"' (30). She therefore considers empathy as a sort of receptivity (a similar argument will be seen in the phenomenological approach to empathy in the next chapter). This empathetic receptivity, or what Noddings calls 'engrossment', is not initiated with an attempt to analyze or to interpret the other's circumstances as objective data (although we may learn to do this during the process of empathetic engagement) (ibid.). Rather, it begins with attending to, and sharing, the other's feeling. Noddings's discussion resembles the difference Coplan makes between empathy and scientific explanation. It nevertheless risks being criticized for suggesting a nonreciprocal caring relationship; that is, the carer gives what is good for the person who is cared for, without receiving care in return, a point that is well evidenced by Noddings's choice of the unidirectional mothering as an ideal model of caring. For discussion of Noddings's relational ethics, see also Hoagland (1991).

(38). During his visit at the Parkinson's (Grace's first employer), Jeremiah gives Grace an extra button for the four she has already purchased, because four is considered as 'an unlucky number' while 'five [is] for luck' (155). He also reminds Grace that 'there are sharp rocks ahead' (ibid.). In hindsight, these words sound prophetic, since shortly after this Mary (Grace's friend) becomes pregnant and dies of an abortion. This is not the only time Jeremiah informs Grace of the forthcoming tragedy in her life. After Grace starts working at Mr Kinnear's, she meets Jeremiah again in the kitchen and shares with him Mary's death and her experience at the new residence. Jeremiah suggests that Grace should 'come away' with him, because she would 'be safer with [him]' (267, 268). Jeremiah's ability to foresee Grace's future and his concern with Grace's safety seem to suggest that he is 'one of *us*', the extradiegetic readers, who have a responsibility of care towards Grace after reading her miserable early life experience (155, emphasis added). As Jeremiah says to Grace: 'For I wish you well, and am willing to help you, and care for you. And I tell you truly that you are surrounded by dangers here' (269).

To a large extent, Jeremiah is the only symbol of hope in Grace's life, since he never comes to Grace *for* anything. Rather, as Grace says herself, as an 'old friend', Jeremiah represents all the past 'better times' in her life (264). On many occasions, Jeremiah is also an embodiment of the reader's desire to save Grace. When Grace is sexually harassed by her neighbour from the coach during her trip to Richmond Hill (where Mr Kinnear inhabits), Jeremiah happens to be there and rescues her from further abuse. As Grace recalls:

> Jeremiah took his stick, and brought it down on the man's arm, and he let go of me; and then Jeremiah pushed him, and he staggered backwards against the wall of the inn, and sat down in a pat of horse dung; at which the others now jeered at him, as that sort will always jeer at those who are getting the worst of it. (206–7)

In contrast to what other male characters in this text would do (i.e. Dr Simon Jordan, Mr Kinnear, Jamie Walsh), Jeremiah does not take any prurient pleasure from Grace's suffering. When witnessing Grace's plight, Jeremiah 'was trying to look into [her] mind; but in a kindly way', a gesture that points to another model of interpretation, one that is featured by a caring and sympathetic – as opposed to intrusive and self-fulfilling – attitude towards the (textual) other

(265). In her elaboration on the symbolic meanings of the 'bone button' that Jeremiah sends her after the Hypnotism, Grace further reflects on the differences between suspicious and reparative models of interpretation. She considers a button as something for 'keeping things closed up' and interprets Jeremiah's behaviour as telling her 'to keep silent' (428). By comparing the hermeneutics of suspicion, as exemplified by Simon's belief in the existence of 'hidden' meaning behind any 'common and unregarded objects', with Jeremiah's empathetic silence and lack of judgement – a kind of silence that is 'out of affection and fellow-feeling' (428) – the account signals the value of empathetic openness as an alternative to the hermeneutics of exposure, and the difficulties of 'knowing, acknowledging, and responding to others' on certain occasions (Jurecic 2011: 24). Also, by positioning Jeremiah as the attentive listener, Grace's account illustrates the ethical possibility genuine empathy inaugurates, in which the empathizer views the other as what Sedgwick describes 'at once good, damaged, integral, and requiring and eliciting love and care' (2003: 137). Following Jeremiah's lead, the way to empathize with Grace is 'to surrender the knowing, anxious paranoid determination' (Sedgwick 2003: 146), and to acknowledge her suffering, including her isolation and starvation in jail, her traumatic experience of sexual harassment, her vulnerability to objectification and prurient consumption. Grace's remark that guilt comes 'from the things that others have done to you' suggests that empathy now replaces suspicion and becomes an efficient means in identifying the 'guilty party' (379; Felski 2011: 215). Only by doing so can readers avoid repeating the same traumatic stories (as those featured in the text) and move towards a different – even if not necessarily better – future.

Conclusion

In *Feeling Backward*, Heather Love points out 'a central paradox' of what she calls 'transformative criticism'; that is, 'its dreams for the future are founded on a history of suffering, stigma, and violence' ([2007] 2009: 1). In this reflection on the way in which future hope is often inextricably tied up with the past, Love's observation neatly summarizes the ethical and political agenda of neo-Victorian fiction, a literary genre that prompts and thematizes the issue of reading the unsettling past. The exposure of historical traumas and injustices in neo-Victorian fiction demonstrates how the genre is imbued with 'ideas of reparation, political and economic compensation, the righting of injustice, the demand for witness and apology' (Ho [2012] 2013: 17). However, the genre's (over-)preoccupation with the suffering of the historically disadvantaged other may also seem to impair its transformative power. Back in 2001, Christian Gutleben has expressed his concern about the exploitation of characters from marginal communities in neo-Victorian fiction by remarking – in a quite parodic manner – that the ideal neo-Victorian protagonist is 'a destitute, handicapped, black, female homosexual' (168). To Gutleben, the stereotypical or generic presentation of the *other* Victorians in contemporary literary imagination complies 'with the hegemony of the politically correct' (66). 'Repeated from one novel to another', Gutleben argues, 'these politically correct perspectives, far from being subversive or innovative, become predictable, not to say redundant' (169).

Indeed, neo-Victorian novels often 'feed to' contemporary reader's voyeuristic desire for the exotic consumption of the 'non-normative' experience of the other Victorians through the use of the first-person perspective and epistolary narrative, resulting in what Marie-Luise Kohlke terms neo-Victorian 'sexsation' or 'the new Orientalism' (2008: 67). The publishing industry also plays an important role in establishing certain readerly expectations for the neo-Victorian genre, as evidenced by their choice of similar book covers for these novels. The 2007 UK paperback edition of Jane Harris's *The Observations*, for example, uses the image of a yellow and sealed envelope that is bonded by a red ribbon, with a vintage skeleton key attached to it, a cover design that embodies the voyeuristic and cryptic reading pleasures afforded by the novel. Similar designs can also be found in the paperback copy of Belinda Starling's *The Journal of Dora Damage* (2007). The presentation of a woman's body that is tied into a corset on the cover graphically associates the act of reading/opening the book with the sensuous experience of exposure and occupation.

Yet Gutleben's critique of the inherently conservative ideology and the 'politically-correct opportunism' of neo-Victorian fiction is problematic for its sweeping generalization (Robinson 2011: 23). In fact, the issues that he is concerned with are staged self-consciously in the novels that I explore in this chapter (and also chapters that follow). Imbued with the ethos of suspicion, neo-Victorian fiction – as a contemporary literary genre – engages with the pleasures and the ethical as well as political controversies associated with the hermeneutics of exposure. Whilst *The Observations* prompts the reader to reflect upon their complicity in the exploitation of the vulnerable other through its provocative and unreliable narrator, *Alias Grace* demonstrates the dynamic pull and push between the reader's empathetic tendencies and the textual pleasures associated with mystery, suspense and problem-solving through its intradiegetic examples. By telling stories that are full of intrigues and gaps in a retrospective manner, both novels implicate their readers in a hermeneutic puzzle that is ultimately impossible to solve, and in so doing, prompt the reader to critically reflect upon their privileged position as the suspicious 'revealer'. The call for readerly empathy – in the form of non-judgemental companion and other-orientated perspective-taking – that we witness at the end of the work of Harris and Atwood, respectively, steers the reader's attention to further questions about their participation in the envision of different futures for both textual and real worlds. Through its imaginative reconstruction of the (un)familiar past and strategic engagement with readerly expectations, neo-Victorian fiction allows for the possibility of a different future. Indeed, as Anne Whitehead contends, 'transformative possibility is predicated […] in the unexpected and unforeseen encounter, that can move us forward in different ways, and open up surprising new directions' (2017: 129).

In the next chapter, I continue the discussion of the transformative potential of neo-Victorian fiction by moving to the examination of how the genre's exploration of the 'shameful' or 'shameless' past invokes, tests and challenges the reader's empathetic and reparative tendency. As a strong affect, shame is not only an important thematic concern in contemporary literary imagination of the life experience of the 'deviant' other in Victorian England, but also informs the narrative structure of the first two novels of Sarah Waters's neo-Victorian trio: *Tipping the Velvet* (1998) and *Affinity* (1999).

2

Reading (with) shame

In a 2013 interview with Kaye Mitchell, Sarah Waters mentioned a shift of focus in her writing interest about the Victorians: 'I've found myself becoming much more interested in character and motivation and emotional dynamics, which means that I'm *less* interested in writing a kind of metafiction, I am less interested in *playing* with history than with creating a kind of *emotional experience* for my reader' (qtd in Mitchell 131, original emphasis). As one of the mostly discussed writers in the field of neo-Victorian studies, Waters's reflection on her writing career is remarkable since it resonates with current debates about different models of literary criticism led by critics including Eve Sedgwick, Rita Felski, Heather Love, Sharon Marcus, and so on (see introduction). The fact that Waters's books, quoting from herself in another interview, are primarily concerned with issues that 'literary departments are interested in talking about: class and gender, sexuality, and playing around with literary tradition' lead to a further concern about the effectiveness of what Sedgwick calls the 'paranoid inquiry' in diagnosing structural issues, obtaining new knowledge and ushering social and political transformations (qtd in Armitt 2007: 125). Waters's self-awareness of how her works 'lend themselves well to being analysed' (ibid.) brings to the fore the 'reciprocal' relationship between creative production and literary criticism in the phenomenon of neo-Victorianism, an issue that I address in detail in relation to the concept of 'narcissism' in Chapter 3. Indeed, as 'a contemporary workshop', neo-Victorianism 'reflects today's literary scene's Zeitgeist', which, as Christian Gutleben explains, enjoys an 'uneasy and complex relation to postmodernism' (2015: 225). In recognition of the postmodernist impulse at the heart of many neo-Victorian narratives, this chapter, nevertheless, follows the recent lead of Waters and moves to an exploration of the 'emotional experience' afforded by neo-Victorian fiction, with a particular focus on the affect of shame.

Shame plays an important role in contemporary writers' imaginative reconstruction of the nineteenth century, although, as far as I am aware, it has been mentioned only in passing by a small number of critics in the field of neo-Victorian studies.[1] The portrayal of dark family history, sexual deviance, the female body and the racial as well as disabled other in novels such as Sarah Waters's neo-Victorian trio – *Tipping the Velvet* (1998), *Affinity* (1999) and *Fingersmith* (2002) – Margaret Atwood's *Alias Grace* (1996), Sarah Blake's *Grange House* (2000), Darin Strauss's *Chang and Eng: A Novel* (2000), Barbara Chase-Riboud's *Hottentot Venus* (2003), Belinda Starling's *The Journal of Dora Damage* (2007), Laura Fish's *Strange Music* (2008) and Andrea Levy's *The Long Song* (2010) presents readers with different kinds of shame (i.e. sexual, bodily, racial and moral). By revisiting and rewriting these past experiences of shame, neo-Victorian fiction reveals – as well as challenges – the process of how these shame-related issues are discursively constructed. Helen Davies's *Neo-Victorian Freakery* (2015), for example, presents a similar argument in her interrogation of the freak show in both Victorian and neo-Victorian contexts. Davies argues that the imaginative presentation of 'the freak' in neo-Victorian fiction prompts contemporary readers to reflect upon their understanding of the boundary between '"normalcy" and the "abnormal"' (15). In this way the genre raises important questions about historical and social justice, a point that is identified by critics such as Marie-Luise Kohlke and Davies as a key social and political implication of neo-Victorian literature and culture (see Kohlke 2008; Davies 2015).

This focus on the discursive construction of shame sheds light on the process of how subjects are interpellated. It nevertheless risks the danger of ignoring the fact that shame is, first of all, a visceral and bodily experience. As Sara Ahmed observes, shame is 'a self-feeling that is felt by and on the body' (2004: 103).Taking into account the physicality of shame, critics such as Eve Sedgwick, Adam Frank and Elspeth Probyn have followed the lead of the American psychologist Silvan Tomkins in construing shame as a primitive

---

[1] A number of contributors to the collections of essays Kohlke and Gutleben edit mention shame in their discussion of sexuality, race, religion, trauma and the suffering of the child. However, none of them has analyzed the textual portrayal or evocation of shame in substantial details. See *Neo-Victorian Tropes of Trauma* (2010) and *Neo-Victorian Families* (2011). See also note 10 for more examples.

'affect'. Here the word 'affect' is used to highlight the difference in critical interest in the study of shame. Probyn explains that critics who are interested in 'cognition, social expression, and the [cultural] interpretation' of shame tend to use the word 'emotion' in their study; those interested in the 'biological' and 'bodily aspects' prefer 'affect' (2005: xv).[2] For Sedgwick and Frank, Tomkins's work is particularly useful for its difference from poststructuralist approaches to identity. However, their interest is not in establishing or reinforcing the opposition between discursive and biological conceptualizations of shame. Rather, by moving between different models of shame, Sedgwick and Frank examine the transformative politics of shame, and in particular, the capacity of shame to 'restructure social meaning' (Hemmings 2005: 550).

Tomkins's affect theory offers a useful alternative to the moralistic, teleological, and developmental understanding of shame, which is exemplified by Foucault's 'repressive hypothesis', Freud's drive theory and the various self-help and recovery programmes aimed at helping people get rid of shame, respectively. Tomkins' writings also 'startle' and excite Sedgwick and Frank 'for their sharpness and daring, their amplitude, and a descriptive levelheadedness that in the dispiriting context sounds almost surreal' (Sedgwick and Frank 1995: 4–5). Such appreciation of the textuality of Tomkins's work exemplifies what Ellis Hanson calls 'a reparative form of critical love' (2012: 558). Indeed, Sedgwick and Frank's editing of Tomkins's affect theory is featured by a desire to build some affective relationship with the critical object rather than an imperative to correct or possess it. In their introduction to *Shame and Its Sisters: A Silvan Tomkins Reader* (1995), Sedgwick and Frank describe their relationship with Tomkins as one between lovers and explain their purpose of editing in an intimate and empathetic tone: we wish 'to show how perfectly Tomkins understands *us*' (23, original emphasis). This inclusive gesture – signalled by the use of the collective pronoun 'us' – is an affective one; it also extends a warm and tempting invitation to their readers. This chapter thus follows Sedgwick and Frank in its examination of the *productivity* of revisiting

[2] Ruth Leys provides a useful review of the different understandings of the contested relationship between 'affect' and 'emotion' among the most influential affect theorists. She suggests that in spite of the wide difference between Tomkins (and his followers including Paul Ekman – those who believe in the existence of a number of 'structured, evolved categories of innate emotions') and those who follow Spinozist-Deleuzean ideas about affect, affect theorists share a consensus; that is, 'there is a disjunction or gap between the subject's affective processes and his or her cognition or knowledge of the objects that caused them' (Leys 2011: 442, 450).

the shameful or shameless past in two selected neo-Victorian novels – Waters's *Tipping the Velvet* and *Affinity* – both of which adopt a retrospective and autobiographical mode of narration (quasi-Bildungsroman and diary entries, respectively). As we will see, the experience of shame or shamelessness enables the first-person narrator of both texts to reflect upon their subjectivity and sexuality in a structure that is based on both narcissistic mirroring and transformative self-reflection. This 'empathetic' and reparative experience also produces more complex ways of understanding the relationship between the past, the present and the future in neo-Victorian literature.

In what follows, I begin with Jean-Paul Sartre's account of shame in order to contextualize the discussion of the role shame plays in the mediation of subjectivity and intersubjectivity. I then move to the writings of the philosophers Bernard Williams and Martha Nussbaum to demonstrate the process of how shame is constructed as a useful tool in moral development and its related issues, respectively. By challenging the developmental understanding of shame in Nussbaum's work, I take up Sedgwick and Frank's lead in arguing for a non-teleological approach to shame. This will provide a more productive framework for the examination of the ontological and affective relationship between self and other. I finish the theoretical section with a discussion of how shame and empathy are conditioned by a similar self–other relationship by drawing upon the contemporary philosopher Dan Zahavi's phenomenological work on empathy.[3] This similarity, as we shall see, positions empathy as a condition for the evocation of shame.

'An original fall'

In his discussion of the role shame plays in our relationship with the other, Sartre tells a story about a voyeur who is looking through a keyhole behind a door. He feels a sudden sense of shame when he hears footsteps in the hall and realizes that someone else might be looking at him at the same time. Although

---

[3] As Zahavi acknowledges, although phenomenologists such as Max Scheler, Edmund Husserl and Edith Stein have different accounts of empathy, their shared interest in the phenomenology of empathy and in particular, 'the givenness of others', provides us with a model of empathy that is different from mirroring and projection (2014: 111).

the voyeur later finds out that nobody is there, he is ashamed of himself since the imagined other makes him aware that he is the object of the other's consciousness, the object which 'the Other is looking at and judging' (Sartre [1956] 1978: 261). As the most poignant experience of the self by the self, shame is, paradoxically, constituted in – and through – the self's encounter with 'the Other', an abstract figure which needs not be a particular individual, or an embodiment of any particular judgement:

> Pure shame is not a feeling of being this or that guilty object but in general of being *an* object; that is, of *recognizing myself* in this degraded, fixed, and dependent being which I am for the Other. Shame is the feeling of an *original fall*, not because of the fact that I may have committed this or that particular fault but simply that I have 'fallen' into the world in the midst of things and that I need the mediation of the Other in order to be what I am. (288–9, original emphasis)

Zahavi explains that the experience of shame reveals 'our relationality' and 'our being-for-others', which is a painful awareness since 'I' cannot know myself in the same way as others can due to the lack of 'required self-distance' (2014: 213). This unsettling self–other relationship is taken up by Williams and Nussbaum in their respective interrogation of the role shame plays in moral construction and social justice. To Williams, the fact that the voyeur does not necessarily need to be caught in order to be ashamed suggests that shame could be ethically valuable for, or function constructively in, moral development:

> The imaginary observer can enter very early in the progression towards more generalised social shame. Sartre describes a man who is looking through a keyhole and suddenly realises that he is being watched. He might think that it was shameful to do it, not just to be seen doing it, and in that case, an imagined watcher could be enough to trigger the reactions of shame. (1993: 82)

Williams further develops Sartre's work by considering shame as not only 'a matter of being seen, but of being seen by an observer with a certain view' (ibid.). It is a sort of judgement that operates between people of 'heteronomous' values (78). The act of anticipating shame – in order to avoid it – could thus help to guide a future action: the self might change the way s/he behaves by thinking ahead about what the other will see. In this vein, shame is linked with the modern concept of civility, which functions as 'a mechanism for regulating relations between different individuals and groups within society' (Charmé 1991: 42).

Yet shame could have a detrimental influence in social behaviour since it is liable to prejudices and biases. As Ahmed contends, due to the inherent hierarchy or 'asymmetry of power' between different social groups, it is possible that the marginal group might be shamed by the powerful ones for things that they probably should not be ashamed of, such as sexuality, gender and race (2000: 8). This power dynamic between 'the shamer' and 'the shamed' is also an issue that Nussbaum examines in her criticism of the use of shame in law and social justice. For Nussbaum, the use of shame in the public system of law risks the danger of 'divid[ing] society into ranks and hierarchies', which is against the ideology of a liberal democratic society (2004: 232). Also, as Nussbaum warns, the fact that shame – unlike guilt – pertains to one's sense of self rather than specific acts suggests that the use of shame penalties might further depress or aggress an already fragile ego, which would 'lead to more, rather than less, violence' (236).

Nussbaum's argument is built upon Max Scheler's understanding of shame as 'a painful awareness of inadequacy' (Nussbaum 2004: 186). With the help of object-relations theory, Nussbaum considers shame – and in particular, the attempt to get rid of 'primitive shame' – as central to the development of self. Here Nussbaum understands primitive shame as 'the recognition of our own non-omnipotence and lack of control' after we leave the mother's womb and come to the uncontrollable external world (182):

> All infant omnipotence is coupled with helplessness. When an infant realizes that it is dependent on others, and is by this time aware of itself as a definite being who is and ought to be the center of the world, we can therefore expect a primitive and rudimentary emotion of shame to ensue. For shame involves the realization that one is weak and inadequate in some way in which one expects oneself to be adequate. Its reflex is to hide from the eyes of those who will see one's deficiency, to cover it. (183)

Nussbaum makes it clear that although shame could begin in early infancy, the cognitive content of shame exists only when one becomes aware of 'one's own being' (184). Focusing on the interaction between the infant and the caregiver (i.e. the mother), Nussbaum argues that primitive shame is the consequence of the infant's attempt to control the mother who refuses to be controlled, which often results in the ambivalence of the child's early emotions. This state of ambivalence, which originates from the infant's awareness that his/her love and hate is directed towards the same object, is also examined in the work of Melanie Klein. As argued in the introduction, Klein's discussion of the infant's relationship with what she calls 'the good breast' and 'the bad breast' fully illustrates how paranoia and reparation oscillate between each other. However, unlike the non-teleological temporality that is identified in Jackie Stacy's explication of Klein's work, Nussbaum's account of shame involves a developmental and progressive understanding of shame (see Stacey 2014). She believes that one's maturity is marked by their departure from primitive narcissism and shame:

> At a certain point children will be able to renounce envy and jealousy along with other attempts to control. They will use the resources of gratitude and generosity that they have by now developed – and developed in part on account of their guilt and sorrow – to establish the relationship on a footing of equality and mutuality. They acknowledge that they will always need love and security, but they see that this can be pursued without a jealous attempt to possess and control. (224)

The problem with this argument, as Nussbaum herself acknowledges, is that this state of maturity is difficult to achieve since the primitive shame we experience as an infant may only be 'partially overcome by the later development of the child's own separateness and autonomy' (185). Shame is therefore construed as a volatile emotion that is difficult and sometimes impossible to control. It is in this context that Nussbaum argues against the use of shame penalties since they might spoil one's self-esteem and ego and lead to more aggression and depression. As Nussbaum maintains, the process of maturation or equilibrium is 'highly prone to destabilization by forces both personal and social' and is thus 'a precarious achievement' (224).

The imperative to undo shame may also be seen as leaving the self *less* able to cope with shame when it does 'erupt' in adult life. It is arguable that the desire to get rid of shame will inevitably trap the self in shame, since shame – as in Nussbaum's context – is about 'lack of control' (336). As we have seen from Sartre, the sense of incompetence in shame is triggered by the vulnerable feeling of the self being objectified, a process which, to a certain extent, presupposes the existence of an omniscient other. As such, it is merely impossible to get rid of the shameful feeling about non-omnipotence. Jack Katz captures this point nicely in the following account: 'The other can see behind me, underneath me, the way I turn my torso and head to regulate my gaze. What is revealed to oneself in shame [...] is a kind of omniscience about oneself that only the Other can possess' (1999: 150).

Indeed, the more we try to undo shame, the more we will feel ashamed, since the other possesses something we have been desiring but will never be able to obtain. But does this mean that there is nothing we can do with shame? Sedgwick and Frank's conceptualization of shame also takes up the concept of primitive shame from object-relations theory, but, in contrast to Nussbaum, they understand it as an 'origin myth' (1995: 5). This is not to say that Sedgwick and Frank perceive shame as something essentially biological or physiological. For them, the difference between biology and social construction is that 'between differently structured residual essentialisms' (20). This is an essential point in their critique of what is described as 'the hygiene of [...] antiessentialism' in poststructuralist theory (17). As Sedgwick and Frank put it, the question is about why specifying affect as ' "discursively constructed" rather than "natural" should claim the status of a theory' (16). This theoretical decision of privileging the former runs the risk of essentialism as well, since it fails to take into account the 'qualitative [i.e. biological] differences among [...] different affects' (17). By challenging the opposition between cultural and biological explanations of affect, Sedgwick and Frank call for a critical attention to how each individual subject *experiences* affect as profoundly 'embodied' and 'essential' regardless of how it circulates in society. Also, by moving between object-relations theory and affect theory, Sedgwick and Frank offer a new way of understanding shame as being *politically productive*. This, in turn, relates to my later discussion of the ethical and political imperative that appears to be a feature of a number of neo-Victorian fictions. It will also help us distinguish between the different responses to 'shameful content' available to readers of neo-Victorian fiction, such as voyeurism, vicarious consumption and empathetic connection.

The 'affective' turn

Focusing on their innate nature, Tomkins considers affects as 'non-intentional' and 'bodily reactions' (Leys 2011: 437). As Tomkins's disciple – psychologist Donald L. Nathanson – explains, the fact that the infant's first cry has no self-consciousness suggests to Tomkins that there must be some biological or 'preexistent mechanism' that triggers the infant's cry (1987: 12). Tomkins also holds that there exists 'a radical dichotomy between the "real" causes of affect and the individual's own interpretation of these causes' (2008: 137). For cultural theorists such as Sedgwick and Frank, Tomkins's affect theory is particularly intriguing for its difference from the drive system, that as a whole the affect system 'has no single "output"' and 'is indifferent to the means-end difference' (Tomkins 2008: 657). It requires no cognitive element and is 'autotelic': having an end or purpose in itself (Hemmings 2005: 552). The following passage from Tomkins is a good example that describes the self-referentiality of affect: 'It is enjoyable to enjoy. It is exciting to be excited. It is terrorizing to be terrorized and angering to be angered. Affect is self-validating with or without any further referent' (Tomkins 2008: 873). Sedgwick further elaborates on its freedom by suggesting that 'affects can be, and are, attached to things, people, ideas, sensations, relations, activities, ambitions, institutions, and any number of other things, including other affects' (2003: 19). Affect thus enjoys some 'structural potential' that is 'not enjoyed by the drive system' (ibid.).

Tomkins also provides a relational way of understanding different affects.[4] Shame, for example, is positioned in relation to 'interest':

> Like disgust, [shame] operates ordinarily only after interest or enjoyment has been activated, and inhibits one or the other or both. The innate activator of shame is the incomplete reduction of interest or joy. Hence any barrier to further exploration which partially reduces interest or the smile of

---

[4] Sedgwick and Frank draw on Anthony Wilden's work on 'digital' and 'analog' communications to explain the operation of the affect system. The pair of concepts are used by Wilden to refer to 'two-valued' and 'many-valued' model of communication, respectively (qtd in Sedgwick and Frank 1995: 9). Unlike the drive system, which operates in the digital (i.e. on/off) model, the affect system yields a model that encompasses both digital and analog communications. In her reading of Tomkins's work, Probyn suggests that affect operates in an 'and/and/and/and' model (2005: 21). Indeed, as Hemmings asserts, the attraction of affect theory to cultural theorists lies in its advocacy of 'connected and relational' modes of power and community as opposed to 'oppositional modes' (2005: 550).

enjoyment will active the lowering of the head and eyes in shame and reduce further exploration or self-exposure powered by excitement or joy. Such a barrier might be because one is suddenly looked at by one who is strange, or because one wishes to look at or commune with another person but suddenly cannot because he is strange, or one expected him to be familiar but he suddenly appears unfamiliar, or one started to smile but found one was smiling at a stranger. (Tomkins 1995: 134–5)

Tomkins construes shame as an affect that is consequent upon interest in a particular object or occurrence. It is 'a programmed response to an impediment to [the] preexisting affect' – interest or joy – when there still '*remains* a competent stimulus for [it]' (Nathanson [1992] 1994: 138, original emphasis). Taking the residual interest into consideration, Sedgwick suggests that shame may also be considered as 'a desire to reconstitute the interpersonal bridge' (2003: 36).[5] Therefore, shame becomes 'one important (embodied) circuit through which power is felt, imagined, mediated, negotiated and/or contested' (Pedwell 2012a: 176).

Linking shame to interest, Tomkins's model provides us with a useful approach to understanding the way in which neo-Victorian fiction plays with the reader's generic reading expectations and desires. As we will see in my following analysis of Waters's *Tipping the Velvet* and *Affinity*, both novels deploy 'immersive strategies' to provoke the reader's voyeuristic and participatory reading interest at first (Boehm-Schnitker and Gruss 2014: 5). Both then 'disrupt' and – to a certain degree – 'shame' the contemporary reader's desire for more knowledge about lesbian sexuality in the imaginatively reconstructed Victorian underworld, which prompts further discussion about what an 'appropriate' ethical approach to the queer subject might look like.[6] This ethical encounter with the other involves a mechanism of – to paraphrase Sedgwick – 'shame-proneness' (2003: 37), which refers to a kind of 'empathetic receptivity'

---

[5] Aside from the book she co-edits with Adam Frank, Sedgwick has also published an article on shame and queer subjectivity in 1993, a revised version of which is included in her 2003 essay collection *Touching Feeling*.

[6] It is arguable that *Tipping the Velvet* and *Affinity* position heterosexual and lesbian readers in potentially different ways in their celebration of same-sex passion. Also, readers of different sexualities could be engaging with the issue of 'queer shame' variously. However, it is worth reiterating that the kind of readerly fascination that I explore in this chapter is about the contemporary reader's general interest about 'submerged sexuality or sexual underworlds' that Waters imaginatively reconstructs in her text, rather than heterosexual readers' curiosity about lesbian sexuality (Waters qtd in Dennis 2008: 45).

to the other's shame and will be explained in detail in the next section. In other words, the kind of readerly shame that I explore in this chapter is associated with the text's manipulative narratological strategies and is premised on the relational nature of shame, rather than Waters's engagement with what might appear to be a 'deviant' content in the context of the heteronormative discourse of sexuality (which could provoke discussion of the role shame plays in the normalizing of heterosexuality).

By linking the psychologist Michael Franz Basch's object-relations approach to shame with Tomkins's affect theory, Sedgwick positions shame as a productive force in the examination of subjectivity and intersubjectivity. Basch's own writing on the relationship between shame and identity in the circuit of mirroring between the child and the caregiver is worth quoting here: 'The infant's behavioral adaptation is quite totally dependent on maintaining effective communication with the executive and coordinating part of the infant-mother system. The shame-humiliation response, when it appears, represents the failure or absence of the smile of contact, a reaction to the loss of feedback from others, indicating social isolation and signaling the need for relief from that condition' (1976: 765). As Sedgwick explains, the communication between the child and the caregiver – in the form of 'mirroring expressions' – constitutes 'primary narcissism' (2003: 36).[7] Shame, in this scenario, 'floods into being as […] a disruptive moment' (ibid.). However, this disruption does not lead to the termination of identity formation. In fact, shame mediates between self and other. In the context of the traditional object-relations developmental narrative, shame is perceived as what defines 'the space wherein a sense of self will develop' (Sedgwick 2003: 37). As we have also seen from Nussbaum, the object-relations theory considers the mitigation of shame as a sign of maturity. However, in contrast to the progressive understanding of shame, Sedgwick and Frank position shame as a productive force in their interrogation of subjectivity and intersubjectivity. Their aim is not to find ways to help us get rid of shame. Rather, they are interested in exploring the way in which the self will be transformed *in* and *through* shame,

---

[7] In Freudian psychoanalysis, 'primary narcissism' refers to 'the necessary self-love which precedes the capacity to love others, based on the blissful self-absorption of the newborn' (Bateman and Holmes 1995: 55). This concept is questioned by later psychoanalysts for its 'entirely solipsistic quality' (Rüggemeier and Maren Scheurer 2019: 172), a point I will address in detail in Chapter 3.

a critical practice that intends to repair our broken or 'disrupted' relationship with the world. And this is why Tomkins's affect theory interests them. As they notice, Tomkins's writing is not only 'sublimely alien ... to the developmental presumption or prescription of a core self'; it is also 'sublimely *resistant* ... to such a presumption' (1995: 7, original emphasis).

The way shame transforms the self is well illustrated by Sedgwick's analysis of the phrase 'Shame on you', which links to her use of J. L. Austin's speech act theory to explain the ways in which particular utterances are instrumental in conferring identity to the speakers concerned (e.g. 'I do' in the marriage ceremony): 'the very grammatical truncation of "Shame on you" marks it as the product of a history out of which an I, now withdrawn, is *projecting* shame – toward another I, an I deferred, that has yet and with difficulty to come into being, if at all, in the place of the shamed second person' (1993: 4, original emphasis). Sedgwick's analysis of how shame effaces the self suggests that the subjectivity of the shamed being 'remains to be specified' and 'is always belated' (13). The idea of subjectivity as to-be-constituted further explains the role shame plays in the construction – or more precisely, transformation – of identity; shame is a state or moment of 'suspended' being in which the subject is 'without essence' and hence open to future metamorphosis. As Sedgwick states, 'shame and identity remain in very dynamic relation to one another, at once deconstituting and foundational' (2003: 36).

Shame and empathy

In explaining the political productivity of shame, Sedgwick invokes the experiences of 'a shame-prone person':

> One of the strangest features of shame, but perhaps also the one that offers the most conceptual leverage for political projects, is the way bad treatment of someone else, bad treatment *by* someone else, someone else's embarrassment, stigma, debility, bad smell, or strange behavior, seemingly having nothing to do with me, can so readily flood me – assuming I'm a shame-prone person – with this sensation whose very suffusiveness seems to delineate my precise, individual outlines in the most isolating way imaginable. (2003: 36–7, original emphasis)

Although Sedgwick does not explain her use of the term 'shame-prone', her account sketches an individual who is hypersensitive and susceptible to the other's socially awkward behaviours (regardless of whether the other feels ashamed or not). The fact that through the act of witnessing the self could become implicated in – and ashamed of – the other's 'strange' manners or humiliating experiences brings to the fore the role empathy plays in triggering shame. The other's 'oddity' prompts the self to confront its own exteriority – or what Sedgwick calls its 'precise, individual outlines' – in an extremely uncomfortable manner, an experience that, to a certain extent, echoes Sartre's story of voyeurism. As introduced in the previous section, Sartre considers shame as the self's awareness of its being-for-others; or, put differently, the self's 'empathetic' experience of itself from the perspective of the other. Carolyn Pedwell further contends that 'empathy is necessary for shame to occur' (2014: 112). As such, shame-proneness can be considered as an act of empathetic responsiveness, which is 'directed at the affectivity of the other' (Agosta 2014: 4). By being receptively open to the other's experience, shame-proneness lends a useful perspective to exactly *how* readers can ethically engage with literary texts.

Shame and empathy can be linked together since both possess a 'self-concept', a term coined by the psychologist Doris Bischof-Köhler in explaining the process of individualization. Zahavi expounds that 'to possess a self-concept is to have the capacity to objectify oneself and to recognize one's outwardly [sic] appearance, one's exteriority, as (part of) oneself' (2014: 229). Indeed, as we have seen from Sartre, shame is triggered by self-objectification, a process that challenges the self's solipsistic stance and pushes one to see oneself in an intersubjective context. The same holds true for empathy, which, Zahavi stresses, is 'other-centred' (161). In Chapter 1, I have examined the difference between self-orientation and other-orientation in empathy by looking at Amy Coplan's conceptualization of self-orientated and other-orientated perspective-takings. In this chapter, I move to a phenomenological discussion of the ontological and affective intertwinement between self and other in empathy.

Zahavi observes that phenomenologists such as Max Scheler, Edmund Husserl and his PhD student, Edith Stein, consider empathy as an act of perception, a phenomenon that is conditioned by the differences rather than similarities between self and other. For Scheler, empathetic experience is about 'the perception of others', which means, unlike emotional contagion or mirroring, empathy orients towards the other's feelings (Zahavi 2014: 118). A similar view can be found in Husserl's *Phenomenological Psychology* (1962), where he defines empathy as 'the intentionality in one's own ego that leads into the foreign (*fremde*) ego' (qtd in Zahavi 2014: 125). The fact that empathy 'articulates a structure of relatedness' between self and other renders it a crucial step to escape solipsism, although Husserl does not step further by suggesting that the self–other relationship plays an essential role in the formation of subjectivity (Agosta 2014: 100). With a focus on the phenomenon of empathy, Husserl explores the way in which we come to know others. Like Scheler, Husserl considers empathy as a process of how we come to perceive – as opposed to infer – the foreign subjectivity: 'it would be countersensical to say that it is inferred and not experienced when given in this original form of empathic presentation. For every hypothesis concerning a foreign subject already presupposes the "perception" of this subject as foreign, and empathy is precisely this perception' (qtd in Zahavi 2014: 127). Husserl's formulation of empathy as a perception of the other's alterity is taken up and further developed by Stein in her 1917 dissertation *On the Problem of Empathy* (*Zum Problem der Einfühlung*), where Stein holds that empathy is 'a kind of act of perceiving *sui generis*' and 'the experience of foreign consciousness in general' (11).[8] In his reading Agosta specifies the phenomenological take on perception as 'a form of receptivity to the lived expressions of animate life of the other individual', which, to him, positions the self as the object of the other's consciousness at the same time (2014: 103). In this light, Agosta proposes that empathy could develop one's self-understanding, since it helps the self to shift

---

[8] It should also be noted that from a phenomenological perspective, the experience of the empathized and that of the empathizer is fundamentally different: 'While I am living in the other's joy, I do not feel primordial joy. It does not issue live from my "I". Neither does it have the character of once having lived like remembered joy. But still much less is it merely fancied without actual life. This other subject is primordial although I do not experience its primordiality; his joy is primordial although I do not experience is [sic] as primordial. In my non-primordial experience I feel, as it were, led by a primordial one not experienced by me but still there, manifesting itself in my non-primordial experience' (Stein 1964: 11). Stein's example makes it clear that the other's joy (which is his or her primordial experience) is not experienced by the self as primordial, although the vicarious experience of the other's joy is a primordial act for the self. Stein emphasizes that empathy is 'primordial as present experience though non-primordial in content' (10).

between different perspectives, a point that resembles my previous discussion of the mediating role shame plays in subjectivity and intersubjectivity.

Now we can see how both shame and empathy are conditioned by a similar self–other relationship. This link between shame and empathy helps us to better understand Sedgwick's advocacy of shame's capacity for transformation both in the reading process and in the practical world. Sedgwick positions shame as 'a near-inexhaustible source of transformational energy' 'narratively, emotionally, and performatively' (1993: 4, 11). As argued before, shame pushes us to see the self in a relational and 'empathetic' way; that is, to see the self as an object for the other, which means to experience others empathetically as subjects who experience us as objects; and also to see others as being-for-me. Indeed, as Sartre puts it, 'the structures of my being-for-the-Other are identical to those of the Other's being-for-me' ([1956] 1978: 339). Shame, then, involves not only a questioning of the self but also a rethinking of the relationality between self and other and, by extension, one's own otherness. It serves as 'the place where the *question* of identity arises most originarily and most relationally' (Sedgwick 2003: 37, original emphasis). The 'desire to reconstitute the interpersonal bridge' shame signals also renders it an intense force for 'metamorphosis, reframing, refiguration, *trans*figuration, affective and symbolic loading and deformation' (36, 63, original emphasis). This approach to shame is notably featured by a reparative impulse to explore – as opposed to be rid of – the paralyzing affect.

In what follows, I move to the analysis of two selected neo-Victorian novels – *Tipping the Velvet* and *Affinity* – both of which present the issue of shame in relation to subjectivity and intersubjectivity.[9] Waters's imaginative

---

[9] Although this chapter limits the scope of its discussion to the first two novels of Waters, it is important to note that shame – as a powerful affective and political force – permeates most of Waters's writings. *Fingersmith* (2002), e.g. explores how the protagonists, Maud and Sue, reappropriate their shameful experience of oppression and exploitation in 'heteropatriarchal pornography' for same-sex pleasure in Victorian England (O'Callaghan 2015: 561). Aside from her neo-Victorian trio, Waters's following publications engage with the issue of shame in various ways, making valuable contributions to contemporary discussion about the political, social and moral significance of shame. Set in 1940s London, *The Night Watch* (2006) appears to be marked by the absence of the discourse of shame and self-loathing that 'dominated psychoanalytical thinking about homosexuality in this period' (Alden 2013: 80). However, Waters's use of motifs such as 'invisibility and secrets' reveals how the four protagonists of *The Night Watch*, Kay, Helen, Julia and Duncan, 'share a shameful queerness' which originates from their position as both 'sexual and social outsiders' (Escudero-Alías 2014: 227). In a similar vein, Waters's latest novel, *The Paying Guest* (2014), examines 'queer shame' and the repression queer subjects receive in a homophobic society (O'Callaghan 2017: 156). Set in a dilapidated house in Warwickshire in the 1940s, Waters's 2009 novel, *The Little Stranger*, is an interesting exception in that

reconstruction of lesbianism in both texts exemplifies Sedgwick's model of reparative practice (see introduction), a point that is barely recognized and little explored by critics in the field of neo-Victorian studies. In fact, Waters's work is often viewed by critics through what Sedgwick would consider 'paranoid lenses'; her fictive renditions of queer sexuality in Victorian England have been regarded as significant contemporary attempts to demystify hidden patterns of class, gender and sexual violence of the past (see Llewellyn 2004; Wilson 2006; Carroll 2012). Waters's bawdy description of queer sexuality in *Tipping the Velvet* and sophisticated plotting of power and possession in *Affinity*, nevertheless, provide contemporary readers with startling, passionate and arguably 'shameless' reimaginings of nineteenth-century lesbianism. Through the use of autobiographical and retrospective narrative, both texts engage with the transformative potential of shame. While *Tipping the Velvet* illustrates the mediating role shame plays in the formation of queer subjectivity and sexuality, *Affinity* further demonstrates the great need for empathetic recognition behind the queer subject's revisitations of the previous experiences of shame. Taking up the lead of Kaye Mitchell, this chapter demonstrates that shame is not only an important thematic concern of Waters's work, but it also 'disturbs the form of the text' and 'infects its reading and reception' (2020: 32).

Shame, performativity, queerness

Set in Victorian England during the 1890s, Waters's debut novel, *Tipping the Velvet*, tells 'a queer *Bildung*' about the sexual awakening journey of the protagonist Nancy (Nan) Astley (Jeremiah 2007: 136). The story traces the process of how Nan, a young 'oyster' girl (Nan is born in the oyster parlour her father keeps), makes her way to London and develops queer

---

it moves away from the familiar topic of queer sexuality and focuses on the unresolved shame and trauma in post-war Britain through the trope of haunting and spectrality. From this brief review, it is clear that Waters's fiction addresses shame in relation to a number of issues such as identity, gender, sexuality, class and trauma. However, the topic of shame is relatively under analyzed in scholarly writings on Waters's work. Focusing on the textual portrayal of the protagonist's lesbian experience in *Tipping the Velvet* and *Affinity* (Nancy Astley and Margaret Prior, respectively), this chapter also contributes to the study of Waters's work through its examination of the mechanism of shame – and in particular, its volatile relation to (self) pleasure – the role shame plays in the formation of queer subjectivity, and the dynamic that exists between shame and readerly pleasure.

relationships with characters from different backgrounds and social classes. Focusing on the symbolism of music hall and the idea of performance that the novel constantly evokes, I demonstrate how the theatrical presentation of female bodies and queer sexuality provokes, as well as appeals to, the reader's desire to 'feel' and consume the nineteenth century. My approach to the issue of performativity is informed by Sedgwick's explication of the *extroversion* that structures theatrical performance, referring to the actor's outward aiming towards the audience/reader (2003: 7, original emphasis), rather than the deconstructionist model, which, as Helen Davies trenchantly remarks, 'has become a critical commonplace' in scholarly writings on *Tipping the Velvet* (2012: 117). Performativity is, therefore, considered as a useful concept in unpacking the text–reader dynamic that Waters's writing facilitates. In light of Tomkins's formulation of the affect polarity between interest and shame, I also propose that through the use of manipulative narratological strategies, *Tipping the Velvet* implicates the reader in the shame of – and shaming – the textual other. In order to fully unpack the complicated reading pleasures afforded by *Tipping the Velvet*, I begin with a discussion of how the text uses various narrative techniques in immersing the reader in the fictional Victorian England. This will then be followed by a further examination of how the vicarious and voyeuristic reading position transforms into a potentially erotic as well as shameful one.

Narrated retrospectively by Nan in later life, the whole story is presented as the journey of her sexual awakening. Using Nan's 'shameles[s]' narrative voice, the text facilitates the reader's erotic, immersive and voyeuristic consumption of the Victorian(s) in the first part (Waters 1998: 41). Through Nan's provocative question 'Have you ever tasted a Whitstable oyster?' and her sensuous description of oysters in the opening paragraphs, the image of which instantly conjures up erotic associations, the text purposefully mixes the tropes of gustatory and readerly pleasures (3).[10] It also plays with the reader's hermeneutic desire to learn about and explore the fictional world by encouraging them to follow in Nan's steps and identify with the figure of Nan's interlocutor through the use of the unidentified second-person pronoun

---

[10] O'Callaghan further argues that oysters are 'a metaphor for queer identities' since they are 'a queer fish' and 'morphodites' (2012: 23).

'you'. The textual details about the location, smell and decoration of the oyster parlour that Nan's family keeps provide the reader with a fully landscaped Victorian world which, in turn, provokes and caters to the reader's vicarious desire to enter the past.

In fact, readerly desire is a thematic preoccupation in several neo-Victorian fictions. The opening of Michel Faber's *The Crimson Petal and the White* (2002) is a classic example. Here the narrator may be seen to taunt the readers by drawing attention to their desire for 'immersion' in the novel at the same time as reminding them that this is impossible:

> This city I am bringing you to is vast and intricate, and you have not been here before. You may imagine, from other stories you've read, that you know it well, but those stories flattered you, welcoming you as a friend, treating you as if you belonged. The truth is that you are an alien from another time and place altogether. (3)

As Kohlke observes, such texts 'entic[e] the reader to lose her/himself in the night time underworld of Victorian London' but then remind them of the reasons as to why they cannot (2008: 54–5). The reader's consciousness is thus appropriated by the text in a 'deliberate and paradoxical manner', which, as Linda Hutcheon explains, refers to the complicated situation that the reader 'must live within an *acknowledgedly* fictional universe as he reads' ([1980] 1985: 140, original emphasis). Yet, as Hutcheon continues, the text 'constantly demands responses comparable in scope and perhaps even in intensity to those of his life experience' (ibid.). By positioning the act of reading as a process parallel to that of writing, Faber's *The Crimson Petal and the White* exemplifies the ways in which certain neo-Victorian texts put significant demands upon the reader's participation. A similar – but less metafictional – example is Jane Harris's *The Observations*. As we have seen in the previous chapter, the narrator Bessy's account at the beginning frames the whole story as a conversation between Bessy and her unidentified interlocutor: 'But wait on, I am getting ahead of myself. Let me begin nearer the beginning' (vii). This dialogic atmosphere invites the reader to follow Bessy and reinforces the sense of readerly participation by creating a parallel between Bessy's actual journey from Glasgow to Castle Haivers (where she meets her mistress Arabella and becomes attracted to her) and the reader's reading process.

Waters's *Tipping the Velvet* evokes the corporeal experience of the space in rendering the act of reading a virtual journey. During this process the reader needs to 'follo[w] the guides offered by the script' (Boehm-Schnitker and Gruss 2011: 5) and piece together fact and conjecture in order to fully immerse themselves in the contemporary fantasy of a Victorian England that is marked by 'erotic excess' (Kohlke 2008: 54). Nan's recollection about the Canterbury Palace of Varieties, where she used to watch the performance of Kitty Butler, is a good example in this respect:

> When I see [the Palace] in my memories I see [...] the mirror-glass which lined the walls, the crimson plush upon the seats, the plaster cupids, painted gold, which swooped above the curtain. Like our oyster-house, it has its own particular scent – the scent, I know now, of music halls everywhere – the scent of wood and grease-paint and spilling beer, of gas and of tobacco and of hair-oil, all combined. (6)

With a focus on the perceptible and sensory qualities of the theatre, Nan's account presents a multisensory aesthetic experience of the theatrical space, referring to 'the perceptual dimensions through which we experience an environment directly – what we hear, see, and feel with our bodies as we move through it' (Berleant 1997: 42). As Arnold Berleant further points out, 'these sensory qualities combine with our knowledge and beliefs to create a unified experiential situation' (ibid.). Indeed, the textual description of Nan's corporeal experience of the theatre – and in particular, the smell of it – reinforces the sense of experientiality, which helps to facilitate the reader's vicarious consumption of the fictional space, a phenomenon that is termed by Nadine Boehm-Schnitker and Susanne Gruss as 'vicarious synaesthesia' (2011: 5). Through these means, then, the reader of *Tipping the Velvet* is proactively seduced into immersing her/himself into the text until they become what Lynne Pearce calls 'the ghostly reader' who enjoys a vicarious participation in the text's intra-diegetic action (1997: 24).

The fact that the theatrical space featured in *Tipping the Velvet* is also linked with queer sexuality adds another explicitly erotic dimension to the reading pleasures afforded by Waters's fiction.[11] As we see from the text, the relationship

---

[11] In O'Callaghan's historical reading, places such as 'clubs, theatres and boathouses' function as 'a "safe" space to which homosexuals flee as respite from homophobia' (2014: 132). As such, Waters's work challenges the conventional understanding of domesticity.

between Nan and Kitty develops from the time when Kitty performs as a male impersonator at the local theatre to Nan following Kitty to London as the two begin to work with one another as a singing and dancing double act. The text subsequently introduces the idea of reading as a secretive and visceral pleasure through its portrayal of lesbian sexuality under the cover of theatrical performance. Narrated from Nan's perspective, the following account plays with the multiple meanings of – and hence different pleasures afforded by – 'double act':

> A double act is always twice the act the audience thinks it: beyond our songs, our steps, our bits of business with coins and canes and flowers, there was a private language, in which we held an endless, delicate exchange of which the crowd knew nothing. This was a language not of the tongue but of the body, its vocabulary the pressure of a finger or a palm, the nudging of a hip, the holding or breaking of a gaze, that said, *You are too slow – you go too fast – not there, but here – that's good – that's better!* […] But, that *was* our show; only the crowd never knew it. They looked on, and saw another turn entirely. (128, original emphasis)

By drawing attention to the gulf between what the audience sees and what the actors know, the reader is made complicit in the text in a way that is potentially erotically arousing. The use of italics in print in Nan's remark – 'What a show *that* would be!' – further encourages the reader to get actively involved in the furtive and visceral consumption of lesbian sexuality with information that is denied the intra-diegetic audience (i.e. the theatregoers in the narrative) (128). The text thus draws the reader's attention to their privileged reading position and reinforces their clandestine reading pleasure by making it clear that Nan's 'sexual' performance is for private audiences, and sometimes, the reader's eyes only.

Nan's 'performance' in Diana's bathroom (a wealthy Sapphist Nan meets after she leaves Kitty) further involves the reader in her narcissistic and exhibitionistic enjoyment of the female body and queer sexuality. She 'might spend an hour or more' examining herself 'before the glass for marks of beauty or for blemishes', and would use different kinds of unguents to polish her 'eyebrows', 'lashes', 'fingernails', 'mouth', 'nipples' and 'heels', an experience which, Nan exclaims, is 'quite like dressing for the halls again' (264).[12] The

---

[12] The idea of performance also reveals Nan's awareness of herself as the projection of Diana's sexual fantasy, or her '*caprice*' as Diana's Sapphic circle addresses Nan (Waters 1998: 278, original

interactive nature of theatrical performance speaks to Nan's intensely charged relationship with her audience/reader. The reader is, first of all, invited to consume Nan's body and queer sexuality in a visceral and vicarious manner, and then led to be critical – and ashamed – of such prurience. The prurient nature of the readerly fascinations is drawn out in Nan's reflection that displaying her body – by putting her 'in a new costume' and having her 'walk before [...] or among' Diana's guests – has become 'a kind of sport' with Diana and her friends (280). In these scenarios, Nan is involuntarily 'confined to a figurative stage' and 'an object of desire' for the gaze of Diana and her upper-class community (Koolen 2010: 384). As Nan claims, 'I could help none of it. It was all Diana's doing' (281). Nan's experience of dehumanization reveals the uneasy relationship between 'sex and power' (O'Callaghan 2017: 36). Here the reader is made starkly aware of the ways in which a fascination with the socially disadvantaged other can lead into exploitation and, at a metacritical level, can *disrupt* their earlier immersion in the text.

Yet Nan's feeling of vulnerability and impotence stimulates her sexual excitement, an experience that attests to the erotics of shame and is exemplified by her orgasm at the hands of Diana's friends. The voluptuous description of how Nan 'twitched and cried out' when 'the ladies [...] stroke the leather' that straps 'Diana's *Monsieur Dildo*' to her hips further involves the reader in the consumption of a sadomasochistic sexuality (281). The risqué encounter Nan's account creates between the text and the reader is carefully disrupted by Nan's authorial intrusion as a narrator: 'I sound weary of [Diana]. I was not weary of her then' (282). The mention of Nan's sense of weariness now – with the connotation of having one's pleasure exhausted – serves to challenge the reader's participation in Diana's game and undermine their pleasurable consumption of the text. This kind of textual disruption could arguably evoke shame, since shame, as we have seen from Tomkins, is positioned in relation to interest. Tomkins notes that 'once shame has been activated, the original excitement or joy may be increased again and inhibit the shame or the shame may further inhibit and reduce excitement or joy', bringing to the fore the

---

emphasis). In this regard, Nan's experience of dehumanization and exploitation demonstrates how Waters's text complicates the discussion about the relationship between female agency and erotic desire. See also O'Callaghan (2017: 32–8).

dynamic interaction between shame and interest (1995: 135). Before I move to a further discussion of how the residual interest decides 'the malleability of shame' (Escudero-Alías 2014: 226), it is important to note that in my context, 'the preexisting affect' is specified as a form of enjoyment that relates to the reader's immersive consumption of same-sex desire in Waters's novel. The readerly shame is triggered by the text's self-conscious engagement with the contemporary reader's expectation for reimaginings of exuberant lesbian sexuality in Victorian England where 'the concept of lesbianism supposedly did not exist' (Dennis 2008: 41). It is also through the mechanism of shame that the text prompts the reader to become more self-aware and reflective of their reading practice.

By revealing Nan's awareness of the audience's/reader's gaze, *Tipping the Velvet* further explores the erotic potential or pleasure in shame. In her account of the double act, Nan suggests that 'Well, perhaps there were some who caught glimpses...' (128). The use of ellipsis in print indicates a significant sense of trailing off, which reinforces as well as challenges the clandestine pleasures afforded by Nan's narrative. Here the textual reader is positioned as both Nan's interlocutor, whose voyeuristic reading is appropriated by the text, and Nan's collaborator in identifying the gaze of the intra-diegetic audience. In so doing, the text draws attention to the act of reading itself. This significant degree of readerly involvement created by Nan's narration is arguably designed to maximize the potential pleasure of the reading experience, which is, notably, predicated on the activation of shame, a point that Waters's text actively engages with. When Nan realizes that Florence (her subsequent lover) might take her as 'some insolent *voyeur*', she remarks that 'the thought gave me an odd mixture of shame and embarrassment and also, I must confess, pleasure' (221, original emphasis). The association Nan makes between voyeurism, shame and pleasure recalls the aforementioned story Sartre tells in his discussion of shame. As argued previously, shame is a powerful intermediary between different aspects of oneself in the process of identity formation.

The intricate link between shame and pleasure is played out in other, equally provoking, ways in the course of the novel. When Nan recollects the younger self's experience of doing some cleaning in Kitty's dressing room, she admits that these 'ministrations' of love involve 'a kind of *self*-pleasure, for it made

[her] feel strange and hot and almost shameful to perform them' (38, original emphasis). In this scene shame is registered and performed by Nan's tangible physiological reactions, and is triggered by her awareness that the pleasure she perceives is a form of self-pleasure, which presents the self as a subject who consumes itself by objectifying its actions. In light of Sartre and Zahavi, Nan's shame is consequent upon her self-concept, or self-objectification, an 'empathetic' experience that also informs the construction of her queer subjectivity and is where my discussion now turns as I explore, further, the complicated reading pleasures afforded by Waters's text.

In recalling one of the younger self's sexual dream, Nan exploits the fraught erotics of shame and uses it as a way to develop an affectionate relationship with her queer youth:

> How Kitty would have blushed, to know the part she played in my fierce dreamings – to know how *shamelessly* I took my memories of her, and turned them to my own improper advantage! [...] I was used to standing close to her, to fasten her collar-studs or brush her lapels; now, in my reveries, I did what I longed to do then – I leaned to place my lips upon the edges of her hair; I slid my hands beneath her coat, to where her breasts pressed warm against her stiff gent's shirt and rose to meet my strokings ...
> (41, emphasis added)

The narrator Nan's comment on the 'shameless[ness]' of her younger self shames the past self. By projecting shame towards the younger self, the text introduces an *intersubjective* relationship between the present self and the past one, thus making it clear that the narrator Nan does not intend to merge with the shamed figurations of the younger self. The meticulous depiction of the past erotic dream – and in particular, its treatment of lavish details – suggests that Nan's attempt is to mobilize the previous self-pleasure or 'shame' (as experienced by the present self) for further 'shameless' consumption and exploitation. As Nan claims, 'The memory [...] was overlaid, in this new setting, with a keen, expectant pleasure' (235). The display of imagined queer sexuality and erotic female bodies in the form of shameful reverie creates what Sedgwick describes as a 'pleasurable form of exhibitionistic flirtation' between different stages of the character Nan (2003: 42). Following Sedgwick, Nan's revisitation of her previous dream can be read as her attempt to develop a more affectionate and sustainable relationship with the younger self through the act of shaming, a reparative and empathetic experience that exemplifies the mediating role shame plays in Nan's development as a queer subject.

Sedgwick's writings on the role shame plays in the formation of queer subjectivity are particularly useful for my discussion here. As Sedgwick contends, queerness is 'lodged in the refusals of deflections of (or by) the logic of the heterosexual supplement' (2003: 71). Herein queer subjectivity is characterized by a kind of negation and detour, and remains to be constituted and navigated rather than presumed. In response to the indeterminate nature of queer subjectivity, shame can be seen as a productive force, since the way it operates – by continuously 'ushering in new forms of communication and new forms of identity-constitution' – questions, and also constitutes, queer subjectivity (Bennett 2010: 303). The constant attempt to reconstitute the 'identity-constituting identificatory communication' with the other is well illustrated by the use of retrospective autobiographical narrative in the representation of Nan's development as a queer subject in *Tipping the Velvet* (Sedgwick 2003: 36). Indeed, as previously argued, Nan's recollection of her 'sham*eless*' queer youth creates an intersubjective relationship between the different stages of subject development, encapsulating what Sedgwick calls the 'relational positionalities' shame delineates (40).

Nan's self-portrait as 'Narcissus' nicely captures her queerness, one that – for many (though by no means all) queer theorists – has privileged sameness and identification (132). Leo Bersani, for instance, asserts that homosexual desire is 'desire for the same from the perspective of a self already identified as different from itself' (1995: 59). This self-splitting is arguably predicated upon self-concept (a notion that enjoys an intimate relationship with empathy as previously argued), in the sense that part of the subject identifies with – and becomes – the 'other' in same-sex desire. Bersani's model also presents queer identity in the form of 'dialogic encounters' between 'self-differentiated selves' (Pinar 2003: 359). *Tipping the Velvet* engages with this notion of individualization through Nan's self-reflection on her lesbian experience. Her claim that 'I might have been Narcissus, embracing the pond in which I was about to drown' reveals Nan's eagerness for connecting with the differentiated self or the identical other (i.e. her reflection in the water) against the precariousness of such gesture (132). Nan's description of her relationship with Kitty further demonstrates the role identification plays in her development as a queer subject. When they start performing together on stage, Nan realizes that 'I had fallen in love with Kitty; now, *becoming* Kitty, I fell in love a little with myself' (126, original emphasis). The act of 'becoming' refers to both the beginning of Nan's career as a male impersonator in the music halls and her identification with Kitty in her journey of sexual awakening. By positioning Kitty as 'the wider object of [Nan's] self-love', Waters's text accentuates again Nan's dependence on identification in the formation of her queer subjectivity (127). Indeed, as 'a form of love', identification involves 'a desire to take a place where one is not yet' (Ahmed 2004: 126). It therefore, Sara Ahmed contends, '*expands the space of the subject*' (ibid., original emphasis).

Through Nan's emotional entanglement with Kitty, *Tipping the Velvet* further explores shame's role in the disruption and reconstitution of queer identity, which, as we will see, also provides a significant model of readerly engagement. In order to get rid of her queer shame, Kitty decides to marry Walter Bliss, their theatrical manager. This betrayal has the consequence of shaming Nan, as indicated by the 'curious mixture of contempt, complacency, and pity' Nan discerns in Walter's behaviour towards her (173). However, unlike Kitty who struggles with her same-sex desire and seeks instead 'heterocentric protection' through marriage (Yates 2016: 184), Nan's feeling of shame is triggered by the unexpected rupture of her relationship with Kitty: she acknowledges bitterly that Walter – as her 'rival' – has 'defeated' her (173). Overwhelmed by her deep sense of shame, Nan considers, for a second, 'heaving [herself] over' the little bridge she reaches and 'making [her] escape that way' (174). This fleeting suicidal thought of Nan vividly illustrates Sedgwick's description of how shame 'floods into being as [...] a disruptive moment' (2003: 36). Shame is detrimental precisely because it 'judges, ridicules, terrorises whatever pretence we might hold of being autonomous, successful, self-determining subjects' (Biddle 1997: 227).

However, as Sally Munt reminds us, shame is 'predicated on the yearning for reconnection', so the shamed subject 'will not relinquish hope of restitution' (2000: 542). When there occurs a rupture to Nan's development as a queer subject, shame serves as a productive force in ushering new processes of identity constitution. Nan's gender-crossing experience as a male renter on the streets of London after she leaves Kitty and her life in the music halls exemplifies Nan's attempt to reassert her agency as a queer subject. Nan starts her 'performance' when she is approached by some stranger who 'looked quite unmistakably like Walter' (198). By abstracting Walter as the person 'whom Kitty lay with and kissed' and describing her oral service to the stranger as a chance to experience 'how *Walter* tastes', Nan positions herself *as* or *alongside* Kitty during her sexual practice with her male partner (198, 199, original emphasis). Here, the imagined identificatory communication with Kitty echoes Bersani's model of queer identity, which, as introduced before, is constituted through negotiations between 'self-differentiated selves' (Pinar 2003: 353). When she bends down to give fellatio to the stranger, Nan acutely senses that it is 'someone else who was kneeling, not myself' (199).

Nan's desire for the 'knowing' other marks another point in her journey towards a queer subject, and this time, the reader is involved in the process of Nan's identity formation:

> I never felt my own lusts rise, raising theirs. [...] My one regret was that, though I was daily giving such marvelous performances, they had no audience. [...] I would long for just one eye – just one! – to be fixed upon our couplings: a bold and knowing eye that saw how well I played my part, how gulled and humbled was my foolish, trustful partner. (206)

By explicitly staging her longing for an identificatory communication with the 'knowing' other, Nan invites her audience/reader to approach her performance attentively and empathetically, an act which in fact involves them in the textual construction of Nan's sexuality. Again, Nan evokes the idea of performativity in her description of sexuality and celebrates it in a self-aggrandizing manner through her claim that 'I was daily giving such marvelous performances'. The performative nature of Nan's sexuality and the longing for the 'knowing' spectator in satisfying her narcissistic needs present the other's gaze as a 'mirror' through which Nan could confront her 'disrupted' and thus 'ashamed' being. Here shame is not registered by Nan's physiological reactions but her hyperbolic self-display; or, put differently, the effacement of shame in her narrative. Indeed, as Sedgwick maintains, 'shame and exhibitionism are different interlinings of the same glove' (2003: 38).

By constantly involving the reader in Nan's shame and pleasure, *Tipping the Velvet* may be seen to be making a large claim for the significance of readerly participation in textual production and the way in which the things we do and feel as readers relate closely to our affective practices in the practical world. In the same way that the readers of the text have experienced what it is like to be an object of desire or 'mirror' in a lesbian relationship, so do we see how – in the intra-diegetic narrative – such mirroring processes are essential to Nan's journey towards discovering herself as a queer subject. These forms of identity constitution, as my following analysis of *Affinity* further demonstrates, are characterized by a kind of empathetic engagement between the text and the reader.

Shame, voyeurism, empathy

Set in 1870s Victorian England, *Affinity* tells a story about how Margaret Prior, a spinster from an upper-class family, falls in love with a female prisoner and spiritualist medium, Selina Dawes, during her visits to the Millbank Prison. Like *Tipping the Velvet*, *Affinity* also focuses on the issue of queer desire and involves the reader in (the character's) shame. Through its use of diary entries, *Affinity* further exemplifies Tomkins's model of shame by playing with the dynamic between readerly immersion and textual disruption. The interpolation of Margaret's diary into the narrative in *Affinity* serves as a kind of 'empathic narration', a concept I take up from Meghan Marie Hammond in describing the use of diary entries in providing the reader with 'an immediate sense of [the character's] thoughts and feelings' (2014: 4). Indeed, as Kym Brindle, quoting from Thomas Mallon, observes, diary entries are a form of expression that 'emphatically embodies the expresser' and is 'the flesh made word' (2013: 88). By constructing a '"framed" communicative situation' in the textual world, Waters's *Affinity* is arguably designed to facilitate the reader's empathetic engagement with the text (Brindle 2013: 33). It self-consciously plays with the reader's generic expectation of diary narrative by remarking from Margaret's perspective that her diary is 'where [she] wrote all [her] secrets – all [her] passion, all [her] love' (Waters 1999: 339). Also, as Lucie Armitt and Sarah Gamble argue in their reading of the novel, by ascribing authorship to the self, Margaret's account presents her diary as a 'self-affirming' narrative, which does not encourage the reader to actively 'challenge the truth-value of any of the material inscribed in them' (2006: 152).

However, at the same time, the fact that diary represents a 'self-reflexive, inward-turned communion' complicates the relationship between the diarist and the reader: the reader is positioned as a voyeur whose access to the diary slides out of the diarist's view (Brindle 2013: 80). As such, the diary form prompts, and caters for, the reader's voyeuristic and vicarious consumption of the textual other. The voyeuristic nature of the reader's encounter with Margaret's diary is thematically highlighted in Waters's use of the trope of the panopticon in the text. As a type of institutional building designed by the English philosopher Jeremy Bentham, the panopticon is developed by Michel Foucault as a symbol for the disciplinary society of surveillance. The character Margaret's description of the structure of Millbank Prison in *Affinity* clearly echoes Bentham's model of the panopticon. Seen from the map, the prison 'has a curious kind of charm to it, the pentagons appearing as petals on a geometric flower' (8). Inside the prison, there is 'a spiral staircase that [winds] upwards through a tower', which is 'set at the centre of the pentagon yards' (10). The tower is designed in this way 'so that the view from it is all of the walls and barred windows that make up the interior face of the women's building' (ibid.). As Foucault explains, the architectural structure of the panopticon determines that the one who sees and the one who is being seen are in a power hierarchy: 'in the peripheric ring, one is totally seen, without ever seeing; in the central tower, one sees everything without ever being seen' ([1977] 1991: 202). Foucault's analysis of the panoptic gaze also speaks to the reader's experience. The use of diary entries provides the reader with an illusion that s/he is positioned in a privileged place – 'the central tower' – so that s/he could peep into Margaret's inner mind without being noticed. This privileged reading position makes the reader 'initially believe that they maintain an all-seeing scrutiny of the diarist's private thoughts' (Brindle 2013: 34). The binary between empathetic engagement (in the form of identification) and voyeuristic consumption afforded by the use of diary entries in *Affinity* provides more complex ways of understanding the reading pleasures associated with Waters's work. Although, as we have seen, the reader is positioned in a more privileged place, their reading pleasure largely depends on their 'willing suspension of disbelief' and engagement with Margaret in more typically 'realist' terms. It is possible that the text's various narrative devices – such as the reader's access to Selina's journal and the revelation of

Selina's spiritualist 'trick' at the beginning of the text – may cause readers to suspend vigilance during their first reading experience, since these devices intrude upon their involvement with Margaret. In Ann Heilmann's reading of the text, she presents a similar argument by suggesting that the reader is 'likely to be seduced into suspending disbelief in the desire for a happy supernatural ending to the lesbian love story' (2009/10: 26). However, *Affinity* disrupts the reader's vicarious consumption of Margaret's queer desire by disclosing – at the end of the text – that the relationship between Margaret and Selina is a fraud designed and manipulated by the character Ruth Vigers, Selina's secret lover, who occupies a 'ghostly' presence in the text. In so doing, it is arguable that the reader is positioned *as* or *alongside* Margaret. In the same way that Margaret's queer desire is manipulated and exploited by Selina and Ruth in a shameful manner in the intra-diegetic narrative, so do the readers of Waters's text experience how shameful it could be when their clandestine and voyeuristic interest in a lesbian fantasy is disrupted by the text.

The disclosure of the fraud at the end of *Affinity* prompts the reader to reflect upon their readerly desire and reapproach the text in a politically meaningful manner. As Rachel Carroll suggests, this disclosure 'generates a retrospective knowledge which transforms the meaning of preceding events' (2006: 136). Focusing on the text–reader engagement the diary narrative generates, I argue that Margaret's diary accounts not only satisfy the reader's desire for a lesbian fantasy but also bring to the fore the importance of empathetic responsiveness in the construction of lesbian subjectivity. As such, *Affinity* demonstrates the way in which the reader is brought within the processes involved in becoming a queer subject in a manner that echoes – but is also slightly different from – the mechanism we have seen at work in *Tipping the Velvet*.

Margaret's hunger for empathetic responsiveness is well illustrated by her account of her relationship with her diary. As she says to Selina, '*that* book was like my dearest friend. I told it all my closest thoughts, and it kept them secret' (111, original emphasis). The analogy between the diary and the 'dearest friend' reveals Margaret's desire for reciprocal interpersonal communication, the rupture of which, as argued before, is the performativity of shame. In this scene the diary may be seen to play a similar role to the 'knowing' other that Nan searches out in *Tipping the Velvet*. The fact that the diary the readers are confronted with is Margaret's 'second book' further exemplifies Sedgwick's formulation of the role shame plays in the construction and disruption of identity and interpersonal relationships. Margaret starts writing her second diary after the death of her scholarly father and the defection of her lover, Helen, who wound up marrying Margaret's brother. From the contextual information, we know Margaret tried to commit suicide after her father's death. This suicidal behaviour is clearly a desire for 'self-effacement', which is 'the defining trait' of shame (Sedgwick 1993: 4). As Michael L. Morgan explains, the intolerable feeling of shame makes the self feel that one could 'serve others best by disappearing' (2008: 24).

Writing a second diary, a different one, in this context, represents Margaret's repeated attempt to construct a meaningful identity for herself; a move that echoes Nan's retrospective narration in *Tipping the Velvet*. As the opening pages indicate, this time Margaret attempts to write history from a different angle, one that may be contrasted with the histories her father dealt with, such as those of 'the great lives, the great works':

> He would start it, I think, at the gate of Millbank, the point that every visitor must pass when they arrive to make their tour of the gaols. Let me begin my record there, then: I am being greeted by the prison porter, who is marking my name off in some great ledger; now a warder is leading me through a narrow arch, and I am about to step across the grounds towards the prison proper. (7–8)

By drawing a comparison between the way her father writes history and her own narrative, Margaret shifts the focus from 'the great lives' to herself. Her diary entries therefore demonstrate her *attempt* to record how she perceives, experiences and reflects on things through her own eyes, a process which is essential for her identity formation. This sense of 'trying' – almost an experimentation of identity – is well illustrated by the dynamic between a tentative claim – '*Let* me begin my record there' – and a series of first-person accounts – 'I *am* being greeted', 'I *am* about to step across' (emphasis added). One could also say it is phenomenological in method – or, at least in attempt – to recapture the immediacy of the experience in the present tense. This very nuanced sense of uncertainty about Margaret's agency evokes shame, which, as Sedgwick explains, calls forth a present self that is 'deferred', and 'has yet and with difficulty to come into being' (1993: 4).

This focus on Margaret's desire for empathetic responsiveness provides readers with a different approach to understanding her relationship with Selina in the text. Like *Tipping the Velvet*, *Affinity* examines the issue of queer subjectivity in relation to the 'mirroring' experience between self and other, which is part of 'identity-constituting identificatory communication' (Sedgwick 2003: 36). With the help of Ruth's 'intrusion' into Margaret's diary, Selina manipulates and plays with Margaret's queer desire for the 'mirrored' other or what Bersani calls 'sameness' (a point that is discussed in detail in the previous section):

> Not sure? Look at your own fingers. Are you not sure, if they are yours? Look at any part of you – it might be me that you are looking at! We are the same, you and I. We have been cut, two halves, from the same piece of shining matter. Oh, I could say, *I love you* – that is a simple thing to say, the sort of thing your sister might say to her husband. I could say that in a prison letter, four times a year. But my spirit does not love yours – it is *entwined* with it. Our flesh does not love: our flesh is the same, and longs to leap to itself. It must do that, or wither! *You are like me.* (275, original emphasis)

By positioning herself as the 'mirror' or 'object' of Margaret's desire, Selina's account caters to Margaret's longing for empathetic responsiveness – or what O'Callaghan alternatively calls 'personal allegiance' (2017: 57) – which plays an essential role in her identity formation. When Margaret discovers that Ruth – the ghostly manipulator – is Selina's 'real' lover, she is overwhelmed by the sense of shame, the power of which pushes her to question her self-identity again. The way shame questions her identity is vividly illustrated by Margaret's clumsy response to the policeman's inquiry about the robbery she desperately makes up after she finds out that Selina and Ruth have already run away:

> He looked at me strangely. He said, two women? – 'Two women, and one of them my maid. And she is terribly cunning, and has abused me, cruelly! And the other – the other – '
>
> *The other escaped*, I meant to say next, *from Millbank Prison*! But instead of saying it, I took one quick icy breath and put my hand to my mouth.
>
> For how should he suppose that I knew that? [...]
>
> The policeman waited. I said, 'I am not sure, *I am not sure.*' (343, original emphasis)

In discussing the same extract, Armitt and Gamble take a poststructuralist approach to power and focus on the importance of social structures in the formation of identity. They argue that the use of the double 'I' in Margaret's response that 'I am not sure, I am not sure' is indicative of her identity crisis, bringing to the fore the disjunction between nineteenth-century narratives of class, gender and sexuality and Waters's arguably anachronistic positioning of queerness in a Victorian setting (2006: 157). In light of Sedgwick's model of queer subjectivity, Margaret's equivocation could also be understood in a more fundamental and profound manner. The doubling 'I' vividly illustrates how shame 'deconstitut[es]' and then 'reconstitute[s]' identity, and can therefore be construed as one of Margaret's self-affirming attempts (Sedgwick 2003: 36). Indeed, these intra-diegetic narratives about Margaret's relationship with the other – be it her former lover Helen, Selina, her first and second diaries – are good examples of how a queer subject may repeatedly attempt to reconstitute an interpersonal bridge with the other when there occurs an impediment to the previous relationship. In this regard, the ambiguous ending of the text – that the reader does not know whether Margaret jumps into the River Thames or not – need not be read as a 'tragic' one. It is arguable that this indeterminacy creates a sense of 'presentness', which involves the reader in the construction of the text and prompts them to respond empathetically to the text. In so doing, Waters's *Affinity* demonstrates how the past is affectively here in the present, which, at the same time, enfolds the future.

Conclusion

Focusing on the lesbian experience of the character Nan Astley and Margaret Prior in *Tipping the Velvet* and *Affinity*, respectively, this chapter demonstrates that Sedgwick's affective approach to shame and Bersani's model of queer identity (which is, admittedly, one of many formulations of homosexuality) can be usefully brought to bear upon one another in order to unpack the complicated reading pleasures afforded by Waters's work. Notably shame has been 'a code word' for same-sex desire since the late-nineteenth century, when the sexological and pathological discourse of homosexuality first emerged (Mitchell 2012: 313). For any discussion about the reading pleasures of Waters's lesbian fantasies, it would seem necessary to take the readers' sexuality into consideration and interrogate how different types of readers will be positioned differently by the text. Indeed, Waters's depiction of same-sex desire may appear familiar to lesbian readers, whilst for heterosexual – and in particular those of a heteronormative mindset – its 'deviant' content clearly caters to their curiosity and fascination in a different manner. However, it is worth reiterating that my focus is not on the role shame plays in the social construction of morality and the pathologization of homosexuality (which, to a certain extent, would constitute a 'paranoid' practice of demystification). Rather, I am interested in exploring the corporeality and relationality of shame and its relation to a particular model of queerness, one that is characterized by the idea of sameness or identification.

Focusing on the use of a variety of manipulative narrative strategies in both novels, this chapter demonstrates how Waters's work involves the reader in the consumption and construction of queer sexuality, a process that is marked by a textual circuit of desire/pleasure and shame. The malleability of shame renders it a useful affect in prompting the reader to reflect on their readerly desires and interpretative strategies. Through the foregrounding of the importance of empathetic responsiveness in the formation of queer subjectivity, both novels, at a metacritical level, call for the reader's awareness of how the things we do and feel as readers relate closely to our affective practices in the non-fictional world. This is arguably where the political and reparative potentials of Waters's work lie. By positioning the reader as the empathetic other and prompting them to be more reflective about their affective responsibilities towards the other, these neo-Victorian narratives 'change us [...] discontent us with our pasts and offer us new futures' (Waters 1998: 250).

In Chapter 3, I continue the discussion of the complex, and often conflicted, text–reader relationship prompted by neo-Victorian fiction by exploring the dynamic that exists between readerly empathy, contingency and 'nausea': a Sartrean metaphor for the disorientation and meaninglessness that occurs when we lose our sense of the 'ground' or 'purpose' of our existence. I propose that a similar nausea may be seen to be at work in the reading of Cox's *The Meaning of Night* and Burnet's *His Bloody Project*, two neo-Victorian novels that challenge the reading subject's own ability to make sense of the world (both textual and practical) and themselves.

3

Tragic man

In the 'Broken Dishes' chapter of *Alias Grace*, Margaret Atwood uses the image of 'a moth in a bottle [...] sailing back and forth across the hideous dark ocean' to illustrate Grace's sorrow and uneasiness about her mother's tragic death during their transatlantic journey (1996: 122). This image vividly evokes a feeling of disorientation, imprisonment and vulnerability. Interestingly, for readers of *Alias Grace*, this particular image is also suggestive of their reading experience. The textual uncertainty about Grace's involvement in the murder arguably upsets the reader, and traps them in a textual world of profound uncertainty whose unstable foundations – first the argument lists one way, then another – may be compared to seasickness.

This sense of disorientation poses an 'existential' question about the reader's position in the textual world, as well as challenging their affective and ethical investment in the text as argued in Chapter 1. In this chapter, I continue the discussion of the text–reader relationship with regards to neo-Victorian fiction, now focusing on the dynamic that exists between readerly empathy and the existential concerns of contingency and 'nausea': a Sartrean metaphor for the disorientation and meaninglessness that occurs when we lose our sense of groundedness and the purpose of existence. Sartre's conceptualization of existential nausea interrogates the human subject's solipsistic concerns about the nature of existence and the individual subject's purpose (or purposelessness) within it. This concern, which is typically figured as an anxiety about the (absent) meaning of life, is particularly important for neo-Victorian fiction, since it is a genre, as noted in Chapter 1, dominated by the representation of marginal figures whose experiences repeatedly cause them – and the reader – to question the meaning of existence. However, instead of understanding such crises in social and political terms (as much of the contemporary neo-Victorian criticism has done), I propose that we revisit them in this wider philosophical and sometimes explicitly religious context. As we will see in the following analysis, a good deal of neo-Victorian fiction chooses to thematize existential concerns about agency, freedom and responsibility through its depiction of characters who attempt to break free from the chance circumstances they find themselves in and their endeavour to alter the course of 'fate'.

This philosophical focus on the individual and his or her destiny is decidedly at odds with what has become the dominant way of reading neo-Victorian literature in recent years, much of which has been characterized by Foucauldian approaches or applications of Judith Butler's work on gender (see introduction). However, the fact that several neo-Victorian novels have inscribed a theoretical awareness of these issues into their textual worlds raises a question about the need for such criticism. Sarah Waters's neo-Victorian novel *Affinity*, for example, is elaborately constructed by what Martin Paul Eve calls the 'high-Theory reference point through Foucault' (2013: 114). As Eve observes, 'the frames of reference' used in *Affinity*, such as the Panopticon and its related issues of discipline and power, 'have a strong bearing upon academic disciplinarity' (113). Lucie Armitt likewise points out that Waters 'lay[s] out before us in fictional form the pre-existing theoretical concepts for which she knows we are searching' (2016: 30). Waters's work thus plays 'a game of pre-empting and guessing' with its critical readers at the same time as raising questions about whether the process really needs spelling out again in scholarly articles (Eve 2013: 117).

To invoke Sedgwick, this textual game is characterized by paranoia. As my discussion of the proto-psychoanalytic sessions between Grace Marks and Simon Jordan in *Alias Grace* in Chapter 1 has demonstrated, the wrestling between the text (or the object of critical inquiry) and the reader points to the 'reflexive and mimetic' nature of paranoia, which is epitomized by the belief that '*Anything you can do (to me) I can do worse*, and *Anything you can do (to me) I can do first* – to myself' (Sedgwick 2003: 131, original emphasis). In light of Linda Hutcheon's work on metafiction, this kind of text–reader engagement also constitutes a form of readerly 'narcissism' ([1980] 1985: 1). Through her allegorical reading of the myth of Narcissus, Hutcheon uses the adjective 'narcissistic' in a figurative way to designate the embedded 'self-awareness' of metafiction (ibid.). Hutcheon's formulation of narcissistic narrative further reveals the existential dimension of metafiction, which, as Brian McHale explains, refers to its preoccupation with 'the ontology of the literary text itself' and that of 'the world which it projects' (McHale [1987] 2001: 10).[1] Notably, this instability and indeterminacy of meaning in the literary texts spills over into questions of contingency in the practical world.

Some neo-Victorian texts – in particular, the 'canonical' ones – have thematized and contextualized this existential concern about the contingency of existence by highlighting the artificiality of the textual world. Through the use of a range of literary devices – such as the 'found manuscript' plot in A. S. Byatt's *Possession: A Romance* (1990) and Michael Cox's *The Meaning of Night* (2006), narrative anachronism in Margaret Atwood's *Alias Grace*, the flagrant intervention of the authorial voice and direct address to the extradiegetic reader in John Fowles's *The French Lieutenant's Woman* (1969) and Michel Faber's *Crimson Petal and the White* – these texts may be seen to be using the God-like status of the narrator or the implied author to remind readers of their powerlessness at the hands of 'fate'. In a 1976 interview, John Fowles rebukes 'Sartre's dictum that the novelist cannot be God' and claims instead that 'when you write a book you are potentially a tyrant, you are the total dictator, and there's nothing in the book that has to be there if you want to knock it out or change it' (463). Similarly, the underlying desire to (re)write the past in neo-Victorian fiction and the widespread preference for the use of retrospective narrative could be construed as a comment on the human subject's desire to challenge such impotence and to alter the course of events. As we will see from the following discussion of Sartre's philosophical novel *Nausea* ([1963] 2000), this preoccupation with the ability to 'act' (or not) goes to the heart of living existentially.

Hutcheon's conceptualization of narcissistic narrative is further developed by Mark Currie in his study of 'theoretical fiction', which is considered by Currie as a subgenre of metafiction ([1998] 2011: 60). Currie posits the difference between metafiction and theoretical fiction in their different thematic focus. Unlike metafiction which 'implies a difference between normal fiction and its metalanguage', Currie understands theoretical fiction as 'a convergence of

---

[1] Here it should be noted that metafictional techniques are not exclusive to postmodernist fiction. Indeed, some of them can be traced back to early literary texts such as Laurence Sterne's *Tristram Shandy*. However, as Hutcheon suggests, the development of postmodernism 'transform[s] the formal properties of fiction into its subject matter' ([1980] 1985: 18).

theory and fiction' (ibid.). Although I have no intention of placing the neo-Victorian genre under the category of theory fiction, it is arguable that many neo-Victorian novels are theoretically self-conscious. In fact, a great number of neo-Victorian authors – including A. S. Byatt, David Lodge, Sarah Waters, Patricia Duncker, and so on – have a PhD degree in literary studies and/or work in English departments and their theoretical knowledge is featured in their fictional creation, a point that is potently reflected in Mel Steel's review of Waters's debut novel *Tipping the Velvet*: 'imagine Jeanette Winterson on a good day collaborating with Judith Butler to pen a Sapphic Moll Flanders' (1998: n. p.). In her 2006 interview with Lucie Armitt, Waters also admits that she writes with her 'old literary critical background' and her 'academic's head [is] still there in the broadest sense' (qtd in Armitt 2007: 125). It is in this context that I turn to Currie for his trenchant critique of the 'felicitous reciprocity' between critic and narrative in the study of theory-inscribed literary text (152). As Currie questions, 'what can the critic or theorist do to avoid the mere restatement of the novel's own critical and theoretical knowledge, or to save the theory-fiction relationship from the narcissistic self-affirmation of these tautologies?' (153).[2] In response to Hutcheon's and Currie's problematizing of this 'narcissistic' trend within literary criticism, this chapter moves away from what has become an almost 'formulaic' reading of neo-Victorian fiction, one that is based upon an educated reader's presupposed knowledge of theorists like Foucault and Butler. Instead, it focuses on the profound existential dilemmas these texts are also concerned with. By positioning the reader alongside characters who struggle with having control (or not) over their fate, this chapter examines the ways in which neo-Victorian fiction can prompt the reader to reflect on their own existential freedom and responsibility.

This chapter also continues the discussion of reader-empathy. By drawing upon the American psychoanalyst Heinz Kohut's work, it establishes the link between empathy, narcissism and the human subject's attempt to overcome feelings of contingency and impotence. I propose that by being

---

[2] The subgenre of what Frances Kelly coins 'neo-Victorian academic fiction' is also susceptible to such critical concern (2017: 42). The fact that these novels seem to aim at 'an academic readership' raises further epistemological and ontological questions about critical interpretation (44). To a certain extent, the rapid development of neo-Victorianism over the past decades is relevant to some reciprocal engagement between 'literary, cultural and academic industr[ies]' (Ho [2012] 2013: 4).

empathetically receptive to the character's experience of existential crisis in neo-Victorian fiction, the reader's immersive and pleasurable consumption of the contemporary fantasy of the Victorian underworld is disrupted. This disruption pushes the reader to see the present in a future-orientated manner, in this way engaging with the transformative potential of readerly empathy.

I begin the discussion which follows with a review of Sartre's characterization of 'nausea' – a metaphor for the contingency of existence – in his first novel *Nausea*. Then, in light of Kohut's research on narcissism – and in particular, his conceptualization of 'self-object' and the link he makes between narcissism and empathy – I argue that the reader in Sartre's text may be seen to be positioned as Roquentin's 'self-object': a projection which enables Roquentin to escape his feelings of paralyzing groundlessness or 'seasickness'. With this focus on the dialogic and intersubjective nature of *Nausea*, and its use of literary devices such as retrospective narrative, journal entries and direct address to the reader, I further propose that although Sartre's text belongs to a very different literary tradition, its form and content provide us with a useful model for thinking through the relationship between contingency, narcissism and empathy in the neo-Victorian genre. This discussion is then continued with a close reading of two neo-Victorian novels – Cox's *The Meaning of Night* and Burnet's *His Bloody Project* – whose central protagonists, Edward Glyver and Roderick Macrae, respectively, bear many similarities to Roquentin. *The Meaning of Night* and *His Bloody Project* are not, however, identically suggestive in their engagement with the topic of contingency, narcissism and empathy. While Cox's novel illustrates the importance of empathetic response in the salvation of intradiegetic characters, Burnet's raises important questions about the reparative limitations of empathy through its refusal of readerly affection towards characters suffering from existential nausea. It is the former novel, then, that forms the major focus of my analysis in what follows.

Nausea and contingency

Sartre's *Nausea* tells the story of how the thirty-year-old Antoine Roquentin settles in the fictional French town of Bouville and tries to finish his research on the life of an eighteenth-century political figure, Monsieur de Rollebon.

During the winter of 1932, Roquentin experiences a particular 'sweet disgust', a sense of 'nausea' that is triggered by his tactile encounter with a pebble: 'Objects ought not to *touch*, since they are not alive. You use them, you put them back in place, you live among them: they are useful, nothing more. But they touch me, it's unbearable. I am afraid of entering in contact with them, just as if they were living animals' (Sartre [1963] 2000: 22, original emphasis). Roquentin is made to question the nature – and necessity – of his own existence as he holds the pebble in his hand in 'sweet disgust'. The existence of the *inanimate* pebble evokes a questioning about the comparative meaning and value of the inanimate and animate (human) objects which, Sartre represents hyperbolically, as a kind of nausea:

> The essential thing is contingency. I mean that, by definition, existence is not necessity. To exist is simply *to be there*; what exists appears, lets itself be *encountered*, but you can never *deduce* it. […] Everything is gratuitous, that park, this town, and myself. When you realize that, it turns your stomach over and everything starts floating about, […] that is the Nausea. (188, original emphasis)

Here Sartre evokes the feeling of sickness – indeed, something strikingly akin to the experience of *seasickness* – to illustrate what he means by existential nausea. It is a reaction to the 'gratuitousness' or, as Robert Solomon alternatively expresses it, 'the intrusiveness of sheer existence' (2006: 66). This sense of nothingness, or contingency, refers to a void, or 'abyss', in the meaning-production circuit. Like the pebble in the extract cited above, its presence is nauseating because Roquentin realizes that it does not mean anything *for* him, or he *for* it. The existential nausea 'has no *intentionality*' (Solomon 2006: 63, original emphasis). As we will see in the next section, Roquentin's experience of the contingency of reality and his poignant feeling of meaninglessness are shared by many characters from neo-Victorian fiction.

In his reading of the novel, Winfried Menninghaus claims that although the advent of nausea is physiologically unpleasant, it is 'an "event" – *évènement* – of comprehensive revelatory quality' (2003: 356). Indeed, in *Nausea*, the character Roquentin is 'liberated' after his awareness of the contingent nature of his existence, since he realizes that 'existence is not necessity' (143, 188). To Steven Churchill, this kind of liberation suggests that 'the world does not *have* to be as it is, such that things *could* be otherwise; indeed, nothing *need* be, at all' ([2013] 2014: 46. original emphasis). As such, existential nausea brings Roquentin a particular freedom and also a profound political *responsibility*. In the story, what Roquentin tries to liberate himself from is most probably a genealogical understanding of existence, as evidenced by his research subject – the historical figure Monsieur de Rollebon – who is constructed as the 'surrogate' for his own existence. As Roquentin admits, Monsieur de Rollebon 'represents the only justification for my existence' (Sartre [1963] 2000: 105); hence, Roquentin's purpose in life is to reveal the meaningfulness of his 'alter-ego', Rollebon. However, after the 'revelatory' and nauseating event – his encounter with the pebble – Roquentin realizes the futility of undertaking historical research into either his or Rollebon's existence. He claims that while 'history talks about what has existed – an existent can never justify the existence of another existent' (252). Through the voice of the fictional character Roquentin, Sartre thus provides a trenchant critique of the linear and genealogical understanding of existence as derived from Christian theology:

> They explain the new by the old – and the old they have explained by the older still, like those historians who describe Lenin as a Russian Robespierre and Robespierre as a French Cromwell: when all is said and done, they have never understood anything at all … behind their self-importance you can distinguish a morose laziness: they see a procession of semblances pass by, they yawn, they think that there's nothing new under the sun. (102)

The final biblical reference demonstrates Sartre's critique of the theological understanding of human existence as being lazy, rigid, void and self-celebrated, which may be seen to echo Eve Sedgwick's psychological critique of Freudian fatalism as discussed in the introduction. Similarly, Sartre's questioning of the seemingly fixed relationship between Roquentin and his 'surrogate', Rollebon, and by extension, that between 'the new' and 'the old', the present and the past, resembles Saussure's conceptualization of the relation between the signified and the signifier of language being similarly arbitrary. It thus explains the means by which Sartre's existential philosophy was subsequently incorporated into the work of structuralist and poststructuralist thinkers. In Derridean terms, Sartre's critique of how historians understand historical figures, such as Lenin and Robespierre in the previous extract, makes us aware that we structure the meaning of existence by difference and deferral ('Lenin [is] a Russian Robespierre and Robespierre is a French Cromwell'). Sartre further proposes an ontological question about the meaning of being human and the ways in which the self could ground itself *positively*. In the story of *Nausea*, Roquentin becomes aware that trying to 'resuscitate Monsieur de Rollebon' is a 'mistake' since it would not help him justify his own existence (252). Rather, Roquentin promises to write another story at the end of the text, a story of 'an adventure' (ibid.), which is arguably his attempt to make meaning out of his contingent existence in terms of our freedom to 'act' and deliver change (i.e. the basic tenets of political existentialism). The act of writing what Churchill describes a 'semi-biographical fiction' is thus presented as an attempted self-rescue (52–3). As I will demonstrate in the next section, this idea helps us to consider the widespread preference for the use of first-person narrative and the engagement with the form of Bildungsroman in a number of neo-Victorian novels as an expression of the existential concerns of the central protagonists, not just a means of engaging readers and promoting readerly empathy.

Here the promise of another book at the end of *Nausea* suggests that the text we as readers are confronted with is a retrospective account of Roquentin's thought process, or, in metafictional terms, a 'document of its own making' (Wood in Sartre [1963] 2000: vii). Churchill likewise suggests that we can 'read *Nausea* as Roquentin's hypothetical novel, incorporating biographical elements with intrigues worthy of an adventure' (53). Roquentin's research has therefore shifted from that of the historical figure – the eighteenth-century political figure Monsieur de Rollebon – to the (past) self. This shift from a grand history to a personal story can be interpreted in different ways. Geoffrey A. Baker contends that *Nausea* is preoccupied with the existential 'difficulties, responsibilities, and contexts of writing and authorship' (2016: 166). Menninghaus's reading of the novel, by contrast, would seem to be modelled on a political and historical concern about subjectivity and agency. He suggests that Roquentin is liberated from 'the ideological patterns and social practices' that prevent him from 'becoming aware of the (absent) ground of [his] own existence' (Menninghaus 2003: 356). Indeed, Menninghaus's interpretation in this respect resembles what is arguably the dominant approach to the analysis of neo-Victorian fictional characters in recent neo-Victorian criticism. With a focus on the use of 'uncanny echoes and repetitions' in neo-Victorian gothic fiction, Kohlke and Gutleben propose that neo-Victorian literature poses questions about the way in which 'the inauthentic' self is 'interpellated' by the 'burdensome past', referring to 'ideologica[l]' forces that deprive these subjects of 'sincere autonom[y]' in particular (2012: 15–16). This materialist approach to the texts is not altogether adequate, since – if we embrace the questioning of subjectivity evoked by Sartre's *Nausea* – it is limited in historicization. Also, as we have already seen, Sartre's formulation of the existential crisis is predicated upon a more fundamental concern about human existence that, I would suggest, finds its complement in a great many neo-Victorian texts. Shifting away from a socio-economic discussion of these neo-Victorian characters, as my reading in this chapter will hopefully demonstrate, may help us recognize even greater complexity in the reading pleasures afforded by neo-Victorian literature. In order to make my hypothesis here clearer, I would first like to dwell some more on the ending of *Nausea*.

First of all, it should be noted that although I am taking up Sartre's thinking on existential nausea in this chapter, I am not interested in developing a philosophical discussion of Sartre's existential concerns per se. Rather, I am focused on an examination of the first-person narration of this existential crisis, which means that I am more interested in reading *Nausea* as a philosophical *novel*. This focus on the act of *narrating* will advance critical concerns about the solipsism of Sartre's 'nausea'. As we have seen, Sartre's particular ethical and political concern with existential nausea has its origins in the solipsistic subject. As Solomon notes in his reading of *Nausea* and Sartre's later philosophical work, *Being and Nothingness*, the concept of 'Being-for-Others' which dominates the discussion in *Being and Nothingness* plays no role in his fiction *Nausea* (Solomon 2006: 63).[3] Also, for Solomon, the form of the journal entries used in *Nausea* is 'for the most part a solipsistic exercise' (71). Solomon is right in pointing out the absence of 'Being-for-Others' in Sartre's formulation of existential nausea and its solipsism, and presenting it as the catalyst for his later politics. However, he approaches the novel as a philosophical rather than a literary work, and neglects to take into account the *dialogic* nature of the text, and in particular, the role of the implied reader. This textual positioning, I propose, lends something new to our understanding of

---

[3] Sartre's idea of 'Being-for-Others' has been discussed in detail in relation to shame in Chapter 2.

the Roquentin character and reveals the text to be less of an exposition of solipsism than it might, at first, appear.

My proposition is that the anticipation of the reader's response at the end of the text adds a dialogic, if narcissistic, dimension to Roquentin's story.[4] After sketching out Roquentin's plan for another book, Sartre describes Roquentin's anticipation of his future readers' flattering response to his book in a self-celebratory way: 'And there would be people who would read this novel and who would say: "It was Antoine Roquentin who wrote it, he was a red-headed fellow who hung about in cafés", and they would think about my life as I think about the life of that Negress: as about something precious and almost legendary' (252). This reintroduction of 'value' and 'meaningfulness' into Roquentin's life on account of his anticipation of readerly compliments and a recognition that his was, after all, a 'precious' and 'legendary' life, demonstrates Roquentin's narcissistic response to the confrontation with deep existential concerns, and also the human subject's inability to sustain his/her view of existence as one of absolute contingency. Here I am moving between a philosophical discussion of Roquentin's experience and a psychological one in order to better understand the final message the text sends us. The direct address to the reader, as evidenced by the use of the second-person pronoun 'you' in mentioning Roquentin's planning for his next book – '*you* would have to guess [the content of my next novel]' – makes explicit a dialogic relationship between Roquentin and his readers, hence interrogating the purported solipsism of his experience (252, emphasis added).

Notably, this is not the first time that Roquentin turns to the other – 'you'– in the text. Throughout the narration, the text moves seamlessly between first-, second- and third-person narratives. The following discussion about where to keep the past is a good example in this respect: 'Where should I keep mine? You can't put your past in your pocket; you have to have a

---

[4] In their reading of Sartre's *Nausea*, David Klass and William Offenkrantz argue that the narrator Roquentin suffers from narcissistic personality disorder. Drawing upon their clinical experiences, Klass and Offenkrantz point out that Roquentin's ways of stabilizing 'his fragmenting self' – including 'reflection', 'temporality' and 'being-for-others' (terms they borrow from Sartre's *Being and Nothingness*) – are also found in narcissistic patients (1976: 547). Inspired by Sartre's existential exploration of Roquentin's identity formation, Klass and Offenfrankz conclude by suggesting that in the treatment of narcissistic personality disorders the patient needs to feel that he is of 'any warmth, empathy, or compliments', an idea that resembles my discussion of the narratological features of *Nausea* in this chapter (ibid.).

house in which to store it. I possess nothing but my body; a man on his own, with nothing but his body, can't stop memories; they pass through him' (97). This brief passage once again demonstrates the inherently dialogic nature of the text, since the narrative voice shifts between different pronouns smoothly. Although in colloquial English 'you' sometimes substitutes for 'one', choosing 'you' rather than 'one' is often the mark of an inclusively and shared experience. This oscillating between first-, second- and third-person pronouns may be seen as Roquentin's attempt to organize his 'self-experience' in 'a constitutive intersubjective context', a phrase that I borrow from Robert D. Stolorow and George E. Atwood's Kohutian reading and will get back to in the next section (1994: 241). Or, it might be an example of a struggling negotiation between different pieces of oneself, which further suggests Roquentin's inability to exist wholly. As James Woods remarks in his introduction to the novel, Roquentin is 'a sufferer and a militant' who is 'at war with ... pieces of himself' (ix). This poignant sense of struggling can also be found in Roquentin's monologue:

> Now when I say 'I', it seems hollow to me. I can no longer manage to feel myself, I am so forgotten. The only real thing left in me is some existence which can feel itself existing. I give a long, voluptuous yawn. Nobody. Antoine Roquentin exists for Nobody. That amuses me. And exactly what is Antoine Roquentin? An abstraction. A pale little memory of myself wavers in my consciousness. Antoine Roquentin ... And suddenly the I pales, pales and finally goes out. (241)

This questioning of 'I' presents an image of a modern man who suffers from the absence of meaning – which used to be represented by 'myth' or 'God' as discussed before. Roquentin's experience is, paraphrasing the title of Milan Kundera's 1984 novel *The Unbearable Lightness of Being*, the unbearable meaningless of being.

As suggested earlier, Roquentin's anticipation of the readerly compliments to his story at the end of the text reveals his narcissistic responses to the poignant existential crisis he is confronted with. Narcissism, in this context, becomes a means for Roquentin to construct meaning out of his contingent existence rather than a pathological disorder. In what follows, I move to the discussion of Kohut's conceptualization of the 'self-object' in order to better understand the importance of writing in a dialogical way for meaning construction.

Self-object, narcissism, empathy

The concept of 'self-object' is probably Kohut's most important and original contribution to the modern application of psychoanalysis, which is, namely, 'self psychology'.[5] As Mario Jacoby points out, unlike classical Freudian psychoanalysis, self psychology positions 'the self' – as opposed to biological drives – 'as the centre of the psychic universe', and highlights the role of desire for interpersonal communication in the construction of a cohesive self (Jacoby [1990] 2006: 72). With a focus on the dynamic between the infant and the caregiver (i.e. the mother), Kohut argues that narcissistic personality disorder is caused by the mother's 'defective empathy with the child's needs' rather than structural conflicts (as in the Freudian model) ([1971] 2009: 46)). In order to better illustrate the difference between the Freudian conceptualization of narcissism and his empathy-focused model, Kohut suggests that unlike the 'Freudian man' who is ridden with guilt (due to the burden of unacceptable and repressed drives and impulses), patients who suffer from narcissistic personality disorder are 'tragic', since, as Michael Franz Basch observes, they 'experience themselves and/or behave as if there is something missing in [their] psychological armamentarium' (Basch 1994: 1).

For me, the key difference between these different psychological models of narcissism lies in their different interpretation of the *nature* of the relationship between the infant and the caregiver. The infant–mother relationship that Kohut introduces is of particular significance to my discussion of how the reader is positioned to empathize with the textual other in neo-Victorian fiction. According to Kohut, the child does not experience the mother as the autonomous other. Rather, the mother is experienced as a 'self-object', an object that is experienced by the child as 'part of the self' ([1971] 2009: xiv). Her empathetic response is essential for the construction of the child's healthy narcissistic self. However, as Kohut explains, when this 'equilibrium of primary narcissism is disrupted by the unavoidable shortcoming of maternal care', the child may replace 'the previous perfection' s/he builds with the parent by either 'establishing a grandiose and exhibitionistic image of the self: *the grandiose*

---

[5] As Bouson notes, there is an ongoing debate among psychoanalysts as to whether self psychology 'complements, encompasses, or supersedes Freudian drive theory' (1989: 173).

self', or 'giving over the previous perfection to an admired, omnipotent (transitional) self-object: *the idealized parent imago*' (25, original emphasis). Kohut's work potently suggests that without sufficient empathetic investment from the parent, the child may not be able to construct a cohesive self and may therefore feel 'compelled to satisfy these essential needs through external sources', a process which is considered by Kohut as 'transference' (Bouson 1989: 16).

During his clinical experience of working with patients who suffer from narcissistic disturbances, Kohut realizes that their archaic narcissism is remobilized during psychoanalytic sessions. As an analyst, he is not experienced as an 'object' (as in object-relations theory) by his patients. Rather, he serves to promote a 'self-object experience' for the analysand, a term used by Kohut 'to label the particular *function* that the analyst serves for such patients' (Basch 1994: 1, original emphasis). By extracting control over and merging with the analyst, the patient manages to 'maintain their sense of self, their cohesiveness' (ibid., 2). As Kohut notes from his work with Miss F: 'I refused to entertain the possibility that I was not an object for the patient, not an amalgam with the patient's childhood loves and hatreds, but only, as I reluctantly came to see, an impersonal function, without significance except insofar as it related to the kingdom of her own remobilized narcissistic grandeur and exhibitionism' ([1971] 2009: 288). Kohut's observation makes it clear that 'self-object' does not refer to any particular person or object, thus differing from object-relations theory. Rather, it is 'an intrapsychic event, an experience' (Basch 1994: 2). Also, as Kohut explains in his posthumously published work *How Does Analysis Cure?* ([1984] 2013), this intrapsychic – as opposed to interpsychic – experience is 'that dimension of our experience of another person that relates to this person's functions in shoring up our self' (49). Although self-object experience operates in an intersubjective context, it is, nevertheless, a *non*-relational and seemingly solipsistic experience. To a certain extent, this non-relationality disturbs the analyst, since s/he realizes that s/he mainly serves as 'a self-extension or a need-satisfying object' whose existence provides the analysand with 'newfound feelings of self-acceptance and wholeness' (Bouson 1989: 14, 18). As illustrated by Kohut's poignant reflection on his work with Miss F, he is 'reluctant' to see that he is constructed as 'an impersonal function' 'without significance'.

This Kohutian thinking of the analyst–analysand relationship suggests a different understanding of narcissism to that propounded by Freud. By positing the archaic narcissistic deficit as a result of 'the severely disturbed empathic responses of the parents' (Kohut [1977] 2009: 74), Kohutian narcissism is, Merton M. Gill stresses, 'not necessarily pathological' (Gill 1994: 207). Indeed, rather than arguing for a reformative need to replace narcissistic desires with independence and maturity, Kohut understands narcissism as a kind of 'lifelong' wish for 'support and nurturance' (ibid.). As such, the patient's narcissistic needs or desires during psychoanalytic sessions are not necessarily reflections of 'fixation', 'defence' or 'an intensification of self-love' (Bacal 1994: 24). Rather, as Howard A. Bacal suggests, they may be 'attempt[s] at repairing a developmental deficit through a relationship with [the analyst]' (ibid.). This non-pathological and non-teleological approach to narcissism is an inherently reparative practice, which, as explained in the introduction, aims at 'build[ing] or rebuild[ing] some more sustaining relation to the objects' in our 'damaged and dangerous' world (Hanson 2012: 547).

I would now like to propose that Kohut's model provides a way of re-examining Roquentin's turbulent reactions to the confrontation with existential concerns and the text–reader relationship in my reading of Sartre's novel *Nausea*. As I discussed previously, Roquentin's address to the reader presents his confessional account – in the form of journal entries – in an overtly dialogic way. In Kohutian terms, we could indeed argue that we – as readers – are positioned to facilitate Roquentin's self-object experience. Here I am aware that there lies a difference between the 'implied' reader and the actual one. Nevertheless, the text's use of the second-person pronoun 'you' may be seen as an attempt to build a bridge between the reading experience of the implied reader and that of the actual one. Thus it is arguable that we, as actual readers, are brought within a disturbing narcissistic circuit, although as actual readers we do of course have the right or freedom to resist such a textual positioning by choosing not to read the text or to read it 'against the grain'. In *Nausea*, when Roquentin starts talking about his plan for the next book, he admits that he 'do[esn]'t quite know which kind [of book he would write]' (252). Then, in the same sentence, Roquentin quickly turns to the reader and, in making the reader complicit into his narcissistic agenda, observes: 'but you would have to guess' (ibid.). The use of imperative here hints at Roquentin's desire for the reader's response, and also perhaps, an expectation that the reader will be complicit in ensuring the importance of his book. This narratorial self-consciousness thematizes the creative process, relating the act of reading to that of writing. As Hutcheon argues in her study of this kind of 'narcissistic text', given the parallel between the act of creating and that of reading, the reader is put in 'a paradoxical position': 'while the text demands that he acknowledge the fictive and linguistic artifact that is its universe, it also teaches and indeed compels him to respond "vitally", to attribute human significance to the process of creating imaginary worlds in words' ([1980] 1985: 117).

Sartre's *Nausea* is indeed a good example of how a narcissistic text appropriates the reader's response in a deliberate and paradoxical manner. By thematizing the process of creating, the text demands the reader to acknowledge the fictionality of the world s/he reads. While on the other hand, as Hutcheon points out, the text constantly requires 'intellectual and affective responses comparable in scope and intensity to those of the [reader's] life experience' (5). As in *Nausea*, it could be further argued that Roquentin expects the reader to be *empathetic*: to share and get involved in his experience of the existential nausea and hence to feel 'ashamed of [*our*] existence' (252, emphasis added). The implication here is that the reader should share in Roquentin's shame as we belatedly become aware of the superfluousness of our own existence. Or, alternatively, the reader's interpellation could be read as a sign of Roquentin's defensive sense of superiority or arrogance. In both regards, the reader is no longer the objective and impartial observer of Roquentin's life; whether the reader likes it or not, s/he is positioned as his caring other, his partial self, his deficient alter ego, and (inasmuch as the reader may fail to meet his needs) his potential enemy.

Roquentin's plan for another book constitutes a transformative process that will ultimately enable him to become more capable of 'self empathy', both in his capacity to recall the past self and – even more importantly – in his ability to anticipate a future one:

> Naturally, at first it would only be a tedious, tiring job, it wouldn't prevent me from existing or from feeling that I exist. But a time would have to come when the book would be written, would be behind me, and I think that a little of its light would fall over my past. Then, through it, I might be able

to recall my life without repugnance. Perhaps one day, thinking about this very moment, about this dismal moment at which I am waiting, round-shouldered, for it to be time to get on the train, perhaps I might feel my heart beat faster and say to myself: 'It was on that day, at that moment that it all started.' And I might succeed – in the past, simply in the past – in accepting myself. (252–3)

Roquentin expects that writing a life story – as a representation of the narcissistic need for empathetic support and assurance – could transform an 'absorbed' or questioned 'I' ('the I pales, pales and finally goes out' (241)) into an experiential and agentic 'I' ('I might *feel* my heart beat faster' (253, emphasis added)). By remobilizing narcissistic structures through transference/the self-object experience, Roquentin becomes more capable of empathy towards his past and future selves. Narrated from the present, the 'anticipation of retrospection' inherent in this passage, a concept taken from Peter Brooks (see introduction), maps out how a present self anticipates a future where Roquentin's life has agency and meaning. In this regard, this anticipatory retrospection liberates the subject from the nausea of his contingency and demonstrates the need for both an empathetic interlocutor/self-object and a dynamic approach to the relationship between the past, the present, and the future. Also, by 'slipping' back into the past, Roquentin seems to be able to *ground* the past self, as evidenced by his claim that 'I might succeed – in the past, simply in the past – in accepting myself' (253). In Kohutian terms, it could therefore be argued that during this intrapsychic self-object experience – when writing (together *with* the reader) – Roquentin manages to create meaning and intentionality for his existence precisely because the past, the present and the future selves begin to exist *for* each other.

In these opening sections, my reading of Sartre's figuration of Roquentin's nausea in his novel of the same name has focused on the dynamic between contingency, narcissism and empathy within a philosophical and psychological framework. In the next section, I move to another exploration of contingency in Cox's *The Meaning of Night* and Burnet's *His Bloody Project*. With a focus on the contingency the protagonist experiences in both texts, I examine the ways in which neo-Victorian fiction engages with existential concerns about agency, choice, responsibility and the exercise of free will (or, indeed, the absence of it). In doing so, I shift away from the 'dominant' reading position offered by both texts, one that depends upon a psychological assessment of the central character's personality and a social-cultural explanation for his moral corruption or criminality. As I will demonstrate, this existential focus also prompts the reader to reflect upon the significance of their implication in the textual world in relation to transformative reparation.

Contingency and 'fate'

Set in Victorian London in the 1850s, Michael Cox's 600-page-long novel *The Meaning of Night* is a contemporary pastiche of sensation fiction.[6] Structured as a Chinese box – a figure used to describe the form of a narrative inside a narrative – Cox's text presents the reader with two simultaneous works: the first is a 'found' manuscript written by Edward Glyver. Written in the form of confession, this account describes Edward's discovery of his true identity (that he is the rightful heir of Lord Tansor, who is the head of one of the most powerful households in England), and his murder of his rival, the poet-criminal Phoebus Rainsford Daunt, who has mercilessly stolen his identity. Edward's confession is interspersed with the second text; that is, J. J. Antrobus's – a fictionalized professor of 'Post-Authentic Victorian Fiction' at the University of Cambridge– annotated reading of Glyver's narrative (3). The introductory remark from Professor Antrobus – 'The following work, printed here for the first time, is one of the lost curiosities of nineteenth-century literature' – presents him as our literary guide to the Victorian underworld, thus positioning the extradiegetic reader alongside him (1). In this context, the use of Antrobus's 'editorial interpolations and footnotes' (ibid.) throughout the text may be seen as 'mirroring' the contemporary reader's hermeneutic desire to 'demystify' the hidden Victorian past. It also evokes and caters to the reader's voyeuristic consumption of the past, a point that is self-consciously appropriated by Cox's choice of the title: 'The *Meaning* of Night' (emphasis added). Indeed, as argued in Chapter 1, neo-Victorian fiction provides the contemporary reader with a literary voyeuristic excursion into the past.

---

[6] For discussion about how contemporary writers reinvent the Victorian sensation novel, see Jessica Cox (2019).

In light of Hutcheon's discussion of the ontological status of fiction, the use of the Chinese box structure in Cox's *The Meaning of Night* also introduces an existential dimension to the discussion of text–reader relationship in neo-Victorian literature. As Hutcheon points out, the literary text 'has *no* existence apart from that constituted by the inward act of reading which counterpoints the externalized act of writing' ([1980] 1985: 28, original emphasis). In other words, the 'existence' of a literary text depends upon the 'collaboration' between the text and the reader, and the latter's involvement is essential in the construction of the textual world. Hutcheon's depiction of the existential condition of fiction is well illustrated by the different levels of text–reader relationship Cox's text involves. Through the use of the 'found manuscript' plot, the text dramatizes the contingency of Professor Antrobus's encounter with Edward's confessional account, thus presenting Antrobus as *the* reader whose participation – in the form of verifying and editing – is essential in helping 'lay [Edward's] soul bare to posterity' (1). This intradiegetic example may be seen as 'mirroring' the covert requirement the text makes of its extradiegetic reader. Mark Llewellyn observes that through the invention of the name 'Antrobus', the text presents itself as a literary 'trick' (2009: 41). According to Llewellyn's research, the name 'Antrobus' is possibly derived from 'the Latin for front (*anterus*) and the Italian for hollow (*buso*)' (ibid.). The professor is thus presented as 'a "hollow front" to the fiction', with the implication that everything that follows will be built as a façade (ibid.). The covert revelation of the fictive nature of the text demonstrates 'the novelistic mimetic code', which requires and facilitates the reader's participation in the construction of the textual world (Hutcheon [1980] 1985: 41). This reader positioning, as reflected by the intradiegetic example about the relationship between Professor Antrobus and Edward, involves an almost existential responsibility, a point that is also considered by Hutcheon as one of the defining features of the text–reader relationship in metafiction ([1980] 1985: 30).

The Meaning of Night further thematizes these issues about existence and responsibility. Although as a contemporary pastiche of sensation fiction, the text does not engage with the philosophical debate about existentialism directly, its thematic use of the idea of 'contingency' – or 'fate' as the protagonist Edward calls it – directs the reader's attention to the existential concerns he confronts. Revolving around the issue of Edward's stolen identity, the text presents the reader with an intricate story about Edward's choice, responsibility and his attempt to intervene in the course of indifferent fate and destiny. Through the use of a retrospective narrative, the text illustrates how Edward tries to ascribe meaning to contingency through his retreat into fatalism. By playing with the dynamic between the idea of contingency and fate, the text may be seen as – to quote from Margaret Atwood's *Alias Grace* – 'sail[ing] back and forth' figuratively, thus complicating the reader's desire or ability to empathize with the textual other (1996: 122). On one hand, the foregrounding of contingency in Edward's life experience presents him as a pathetic victim, which helps to elicit empathetic response and affective investment from the reader. On the other hand, the textual characterization of Edward's solipsistic responses to his existential crisis renders him a self-aggrandizing perpetrator, posing serious questions about the moral and political implication of readerly empathy.

The discovery of Edward's true identity is a good example of how the awareness of contingency raises deep existential concerns. Like the Roquentin character in Sartre's *Nausea*, whose chance encounter with a pebble evokes an existential concern about the meaning of his existence, Edward is made to question his existence by his chance discovery of his birth. As we see from the perspective of Edward, it is through his chance reading of Mrs Edward Glyver's – whom he thought was his birth mother at that time – journal entries that he becomes suspicious of the friendship she holds with Laura Tansor (the wife of Lord Tansor, who turns out to be Edward's birth mother). Here the text dramatizes the sense of contingency and chance by presenting Edward's reading of Mrs Glyver's diaries as an event that is consequent upon the following conditions: (a) the 'convenient' passing away of his adoptive mother, who happened to have a habit of 'committing her private thoughts to her journals' (151); (b) her insistence on not throwing things away (ibid.) and (c) Edward's idleness. The fact that Edward is left with no family member after the death of his adoptive mother and his unemployed status make it possible for him to stay 'indoors, alone and undisturbed' for most of the time (ibid.).[7] This chance discovery of his birth overturns Edward's previous self-identity and raises serious questions about his existence:

---

[7] Writing for *The Independent*, Roz Kaveney remarks that the use of 'coincidence and surprise' in *The Meaning of Night* is as 'outrageous' as 'any book of Wilkie Collins or Dickens', pointing to the fact that these two elements are generic of the Victorian sensation novel (2011: n.p.).

> I was not the son of Captain and Mrs Edward Glyver. My blood was not theirs. It connected me instead to other places and times, and to another name – an ancient and distinguished name. I had nothing of the man I had thought was my father in me, nothing of the woman I had called my mother. The eyes that were reflected in my mirror on rising every day were not her eyes, as I had always liked to think. But whose were they? Whom did I resemble – my real father, my real mother, or my dead brother? *Who was I?*
>
> The questions went around and round in my head, day and night. I would wake from fitful sleep in a state of extreme agitation, as if the ground had been cut away from under my feet and I was falling through infinite space. (156, original emphasis)

The focus on hereditary likeness demonstrates the importance of genealogy in grounding or establishing Edward's existence. The discovery that his 'blood' actually connects him to 'other places and times' (which are unvisited or unknown to him at this stage) overturns Edward's previous self-identity and leaves him in an insecure situation. The question 'Who was I?', in this context, involves an existential concern about how Edward could possibly position himself, as vividly illustrated by the poignant and disorienting sense of groundlessness he experiences.

This gratuitous feeling consumes Edward and, as a psychosomatic experience, arguably mirrors his consumption of opium on another occasion: 'And then the floor-boards seemed to fall away beneath me and I was tumbling through the air, spinning round and round, descending ever deeper into a great yawning, roaring void' (345). This horrific depiction of how Edward is uncontrollably absorbed into a Nietzschean abyss demonstrates the extent to which the issue of Edward's stolen identity challenges his agency: 'I was adrift on an ocean of mystery, like the blackbird in my dream – powerless, frozen. What dark creatures inhabited the unseen deeps beneath me? What landfall awaited me? Or was this my fate, to be forever pushed and pulled, now this way, now that, by the winds and currents of circumstance, without respite?' (344). The status of 'be[ing] forever pushed and pulled' illustrates again the desperate sense of being out of control that Edward experiences. The reference to the ocean also resembles the passage in *Nausea*, where Roquentin describes the feeling evoked by contingency as something nauseous, something akin to seasickness. Although Edward is not presented as a character who is as philosophically sophisticated as Roquentin, these textual details bring to the fore Edward's psychosomatic turmoil, which, as we have seen from the previous discussion, is triggered by his chance discovery of his birth.

Viewing Edward through this existential lens provides us with a different means of evaluating his unsettling behaviours, and in particular, his merciless murder of a stranger as described at the beginning of the text. Admittedly, the striking opening – 'After killing the red-haired man, I took myself to Quinn's for an oyster supper' (9) – may be seen as encouraging a clinical-psychological analysis of Edward in the reader. The stark contrast between the brutal and extraordinary act of killing and the daily activity of eating would appear to characterize Edward as a stereotypical psychopath, a speculation that is compounded by the subsequent description of Edward's paranoid behaviour (such as his suspicion that he is observed or followed by someone in the darkness (10)). In his review of the novel, Roz Kaveney remarks that Edward is 'a man who inhabits the borderland of sanity' (2011: n.p.). Edward's seemingly pathological action is also linked with the circumstances he is in. Revolving around the issue of Edward's stolen identity and his attempt to take back the family property, the text encourages a very material explanation for Edward's corrupted morality and criminality. Indeed, as I have discussed in relation to Atwood's *Alias Grace* in Chapter 1, neo-Victorian literature often steers the reader towards a historical and materialist interpretation of the character's psychological condition. The existential approach this chapter adopts therefore seeks to add a new dimension to the discussion of the reading pleasures afforded by neo-Victorian fiction. This move away from social and historical explanations is dramatized in Cox's text by the fact that, although the act of killing is premeditated, Edward's choice of his victim is contingent:

> Now I knew that I could do it; but it gave me no pleasure. The poor fellow had done me no harm. Luck had simply been against him. [...] His way that night, inauspiciously, coinciding with mine in Threadneedle-street, had made him the unwitting object of my irrevocable intention to kill someone; but had it not been him, it must have been someone else.
>
> Until the very moment in which the blow had been struck, I had not known definitively that I was capable of such a terrible act, and it was absolutely necessary to put the matter beyond all doubt. For the despatching of the red-haired man was in the nature of a trial, or experiment, to prove to myself

that I could indeed take another human life, and escape the consequences. (10–11)

The focus on Edward's ability to kill makes it clear that for him killing is an exercise of agency and freedom rather than something pleasurable for more complex psychological reasons. Indeed, Edward's imperative to act is linked with very obvious existential concerns, as evidenced by the passing remark that his 'great enterprise' (160) helps him to 'gain ground on [his] feeble self' and ascribes 'purpose and definition' (61) to his gratuitous existence. The following account on Edward's failure to kill his rival, Rainsford Daunt, further demonstrates the centrality of the freedom to act (or not) plays in securing or undermining his existence:

> Shocked to the core by my inability to do what I wished to do above all things, I stumbled off, arriving at last at the opium-master's door in Bluegate-fields. Oh God, what dreams came to me that night – dreams so terrible that I cannot bear to set them down! I ended by raving wildly for an hour or more. [...] Where was I? (545)

The question Edward faces – 'Where was I?' – after the consumption of opium illustrates how the inability to conduct his 'great enterprise' (160) brings Edward to the brink of a true 'existential crisis'. Edward's 'successful' murder of a stranger may therefore be considered as his attempt to 'impose [his] will' (177) on the gratuitousness of human existence, to live existentially.

One of the consequences of this foregrounding of Edward's existential predicament is that it encourages the reader to suspend their moral judgement. By the same token, it also helps to elicit empathetic response and affective investment from the reader. Giles Foden has likewise suggested that we are led to 'sympathise with' Edward (2006: n.p.). Through the use of retrospective narrative, the text directs the reader's attention to the story of how Edward is *acted on* by 'fate' 'inexorably' and how he tries to take back control (151). This reading position is further exemplified by Edward's call for the 'Truth of truth' in one of his darkest moments of despair: 'What we commonly call "true" – that "A" equals "B", or that Death waits quietly for us all – is often but a shadow or replica of something greater. Only when this shadow-truth conjoins with *meaning*, and above all with meaning *experienced*, do we see the substance itself, the Truth of truth' (424, original emphasis). By highlighting the importance of developing embodied meaning out of pure existence, Edward's account echoes Sartre's famous claim that 'existence precedes essence', which, as Sartre himself explains, refers to the existential tenet that 'man first of all exists, encounters himself, surges up in the world – and defines himself afterwards' (1948: 28). For Sartre, the essence of the human being is not determined by God or another external source, a point that I discussed earlier in relation to Roquentin's decision to shift the focus of his writing from his 'alter-ego' – the eighteenth-century political figure Monsieur de Rollebon – to himself. As Sartre argues elsewhere, man is 'what he wills', or what he 'makes of himself' (ibid.). This understanding of the performative nature of existence – what Emil L. Fackenheim calls 'self-making-in-a-situation' (1961: 37) – is also linked, in the above extract, to the use of the plural pronoun 'we', which may be read as a call for the reader's empathy and solidarity: in particular, his or her ability to share in the experience of the indifferent and 'inexorable fate' (to paraphrase Edward).

As we have seen from the discussion of *Nausea* in the previous section, the ability to act – or to prove that one *can* act – is essential in helping Roquentin to overcome his nausea and is considered by Sartre, in his later works, to be the mark of existential freedom. A similar existential scenario is explored in Cox's characterization of Edward's violent actions in *The Meaning of Night*. However, the fact that Edward's attempt to secure his own existence depends upon the act of violence against the innocent bystander also invokes Sartre's concern about actions which reject the autonomy and freedom of others:

> Obviously, freedom as the definition of a man does not depend upon others, but as soon as there is a commitment, I am obliged to will the liberty of others at the same time as mine. I cannot make liberty my aim unless I make that of others equally my aim. Consequently, when I recognise, as entirely authentic, that man is a being whose existence precedes essence, and that he is a free being who cannot, in any circumstances, but will his freedom, at the same time I realise that I cannot will the freedom of others. Thus, in the name of that will to freedom which is implied in freedom itself, I can form judgments upon those who seek to hide from themselves the wholly voluntary nature of their existence and its complete freedom. (1948: 52)

Sartre contends that to act in good faith one should 'will' the freedom of both the self and the other; not – as in Edward's case – seek to prove the existence of the self *at the expense of* the other. This Sartrean understanding of freedom, Kevin L. Stoehr argues, suggests that violence against the innocent other is 'an implicit extension of the "violence" done to oneself when an individual denies his own radical freedom' (2011: 41). Viewed in this way, Edward's ruthless murder of an innocent stranger is arguably an act of self-deception and self-negation. The following way in which Edward presents himself as the victim of a fate beyond his control vividly illustrates the Sartean notion of self-deception and self-negation:

> I was but a man, a good man at heart, if the truth be told, driven to set right the wrong that had been done to me, absolved – even of murder – by the implacable fatalities to which I was then convinced my life had been subject. To me, this power was the Iron master, forever forging the chains that bound me to actions I *must* take. My destiny, I believed, was to take back what was rightfully mine, whatever the consequences. (24, original emphasis)

By ascribing his actions to the 'power [of] the Iron master', Edward presents himself as a mere puppet of 'destiny' rather than an autonomous human being with free will and agency. This retreat into fatalism demonstrates Edward's inability to take responsibility for the consequences of his acts. It also negates the very kind of radical freedom brought by the contingency of existence and reality, as a result of which Edward fails to make meaning out of his existence. Even after Edward's 'successful' murder of his rival Phoebus Daunt, he fails to secure his true identity, which traps him further in a despairing spiral of meaninglessness and nothingness, as illustrated by Edward's internal monologue:

> *What do you know?* Nothing.
>
> *What have you achieved?* Nothing.
>
> *Who are you?* Nobody. (528, original emphasis)

These bleak existential questions demonstrate that acts of violence against the (innocent) other negate not only the autonomy and freedom of the victim, but also that of the perpetrator. In Sartrean terms, Edward is a character who is 'inauthentic' and acts with 'bad faith'.[8]

---

[8] Sartre refers to self-negation as a form of 'bad faith' (*mauvaise foi*). For details, see his discussion about how we judge the actions of others in *Existentialism and Humanism* (1948: 50–4).

This portrayal of Edward's 'inauthentic life' raises ethical concerns about his solipsistic and violent 'self-making' process, which also challenges the reader's ability to empathize with him. The fact that Edward's choice of the victim is contingent pushes the reader to question the stability and intelligibility of their own lives. By revealing the horrifying fact that there is no guarantee for their existence, Cox's *The Meaning of Night* prompts the reader to confront – with reference to Nietzsche – 'the horror of the abyss', which brings about a 'nauseous' *reading* experience. Nevertheless, the constant appeal to the reader also makes clear that Edward requires an interlocutor of some kind in order to be redeemed and to discover the meaning in his existence. Like the Roquentin character in *Nausea*, Edward chooses to write journal entries – for his 'UNKNOWN READER' (6, original emphasis) – in order to help him get rid of the 'dreadful feeling of abandonment' (156), and to record – that is, to 'verify' – his existence: 'I had decided [...] that I would begin recording, in brief, the daily course of my life, partly in emulation of my foster-mother's habit, but with the additional purpose of providing myself, and perhaps posterity, with an accurate digest of events as I embarked on what I had become convinced would be a critical phase of my great project' (369). Edward's anticipation of retrospection reveals the crucial importance of his 'project' to the validation of his existence. As for Roquentin, it is a project that requires the *illocutory* presence of a reader, even if this implicit or idealized figure is situated way into the future. By repeatedly assuring 'his unknown reader' that he is communicating his existence and his struggles 'in full and complete form' (78), Edward calls for their 'full-hearted sympathy and support' (75) and demands their unconditional trust ('you must take it [his account] on trust' (26)). In this context, the textual characterization of Edward as both an active agent and a passive victim in the hands of fate invites the reader's recognition of – and empathetic engagement with – his existential dilemma, and the way he has 'heroically' survived his encounter with the abyss.

In light of my discussion of Kohut's formulation of the self-object in the previous section, the reader may be seen as Edward's self-object, whose existence provides Edward with 'newfound feelings of self-acceptance and wholeness' (Bouson 1989: 18). Indeed, as we see from Edward's critical reflection on his recourse to fatalism in his final confession, Edward manages to position himself as both subject and object, agent and acted upon simultaneously: 'I felt impelled by a relentless and misguided sense of fatality, which I interpreted as justifying whatever actions I chose to take' (590). The overt willingness or ability to take ownership of his actions therefore presents Edward's act of writing – together with the presence of the empathetic reader – as his road to the restoration of his agency and existential freedom. *The Meaning of Night* thus tells a double story: one is about Edward's 'inauthentic life', which involves his violent and selfish acts in the name of fatalism; the other is about how Edward tries to live existentially through the act of 'dialogic' writing. This kind of double story chimes with the philosophy of existentialism, and in particular, Sartre's challenging of the notion of predetermined human nature and his foregrounding of the individual actions and commitments in the construction of human essence, which also pushes the reader to reflect upon their own existential freedom, responsibility and 'seasickness'. Further, this existential awareness disrupts the reader's immersive consumption of the contemporary fantasy of the Victorian underworld, and prompts them to be more critically aware of the significance of their implication in the textual world.

Against empathy

In this section, I turn to a brief discussion of Graeme Macrae Burnet's second novel *His Bloody Project*, a text that tells an extremely uncomfortable story of meaningless violence and nihilistic horror. Revolving around a brutal triple murder in a remote Scottish crofting community in 1869, *His Bloody Project* is presented as a collection of documents discovered and further edited by the author whilst he is researching his own Highland roots, a literary trick that thematizes the issue of authenticity (as those I mentioned at the beginning of the chapter) or what Robert Wirth terms 'deceptive communication' (see Wirth 2019). These documents include a series of police statements taken from the residents of the village of Culduie, which offer contradictory statements on the personality of the accused – the seventeen-year-old Roderick Macrae – and his own retrospective account of how a certain 'chain of events' lead to his ruthless murder of three people (25). These documents are followed by post-mortem reports on the victims, psychological evaluations of Roderick's state of mind (in particular, whether he was sane and rational at the time of the killings) and transcript from the trial. Similar to Atwood's *Alias Grace*, Burnet's multilayered narrative in *His Bloody Project* may also be seen as positioning the extradiegetic reader alongside the jury, inviting judgement on the character Roderick's behaviours. Also, its detailed description of the harsh realities of crofting life in the Scottish Highlands in the nineteenth century and inclusion of psychiatric evaluations of Roderick's personality clearly steer the reader towards a social and psychological explanation for Roderick's seemingly pathological behaviour and criminality. As I have argued in Chapter 1, this materialist or Foucauldian reading position may be considered as the dominant one offered by neo-Victorian fiction. However, in light of this chapter's discussion of existentialism, I would like to propose that like *The Meaning of Night*, *His Bloody Project* is a novel that thematizes the idea of contingency, or the 'ill fortunate', as the text puts it, raising questions, once again, about the meaning, or meaninglessness, of human existence (21). The reader is therefore prompted to think about Roderick's criminal actions from the existential as well as an historical and psychological perspective.

The account of Roderick's chance discovery of a dying sheep in a boggy hillside at the beginning of his memoir resonates with the depiction of existential 'nausea' in Sartre's and Cox's novels:

> When I emerged over the bridge, I found a distressed ram, lying on its side, half submerged in the mire. [...] The animal flailed its free limbs uselessly, succeeding only in working itself further into the slough. As I neared the stricken beast, keeping to the heathery outcrops upon which it was safe to stand, I whispered soothing sounds in an attempt to calm it. The sheep turned in my direction, like a sick old woman too weak to raise her head from the pillow. I felt no pity for the beast, only a kind of loathing for its stupidity. (32)

Similar to the way in which Roquentin's chance contact with an inanimate pebble makes him aware of the gratuitousness of his own existence and prompts him to act in a desperate and violent manner, so too is Roderick forced to take action on account of his chance witnessing of how the sheep strays into the bog and is 'devoured by' it (32). Roderick's interpretation of the 'caw' of the crow nearby as 'the mockery of [his] efforts' reveals his desire to take control and break himself free from the chance circumstance he finds himself in (33). His eventual decision to kill the sheep can therefore be read as a desperate attempt to assert his agency over the horror of the abyss or void that is symbolically invoked by the bog itself. In the memoir, his act is also given a religious inflection by his claim that he is the 'redeemer' who has the 'duty to end the life of the stricken beast' (28, 33).

In many respects, the experience of the dying sheep whose existence appears to be gratuitous 'mirrors' Roderick's own life. Written in the form of a retrospective narrative, Roderick's account tells a story of how his family has been acted upon by different kinds of 'ill fortune' and 'unchancy beings' (21). Born into a family of crofters, Roderick is presented as a vulnerable character who does not have much choice over the course of his life or its misery: circumstances which initially help to elicit an empathetic response from the reader. Although the schoolmaster Mr Gillies suggests that Roderick has 'the necessary ability to become a teacher or a minister or anything [he] choose[s]', he is unable to continue his education since he is 'required for the croft' (25). Also, Roderick's contingent decision to kill the dying sheep links the fate of his family with that of Lachlan Mackenzie, the owner of the sheep that died at Roderick's hands. From Roderick's narrative, we see that Lachlan is a vengeful character whose election as the village constable brings a good deal of trouble to Roderick's family, including Lachlan's decision to reduce the portion of the croft Roderick's family is given to work on, which leaves them in a financially desperate situation. Lachlan also exercises his power by the vicious rape of Roderick's sister, Jetta, on several occasions. In this context, the account of how Roderick and his father try – and then fail – to get any assistance or form of justice from the factor (the estate manager) demonstrates the extent to which Roderick's family is exploited: narrative details which inevitably steer the reader towards a historical and sociopolitical interpretation of Roderick's behaviours. However, as my previous discussion of Roderick's killing of the sheep at the beginning of the text suggests, his actions may also be seen as 'responsive' to the situation he finds himself in unexpectedly or 'by chance'. Indeed, viewing Roderick's 'crimes' through this existential frame arguably makes better sense of them than a reading which tries (like the jury at his trial) to explain them in more straightforward psychological or political terms.

Like Edward in *The Meaning of Night*, Roderick's violent killing of Lachlan's family is a combination of premeditated revenge – his 'project' as he calls it – and a contingent response to what he finds in the house (151). Although Roderick's initial plan is to kill Lachlan in order to pay back 'the tribulations' Lachlan had caused his family, his first two victims are Flora and Donnie (Lachlan's two children), who simply happen to be at home when Roderick gets there (145). The appalling depiction of how Roderick 'brought the back of the blade firmly down on [Flora's] skull' and then 'hit [Donnie] on the side of the head with [his] flaughter' provocatively challenges the reader's ability to empathize with him (148, 149). It also evokes a kind of nihilistic horror, which may cause readers to confront and question the very gratuitousness that pervades their own existence. Indeed, Roderick's spontaneous killing of Flora and Donnie is difficult, if not impossible, to rationalize either psychologically or politically no matter how acutely his family has suffered.[9] As John Armstrong asserts, these killings 'are impossible to incorporate into a straight tale of revenge' (2018: 66). The very contingency underlying Roderick's killing of Flora and Donnie may therefore be seen as stemming from an irrationality that is best understood as a denial of the value of life itself. With reference back to Stoehr's explication of existential freedom, Roderick's violent action presents itself as a kind of 'life-negating freedom', which – following Stoehr – destroys the possibilities of 'life-affirming freedom' (2011: 43).

Significantly, Roderick's account is permeated by a sense of indifference that extends to both his intradiegetic interlocutor (the advocate, Andrew Sinclair) and any future readers of his journal. In contrast to Sartre's *Nausea* or Cox's *The Meaning of Night* – where the protagonist tries to construct a kind of self-object experience (in Kohutian terms) with their interlocutor/reader in order to construct meaning out of their contingent existence – the character in Burnet's *His Bloody Project* displays no interest in building a productive relationship with anyone, present or future, who might read what

---

[9] Roderick is also presented as an unreliable narrator. The post-mortem of Flora reveals that she was sexually assaulted during the murder, a detail that is not mentioned in Roderick's own account. Roderick's denial of inflicting such injuries leaves the reader wonder 'whether his crimes were sexually motivated all long' since Flora had refused Roderick's advances before (Armstrong 2018: 66). The text's refusal to provide a definite answer to this issue can be seen as evoking as well as frustrating the reader's desire for the 'truth'.

he writes. In fact, he repeatedly states that he *does not* intend to 'rouse the pity of the reader' (26). Nor is he interested in absolving himself 'of responsibility for what [he has] done' (43). Rather, he agrees to write down his experience simply because his advocate Mr Andrew Sinclair requires him to do so and he wants to 'repay [his] advocate's kindness' (15). Roderick's insistence on reciprocity leads to a troubling question about empathy: what if the other refuses to be empathized? This question also points to the problematic structure of empathy. As Daryl Koehn notes, 'we may marshall all of our understanding to grasp a particular feature only to find out that the party on the other end does not think this trait is especially important or revelatory of her character or being' (1998: 60). In this regard, Clare Hemmings warns, 'To be empathised with could be a horrific prospect', since it might lead to 'the dissolution of the other's sense of self' (2012: 153). The peril of empathy is also reflected in the slips between empathy and pity in Roderick's account. In light of Terry Eagleton's suggestion that pity is 'a spectator sport' (2003: 160), Roderick's refusal of readerly empathy is indicative of his assertion of a strong self whose experience cannot be easily appropriated by the other. This defensive gesture reveals Roderick's insistence on his singularity, which, interestingly, can also be considered as his coping strategy with his existential crisis. Roderick's experience thus brings to the fore the limit of readerly empathy: it risks 'destabliz[ing] meaning from the personal to the allegorical' (Shuman 2005: 4).

Burnet's *His Bloody Project* provides the reader with an extremely uncomfortable reading experience all round: not only is this a story about how human freedom is exercised at its most radically *negative*, but it is also one that refuses the usual explanations ('madness' or sociopolitical injustice and oppression) which induce, or at least *permit*, sympathy or empathy. Through its repudiation of the reader's empathetic understanding (which, as argued previously, is positioned by Cox's text as the means to help Edward get through his 'existential' crisis), Burnet's text also refuses to provide the reader with a 'satisfactory' closure to the unsettling story about Roderick's brutal behaviours, with the result of frustrating the reader's desire to 'redeem' the 'unpleasurable' past. Indeed, as Anne Whitehead reminds us, '"being moved" can too readily blur into "moving on"' (2012: 193). By demonstrating how extremely 'uncomfortable' reading neo-Victorian fiction can be, *His Bloody Project* also directs the reader's attention to a further reflection on the personal, historical and political reasons behind the other's refusal to be empathized with. The lack of emotional closure in Burnet's novel hence becomes an effective means in implicating the reader in the (re)construction of the past, the present and the future.

Conclusion

In a 1969 article, John Fowles ascribes his interest in the Victorians to their preoccupation with concerns such as 'purpose' and 'morality': 'the Victorian age, especially from 1850 on, was highly existentialist in many of its personal dilemmas. One can almost invert the reality and say that Camus and Sartre have been trying to lead us, in their fashion, to a Victorian seriousness of purpose and moral sensitivity' (1977: 140). Speaking from the modern perspective, Fowles suggests that the Victorian 'personal dilemmas' about 'purpose' and 'moral sensitivity' are 'existentialist'. Although as a cultural movement existentialism flourished in Europe in the 1940s and 1950s, some of its key ideas – such as its challenge to the existence of God and subversion of the conception of 'ready-made' human nature – are clearly associated with the development of science and technology in the Victorian period, and in particular, Darwin's theory of evolution. As Sally Shuttleworth observes, there was 'a decisive crisis of faith' (1998: 260) in the Victorian period 'when the certainties of natural history and theology were shattered by the emergence of evolutionary biology' (253). This crisis of faith, Shuttleworth explains, is 'existential' (260). Also, the nineteenth-century philosopher Friedrich Nietzsche is widely considered to be the precursor to twentieth-century existentialism. Fowles's own existential interest in the Victorians has been made famous by his novel *The French Lieutenant's Woman*. As a novel that self-consciously engages with Victorian literary convention, gender politics and morality, *The French Lieutenant's Woman* is a text that 'themati[zes]' and 'structur[es]' the issue of existential freedom (Hutcheon [1980] 1985: 60). Its blurring of the boundary between fiction and reality and inclusion of multiple endings may be seen as playing with Sartre's famous claim that 'existence precedes essence', which, to many critics including Hutcheon, undermines the power of the God-like narrator and ascribes the meaning of existence to what one does or what one chooses.[10]

Fowles's preoccupation with existentialism in *The French Lieutenant's Woman* can be found in a great number of neo-Victorian novels. Works such as Graham Swift's *Ever After* (1992) and A. S. Byatt's *Angels and Insects* (1992) feature Victorian characters who 'pose the question of whether future generations would shrug at the vista of meaninglessness which so appalled them' (Shuttleworth 1998: 216). Given these texts' shared interest in existential crisis and the importance of existential concerns in the study of metafiction (i.e. the ontological status of textual world and the role and responsibility of the reader), it is a bit surprising to see that very little has been written on neo-Victorian fiction – a genre that can be positioned within the parameters of highbrow literature and popular fiction – from an existential perspective. Taking up Fowles's lead, this chapter has moved away from the well-established critical fascination of detecting the similarities and/or differences between the Victorians and ourselves in the twenty-first century (which, as argued in the introduction, often involves what Sedgwick calls a 'paranoid' impulse), and has chosen to examine the representation of personal dilemmas in neo-Victorian fiction from a philosophical and ahistorical perspective instead. It tries to demonstrate that although as a cultural movement, existentialism may belong in the twentieth century, its core ideas – such as personal freedom, agency and responsibility – are still useful for, and relevant to, the discussion of reader-response theory and the issue of empathy. By bringing Sartre's philosophical discussion of existentialism together with Kohut's theory of self psychology, this chapter has mapped out a different model of text–reader relationship: one that concerns the importance of the interlocutor in helping subjects negotiate the contingency of their existence. The fact that texts like *Nausea* and *The Meaning of Night* appear to position the reader as someone of crucial importance in the reparative transformation of intradiegetic characters

---

[10] There is an ongoing debate about whether or to what extent the inclusion of multiple endings in Fowles's text extends the reader's freedom and control. Unlike other critics, A. S. Byatt argues that Fowles's choice undermines – rather than extends – the reader's freedom. She writes that 'for the writer, whilst the plural endings are possibilities in the head, they intensify the reality of the future world. For the reader, now, they reduce it to paperiness again' (Byatt 1991: 174). For my purpose here, I think it is fair to suggest that the use of different endings engages with the Sartrean concept of existential freedom.

serves to implicate him/her in a very particular way and create what are often extremely uncomfortable reading experiences. *His Bloody Project*, by contrast, refuses to position the reader as an empathetic ear to the character's suffering, thus further advancing current discussion about the political and ethical values of readerly empathy.

In the next chapter, I move from a discussion of how the reader empathizes with the textual other to an examination of the reader's empathetic engagement with a non-human subject; that is, the landscape. By tracing the concept of empathy back to its aesthetic origins, I consider how neo-Victorian literature locates its characters in space and place and how their (dis)orientations sometimes mirror the reader's own experience.

4

Affective embodiment

In 2001, the Shanghai Municipal Planning Bureau launched a project called 'One City, Nine Towns'. Its core idea was to urbanize and develop the peripheral ten towns of Shanghai – which were known as 'one city and nine towns' – into its satellite towns. As the Shanghai Municipality No. 1 Decree of 2001 stated, in order to redevelop these suburbs into places that 'attract urban residents through an agreeable natural environment, distinctive townscapes, and a modern way of living', the government decided to 'copy' European architectural styles, which, to them, would help 'to project an image of cosmopolitanism' (Shen and Wu 2012: 190). The towns were built in the 'stereotypical' architecture of Britain, Italy, the Netherlands, Germany, Spain, Scandinavia and North America, respectively. By recreating the most picturesque elements of Western townscapes, this project epitomizes a Baudrillardian postmodern world (see Baudrillard 1988). It also fulfils the Chinese consumer's experience of the exotic.

Taking the scheme of 'Thames Town' as an example, this chapter continues the discussion of the pleasures afforded by neo-Victorian literature and culture, now focusing on the dynamic that exists between space, place and empathy.[1] Although the architectural replicas in Thames Town are not exclusively neo-Victorian, the 'immersive' tourist experience it affords is analogous to the consumer's experience of neo-Victorian fiction and film. It also resembles the nineteenth-century German aesthetic perception of *Einfühlung*, which, as noted in the introduction, is the etymological origin of the English term empathy. As I will explain in more detail below, neo-Victorian cultural practices,

---

[1] As Edward Relph explains, space is 'amorphous and intangible and not an entity that can be directly described and analysed' (1976: 8). Place, instead, refers to 'the lived-world of our everyday experiences' and landscape is its 'physical, visual form' (6, 30).

such as heritage tourism and film and TV adaptations, invoke and cater to the contemporary – and in particular, international – customer's empathetic engagement with the fully landscaped 'Victorian' world, and also function as a highly evocative *paratext* for them.[2] Nevertheless, neo-Victorian literature often mobilizes space and place for different purposes. Margaret Atwood's *Alias Grace*, for instance, presents the character Grace's 'over-identification' with the phenomenal world as part of her troubled psychological condition. By contrast, Julian Barnes's *Arthur & George* features characters who struggle with building intimate or affective relationships with their surroundings, a strategy that frustrates the reader's desire to empathize with the simulated landscape of Victorian and Edwardian England. In this context, I propose that many readers – international and otherwise – would overcome this obstacle or frustration by bringing their paratextual imagination (which is often drawn from their experience of film and other media) to bear upon the text and fill in any absence of material landscape in the novel.

I begin the discussion which follows with a brief review of the scheme of Thames Town. With a focus on its aesthetic features, I explore how the idea of 'Englishness' and English landscape translates into the Chinese context and the ways in which the 'semi-colonial' history of Shanghai comes to form part of a design vocabulary for cosmopolitanism.[3] Through the comparison

---

[2] Llewellyn and Heilmann are uneasy about the 'implied imperialism' of expressions containing 'Victorian' in the global context (2013: 26). Critics have since been trying to address this issue by inventing new terminologies. Nadine Boehm-Schnitker and Susanne Gruss, for instance, propose that 'a more descriptive term such as "Neo-Nineteenth Century" might […] prove more useful' when we extend the scope of study to the world (2014: 14). In spite of its seeming plausibility, Antonija Primorac and Monika Pietrzak-Franger point out, such typological distinction 'risks maintaining the system of values' that troubles postcolonial study and literature; that is: 'a system of appraisal rooted in (imagined) geographical distinctions that divide the world along the binaries of the centre and the periphery' (2015: 8). In this chapter, I stick with the term 'neo-Victorian' for the compelling reason Priya Joshi offers: '"Victorian" refers today not only to historical boundaries, but more cogently to a set of interrelated cultural, intellectual, and social preoccupations that far outlive the originary moment. "Victorian" persists as a contact zone: a space of encounter, (mis) recognition, and, sometimes, refusal' (2011: 39). More importantly, my main focus in this chapter is on what is distinctive about the ways in which readers/audiences of these neo-Victorians texts are positioned, rather than a postcolonial discussion of how the neo-Victorian genre negotiates the imperial legacies.

[3] There is a long-term debate about the difference between 'Englishness' and 'Britishness' in the context of the dissolution of the British Empire (see Nairn 1981). In this chapter, I use the word 'British' when the focus is on the idea of the nation state. It is also important to note that the term 'semi-colonialism' is used by historians to highlight the differences between the history of imperialism in mainland China and the 'standard' model of colonialism elsewhere. As Jürgen Osterhammel explains, during the period of foreign imperialism in China, China was still recognized as 'a sovereign member of the international community' (1986: 290). The term 'semi-colonialism' is therefore used to describe 'a somewhat deficient colonialism, short of overt political domination' (296).

of Thames Town and the project of *1881: Heritage* in Hong Kong, this section further contributes to current debate about the global reach and relevance of neo-Victorianism. I then draw upon the German philosopher Robert Vischer's work on *aesthetic empathy* in the examination of the dynamic between space, place and empathy. Although Vischer's model of empathy appears to be an egoistic form of projection at first sight, it involves some fundamental concern about the relationship between human beings and the universe. Its preoccupation with the embodied experience of the object also anticipates the recent 'corporeal turn' in the field of arts, humanities and science. Maxine Sheets-Johnstone uses the term to describe an interdisciplinary field of study that attests to 'the importance of exploring the living realities of corporeal life' (2009: 3) in 'correcting' the 'Cartesian legacy' which positions the body 'as mere material handmaiden of an all-powerful mind' (2). Published in 1873, Vischer's doctoral thesis *Über das optische Formgefühl* ('On the Optical Sense of Form') explores the bodily perception of the phenomenal world. His focus on the role physiological reactions play in the evocation of feelings also lays the foundation for this chapter's reparative exploration of – to borrow the phrase from Robyn Wiegman – our 'worldly inhabitations and needs' (2014: 7). In light of Vischer's work, I examine the intradiegetic examples of the relationship between character and landscape in Atwood's *Alias Grace* and Barnes's *Arthur & George* as well as its 2015 TV adaptation in order to discuss the different ways in which neo-Victorian literature and culture facilitate or frustrate the contemporary reader's/viewer's desire to empathize with the simulated landscape of the past, and its affective, ethical as well as political implications.

Thames town in Shanghai

Thames Town is the English name for a new town in the western quadrant of Songjiang District, Shanghai, and is clearly named after the River Thames in London.[4] The construction of Thames Town, as Jonathan Watts

---

[4] In terms of administrative planning, Shanghai used to be a regional area of Songjiang until the early-twentieth century. In 1958, Songjiang became a city district of Shanghai County.

from *The Guardian* remarks, is an 'ambitiou[s]' plan since it 'squeez[es] 500 years of British architectural development into a five-year [...] project' (2016: n.p.). As a mash-up of Tudor, Georgian and Victorian architectural styles, Thames Town is advertised as a recreation of the 'authentic' British townscape. It has mobilized a number of signs and symbols of British culture, including a fake turreted castle; a fake church (which is modelled on Anglican Christ Church, Clifton Down in Bristol); a pub and a fish and chip shop as copied from buildings in Lyme Regis Dorset; a covered market reminiscent of Covent Garden and the red telephone boxes which could be found throughout Britain until quite recently. There are also bronze statues of British public figures around the town, featuring historical personages such as William Shakespeare, Florence Nightingale, Winston Churchill and Princess Diana.

As a palimpsest of British architectural styles of different historical eras, Thames Town evokes, caters to and facilitates the Chinese visitor's desire to consume and get immersed in what they consider an 'authentic' British townscape. Constructed by and for the Chinese, Thames Town, to paraphrase Elizabeth Ho, immerses the visitor in 'lush [English] exotica' 'much like Victoriana' (2011: 195). It is an interesting example of how British history and heritage are restructured as the exotic other for the consumption of the East. Designed as 'a major tourist attraction' and 'high-quality living environment' in Shanghai, the scheme of Thames Town reveals how British landscape and culture are associated with ideas of class, taste, moral order and identity (Shen and Wu 2012: 191). It could therefore be considered as an example of Orientalism in reverse, whereby the 'Other' role is taken by the British – or the West by extension – rather than the East. This kind of 'reverse Orientalism' can also be seen in places such as Hong Kong. In their reading of Ho's analysis of the urban politics and aesthetics in Hong Kong, Kohlke and Gutleben note that 'the notion of Otherness is transferred from the one-time colonised's to the former coloniser's past' and 'the ex-colonised becomes both ideal consumer of and ideal tourist in the ex-imperial cityscape' (Kohlke and Gutleben 2015: 32). Although both projects – Thames Town and *1881: Heritage* (Ho's example) – exemplify the exotic pleasures afforded by the British landscape, the way they engage with imperial memory and legacy is quite different, a point I will elaborate in the next section.

The fact that Thames Town is planned and designed by the British architectural firm, Atkins, also presents the project as an example of the global reach of – to paraphrase Julian Barnes – 'invent[ed]' English traditions (qtd in Denning 1998: n.p.). Here Barnes is talking about the issue of English culture and history in relation to his 1998 novel *England, England*. The text interrogates the constructed nature of English identity through its imaginative replication of England in a theme park on the Isle of Wight: a fictional enterprise which resembles the project of Thames Town. Notably, Barnes's list of 'the Fifty Quintessences of Englishness' in the text includes several of the elements we see in Thames Town, such as 'the Royal Family', 'pubs', 'Shakespeare' and 'shopping' (83–5). This overlap attests to the process of how certain symbols and character traits are selected and used in the construction of a continuous and historical English identity. Also, like the fictional theme park in *England, England*, Thames Town provides its visitors with a 'psycho-semiotic model' of England, or 'a fantasy space' into which individuals can project their desires and feelings (Bentley 2007: 486). It thus delivers to the public, to quote from Ann Heilmann and Mark Llewellyn, 'a representation of a representation' (2010: 214). However, unlike Barnes's text which explores, parodies and deconstructs the process of identity construction, Thames Town celebrates a particular version of Englishness and facilitates the Chinese visitor's consumption in less critical manners.

The exotic pleasure derived from this quaint and hyperbolic simulacrum of the British borough is well illustrated by the fact that Thames Town has become an iconic place for wedding photography for some Chinese young people. It also provides people with a chance to experience the British townscape economically. As Ruth Morris, from the BBC, quotes from her interview with a Chinese office administrator who chooses to have a family day out in Thames Town, 'I really hope I can visit the real Thames River one day, sit along the banks, drink a cup of coffee and enjoy the British sunshine' (2013: n.p.). But she cannot afford to travel to England now. The particular interest the interviewee displays in the corporeal experience of the landscape also points towards the embodied pleasures Thames Town affords vicariously. In his study on tourism, Tim Edensor emphasizes this kind of experience as highly 'performative' (see Edensor 2001). Indeed, by modelling the town on the stereotypical British townscape, the scheme of Thames Town involves its residents and visitors in something like 'The Truman Show', a reference to the 1998 movie chronicling a man who unwittingly lives his life in a fake town (Morris 2013: n.p.).

Across several disciplines, scholars have observed that human activities – and, in particular, movements – are what animate the constructed environment. In his study of theme parks, Arnold Berleant argues that the character of a theme park is 'decided largely by [its] prominent aesthetic features', referring to 'the perceptual dimensions through which we experience an environment directly – what we hear, see, and feel with our bodies as we move through it', and 'how these sensory qualities combine with our knowledge and beliefs to create a unified experiential situation' (1977: 42). Berleant's argument associates the aesthetics of theme parks with the embodied experience, knowledge and expectation of the visitors. By highlighting the link between the corporeal, kinaesthetic and sensual experience of the space and the visitor's previous knowledge and expectation, Berleant delineates a dynamic engagement between designed landscapes such as theme parks and human subjects.[5] Seen in this light, it is clear that Thames Town facilitates the Chinese's visitor's desire to consume and experience British exotica in an embodied and participatory manner. The human–landscape dynamic Berleant maps out also echoes Vischer's understanding of empathy, a point I will elaborate in the next section.

However, given the fact that the history of Western imperialism in China began with the First Opium War (1839–42) and Shanghai was one of the five cities that were forced to allow the British to reside and carry on 'their mercantile pursuits [...] without molestation or restraint' (Mayers 1906: 1), the idea of recreating an 'authentic' British town in Shanghai has generated some unsettling questions about the city's engagement with its semi-colonial history and British imperial legacy. As Thomas J. Campanella puts it, 'It is somewhat ironic that a city once subjugated by Western imperialism should choose to build simulacra of Western cities as part of a regional growth strategy, especially

---

[5] In his discussion of *Dismaland*, a temporary art exhibition that is organized by the street artist Banksy and parodies Disneyland, Saverio Tomaiuolo demonstrates the critical potentials of theme parks. Tomaiuolo contends that *Dismaland* employs a number of 'aesthetic strategies' to explore social and political issues such as 'environment crisis', 'protest movements', 'the refugee crisis', 'domestic violence', etc. (2018: 14).

since many of the towns selected for redevelopment are many times older than Shanghai itself' (2008: 88). Campanella's wry observation brings to the fore the role the colonial past plays in the discourse of the city's future prosperity and its related ethical concerns.[6] The fact that Thames Town encourages its visitors to consume the British landscape in an ahistorical manner suggests a more complex model of engagement between different temporalities. In his work on the cultural industry of 'Shanghai Nostalgia', Tianshu Pan asserts that the idealization and adaptation of the colonial past helps to reimagine a 'pre-Communist colonial' Shanghai, which is part of 'the social and political agenda for Shanghai's transition towards a global city' (2004: 110). As a mash-up of architectural styles of different historical periods, Thames Town indicates the self-identity of Shanghai as a cosmopolitan city that is willing to embrace global capital and celebrate its mercantile background.

A similar, but also fundamentally different, practice may be found in the project, *1881: Heritage*, in Hong Kong. Unlike Thames Town, which is a self-consciously constructed replica, *1881: Heritage* is an example of the 'adaptive re-use' of colonial architecture in the former colony of the British Empire (Ho 2015: 331). It appropriates the Victorian space 'in and for the present' through 'the transformation of the former Marine Police Headquarters into a heritage hotel, museum and luxury shopping center' (ibid.). This model of adaptation presents the past and the present in 'a "parallel dimension"', a term Julian Wolfreys borrows from Ian Sinclair in describing how 'the present-day territory' is overlaid with 'its earlier selves' in neo-Victorian spatial practice (2015: 134). In a similar vein, Kohlke and Gutleben suggest that neo-Victorian space is '*quintessentially gothic*', since it provides a prism through which 'today's cities' and 'their reimagined nineteenth-century referents' haunt each other (2015: 8, original emphasis). As a postmodern artefact and historical replica, the project of Thames Town, nevertheless, is more concerned with the boundary between authenticity and artificiality rather than the dynamic between the past and the present (although, as my discussion in the previous section has demonstrated, it is important to examine the project in the context

---

[6] China signed the Treaty of Nanjing with Britain after its defeat in the First Opium War. According to this treaty, China had to reduce its authority on unilateral tariffs on the articles of trade in the cities of Shanghai, Canton (now Shantou), Amoy (now Xiamen), Fuchau-fu (now Fuzhou) and Ningbo, and cede the territory of Hong Kong to the British.

of Shanghai's semi-colonial history). Also, as argued before, by evoking a particular sense of timelessness, Thames Town facilitates the Chinese visitor's immersive and ahistorical consumption of the simulated British landscape.

Drawing upon Harry Francis Mallgrave and Eleftherios Ikonomou's valuable editing and translation of Vischer's work on aesthetic perception, I propose that the human–space dynamic afforded by Thames Town resembles the model of aesthetic empathy, or *Einfühlung*, the German word used by nineteenth-century German aestheticians to describe the affective and embodied engagement between human subjects and artwork. The concept of *Einfühlung* suggests a more complex model of aesthetic perception than the modern sense of projection and anticipates the later phenomenological study of embodied spatial practices in the field of human geography. Thus, it provides a useful framework for this chapter's examination of the relationship between mobility, empathy and space in neo-Victorian literature and culture.

Einfühlung and embodied simulation

Literally translated as 'feeling oneself into' or 'in-feeling', the idea of *Einfühlung* is introduced and widely explored in Vischer's 1873 essay *On the Optical Sense of Form*. As the title suggests, Vischer's research placed great emphasis on physiology, which, to him, 'condition[ed] sensory and emotive responses' in aesthetic contemplation (Vischer qtd in Mallgrave and Ikonomou 1994: 22). Taking the viewer's perspective into consideration, Vischer argued that for the appreciation of visual arts, the key issue is not the content or form but 'the power of the image' and 'its phenomenality' (27).

Vischer's conceptualization of *Einfühlung* is inspired by his reading of Karl Albert Scherner's 1861 book on dream interpretation – *Das Leben des Traums* (*The Life of the Dream*) – which predates Sigmund Freud's seminal work *The Interpretation of Dreams* (1899). In a reference to Scherner's chapter on 'Basic Symbolic Formations for Bodily Stimuli', Vischer remarked: 'Here it was shown how the body, in responding to certain stimuli in dreams, objectifies itself in spatial forms. Thus it unconsciously projects its own bodily form – and with this also the soul – into the form of the object. From this I derived the notion that I call "empathy" [*Einfühlung*]' (92). Vischer's interpretation of dreams chimes with Freud's theorization of the unconscious. Indeed, as Mallgrave and Ikonomou note, Freud developed certain examples of Scherner's – such as 'wish fulfilment' and 'erotic longing' – in his own work (24). Also, Vischer took up Scherner's discussion of the way 'the mind [translates] ideas into visual impressions or symbols' in dreams in his explanation of the dynamic that exists between the external stimuli and the sensory response of the body (ibid.). Vischer's model of empathy provides the reader with a different approach to the following examination of Grace's mentality in Atwood's *Alias Grace*, one that positions her 'empathetic tendency' – which is specified as her 'over-identification' with her physical surroundings – as part of her pathological disorder.

For Vischer, 'the unconscious need for a surrogate for our body-ego' he derived from Scherner carries over into everyday experience: 'As in a dream, I stimulate, on the basis of simple nerve sensations, a fixed form that symbolizes my body or an organ of it. Conversely, an objective but accidentally experienced phenomenon always provokes a related idea of the self in sensory or motor form' (101). *Einfühlung* involves a form of transference that is more dynamic and influential than the projection of emotions into the object.[7] In their reading Mallgrave and Ikonomou interpret this transference as one 'in which our whole personality (consciously or unconsciously) merges with the object' (25). As Vischer himself observed, when we empathize with an image, we 'penetrat[e] *into* the phenomenon' (101, original emphasis). Here Vischer invoked a highly sensory and corporeal experience to stress the intensity of such encounter; that in viewing the specific object 'I wrap myself with its contours as in a garment' (ibid.). *Einfühlung* thus entails a strong embodied experience of the other, one that is featured by affection, generosity and desire. Vischer also placed great emphasis on the role of imagination in crystallizing the physical or bodily sensation: 'A kinesthetic stimulus does not always and necessarily lead to actual movement but always to the idea of it. Imagination is an act by which we mentally simulate something that previously existed as a

---

[7] Timothy C. Vincent provides a nuanced reflection on the difference between Vischer's framework and the mechanism of projection. Defining it as 'empathetic identification', Vincent explains that Vischer's conceptualization of *Einfühlung* 'acknowledges the separateness of the object [world and the individual] while at the same time acknowledging the role of psychological projection in the creation of reality and avoiding the problem of solipsism' (Vincent 2012: 6).

vague content of our sensation as sensuous, concrete form' (99). The difference between sensation and feeling is key to Vischer's conception of *Einfühlung*. Imagination is what changes the physiological reactions into concrete forms or ideas, which, when combined with images of ourselves, could evoke an advanced level of feeling; that is, empathy: 'I might imagine myself moving along the line of a range of hills guided by kinesthetic imagination (be it direct or mediated by the reflex stimuli of sensitized nerves). In the same way, fleeting clouds might carry me far away' (101). Here it is striking that Vischer focused on the way in which the body experiences itself kinaesthetically; *mobility* is the crucial link between what we see and what we feel. The embodied simulation of the form and movement of hills and clouds provokes a kinaesthetic awareness and imitation in the body. This focus on kinaesthesia and embodied simulation is also shared by Henri Bergson in his discussion of aesthetic perception and is likewise considered by him as essential in transmitting the emotions of the artist to the viewers.[8]

Equally significant, Vischer's discussion of imagination involves the human subject's fundamental desire to unite with – and position oneself in – the universe. As Vischer stated, imagination is 'a fluid medium in which contradictions of the world – repose and motion, self and nonself – merge into a mysterious whole' (102). Vischer specified this impulse to merge through empathetic imagination as a 'pantheistic urge for union with the world', which 'must, consciously or unconsciously, be directed toward the universe' (109). For Mallgrave and Ikonomou, this imperative can also be read as the human subject's 'psychological attempt to bridge the essential "otherness" of nature', as illustrated by the metaphor Vischer used, that 'he can tolerate no obstacle; he wants to roam the whole world and feel himself as one with it' (26). Taking the perspective of the phenomenal object into consideration, Mallgrave and Ikonomou are more concerned with how the world 'exerts a pull or attraction against human subjectivity' that the human wants to 'merge with the universe' (26). This experience, Vischer stressed, has the potential to transform the self: 'I project my own life into the lifeless form, just as I quite

---

[8] As Susan Leigh Foster points out, the term 'kinesthesia' was coined in 1880 to help establish 'the existence of nerve sensors in the muscles and joints that provide awareness of the body's potions and movements' (2010: 7). In other words, the notion of kinaesthesia highlights the importance of sensory awareness. I treat the term kinaesthesia and movement as near synonyms.

justifiably do with another person. Only ostensibly do I keep my own identity although the object remains distinct. I seem merely to adapt and attach myself to it as one hand clasps another, and yet I am mysteriously transplanted and magically transformed into this Other (104)'. Vischer's reflection on the subtle yet substantial interaction between the object world and the individual also anticipates Gaston Bachelard's recognition of the autonomy of nature and the attraction it exerts against the human subject. Nature, Bachelard notes, 'forces us to contemplation'; in the meanwhile, 'everything which shows, sees' (1983: 30). For Bachelard, as for Vischer, empathetic imagination is essential in humanizing the 'objective' world (see also Kaplan 1972).[9] In the words of Bachelard, 'it is an attempt to *inscribe* human love at the heart of things' (1964: 51, original emphasis). Alongside the desire for 'aggressive' penetration, the writings of Vischer and Bachelard are also full of reparative impulses. Their shared affection and confidence reveal the human subject's fundamental urge for inclusiveness and companionship.

In the context of aesthetic perception, the phenomenal object is specified as the 'art work' or 'artefact' rather than the natural landscape or universe. I now turn to Bergson's discussion of art appreciation to demonstrate the way in which literary and filmic representation of the landscape involves the reader/audience affectively. Like Vischer, Bergson is more concerned with the 'phenomenality' (in Vischer's word) of artwork, as evidenced by his claim that 'art aims at impressing feelings on us (the viewers) rather than expressing them' ([1913] 2001: 16). In addressing the epistemological issue about 'how and what art means', Bergson examines, first of all, the process of how artwork is encoded with feelings and thoughts of its creator(s) (Jones 2012: 11). Bergson contends that in order to share his or her personal emotion with the viewers, the artist needs to 'bring about by choosing, among the outward signs of his emotions, those which our body is likely to imitate mechanically, though slightly, as soon as it perceives them' (18). Bergson's focus on corporeal imitation resembles Vischer's model of *Einfühlung*, one that is preoccupied with the kinaesthetic experience of the body. It also highlights the role

---

[9] As Lynne Pearce points out, Bachelard works at 'the interface of Freudian psychology and philosophy/phenomenology', which, to a certain extent, echoes Vischer's interests in the phenomenal world and the human mind (2016: 159).

kinaesthesia plays in involving the viewers in the affective landscape of the artwork.

As by now it has become obvious, Bergson's work on aesthetic perception has particular implications for my discussion of neo-Victorianism. The kind of place that I will look at in the neo-Victorian literary and filmic texts in the next section is not place per se. Rather, the focus is on the literary or artistic representation of place and its associated affective impact upon the reader/audience. My discussion of Thames Town – as an example of the self-consciously constructed and mediated landscape – at the beginning of this chapter reveals how a certain kind of place is designed to facilitate a fairly straightforward empathetic engagement between the landscape and its visitors. By contrast, the two neo-Victorian novels that I have selected for this chapter – Atwood's *Alias Grace* and Barnes's *Arthur & George* – mobilize landscape for different purposes, such as character development, critical reflection on the Victorian literary tradition and the construction of English identity. In the following section, I move to the discussion of the intradiegetic examples about the human–landscape dynamic in these two neo-Victorian novels which, as I will argue, 'mirror' the extradiegetic reader's relationship with the simulated landscape of the past.

'Abnormal' empathy

Since *Alias Grace* has already been examined in detail in Chapter 1, here I focus only on the textual representation of the relationship between the two main characters, Grace and Dr Simon Jordan, and the different kinds of places they encounter. In light of Scherner's work on dream interpretation and Vischer's conceptualization of *Einfühlung*, I approach the human–landscape dynamic in the novel from the following two perspectives: one is about how the mind embodies itself in spatial terms; the other involves a discussion of the significance of kinaesthesia in involving the reader affectively in the textual landscape.

As noted before, Vischer derived the notion of empathy from Scherner's work on dreams. For Vischer, Scherner's discussion of dreams illustrates the process of how the human body projects its bodily form and psyche into spatial objects in an unconscious manner. In talking about sexual dreams, for example, Scherner gave a scenario of 'the dreamer [who] stands talking with women in a narrow court' (Massey 1990: 572). As Irving Massey notes, Scherner interprets the image of a narrow court as 'the narrow space between the thighs' (ibid.). This example illustrates how dream images reflect the subtle somatic events that are ignored by the daytime consciousness. The writings of Scherner and Vischer are therefore useful for understanding Grace's intimate relationship with her (illusory) surroundings.

Set in mid-nineteenth-century Canada, *Alias Grace* provides the reader with an interesting account of pre-Freudian understandings of the human mind. The fact that the doctors and public figures who attend to Grace do not have a working knowledge of the 'unconscious' means that they struggle to make sense of her complex psychological profile, including the significance of her 'hallucinations'. Atwood extends this nineteenth-century viewpoint to her description of Grace's hallucinations which are marked by what is seen to be her idiosyncratic sensitivity to her physical surroundings. The nature of these hallucinations – and in particular, Grace's affective engagement with certain landscapes – may be seen as key to her distinctive psychological problems, including her disorientation and difficulty in remembering her actions. It is arguable that Grace is presented as a character who is *too* empathetic towards her surroundings.

In the scene at the beginning of the novel where Grace walks around the yard of the Governor's house, the representation of Grace's projected thoughts – communicated here by free indirect discourse – is a good example of the model of empathy associated with the work of Scherner and Vischer: 'Out of the gravel there are peonies growing. They come up through the loose grey pebbles, their buds testing the air like snails' eyes, then swelling and opening, huge dark-red flowers all shining and glossy like satin. Then they burst and fall to the ground' (5). The use of performative verbs such as 'testing' and 'opening' are indicative of Grace's unconscious attempt to project human subjectivity into these peonies, which are presented as animated creatures who have the autonomy and ability to act. As noted before, this process of projection involves an urge to 'bridge the essential "otherness" of nature' (Mallgrave and Ikonomou 1994: 26). Indeed, these peonies are presented as symbols of temptation. Their peculiar stain-like texture, Kym Brindle remarks, is 'slippery and seductive' (2013: 107). Grace's attempt to 'reach out [her] hand to touch one' of the peonies and her animated description of them hence demonstrate the way she tries to merge with – and exert control over – her surroundings (6).

However, as we quickly learn from the text, these flowers are not 'real'. Grace's subsequent reflection that 'its April, and peonies don't bloom in April' reveals her troubled psychological condition in which she seems to oscillate between hallucination and rationality (6). In this context, her empathetic engagement with the physical world seems to undermine the integrity of her subjectivity, which also directs the reader's attention to the power dynamic between the self and the other in the mechanism of empathy. The account of how Grace imagines red peonies growing slowly on the empty prison wall while she is out of the prison yard further dramatizes the tension between the conscious and the unconscious, the desire to escape and the sense of imprisonment. The movement of these peonies – that they 'burst and fall to the ground' – may be read as the embodiment of Grace's bodily sensation (5). As Hilde Staels argues, 'the 'condensed and synaesthetic metaphor of red silken peonies' embodies 'the sensations of sorrow and of physical pain', which also reflect the process of how Grace's psyche objectifies itself in spatial forms in response to the external stimulus (2000: 437). By linking the idea of captivity – as exemplified by institutions such as the prison – with the nature imaginary of dark-red peonies vibrantly bursting in the air and petals falling to the ground, the text illustrates Grace's bodily desire for freedom and escape, as a response to the imprisoning actions of others.

From a metacritical perspective, this dynamic between freedom and captivity also adds an ethical and gendered dimension to the discussion of readerly empathy. As we see from the following account of the Parkinson residence (where Grace used to work with her friend Mary, who died from a scandalous abortion), the text plays with the reader's desire to 'penetrate into' or empathize with the place that is associated with Grace's tragic life experience by, first of all, evoking the reader's kinaesthetic experience of it:

> At the very top of the house was a large attic, divided up; and if you climbed the stairs, and then went along past the room where we slept, and down some other stairs, you were in the drying room. It was strung with lines, and had several small windows that opened out under the eaves. And the chimney from the kitchen ran up through this room. (159)

Through the use of the second-person pronoun 'you', the text may be seen as inviting the reader to identify with the figure as Grace's interlocutor. The textual focus on the structure of the house facilitates the reader's kinaesthetic experience of it, which, as we have seen from the previous discussion of Vischer and Bergson, involves the reader affectively in the textual landscape and fulfils their desire to empathize with the interior space. The fact that the places presented here, such as the attic and drying room, are representative of feminine, domestic and private space also fosters a gendered critique of the reader's empathy; a reading position that is arguably 'mirrored' by the intradiegetic example of the character Simon's erotic consumption of the laundry room of his childhood (which is another example of feminine space):

> The sheets and linens move in the wind, as if worn by invisible swelling hips; as if alive. As he watches – he must be a boy, he's short enough to be looking upwards – a scarf or veil of white muslin is blown from the line and undulates gracefully through the air like a long bandage unrolling, or like paint in water. He runs to catch it, out of the yard, down the road – he's in the country, then – and into a field. (194)

Simon animates and projects his erotic fantasy into the laundry room through the link he makes between the movements of the sheets and linens and 'swelling hips'. The moving sheets and linens are arguably the embodiment of the female body Simon desires. The subsequent description of his physical sensation further illustrates how an empathetic engagement with this feminine space greatly satisfies Simon's erotic desire, that when he 'tugs [the cloth] down' in the dream 'he struggles; he is being closely embraced; he can scarcely breathe' and for him 'the sensation is painful and almost unbearably erotic' (195). Focusing on the power and erotic dynamic between the observing subject and the object, the text also prompts the reader to reflect critically upon the act of empathy, and in particular, the 'perversity' of it.

In this section, I have used the work of Scherner, Vischer and Bergson to further examine Grace's psychology and the text–reader relationship in *Alias Grace*. As I have argued, Grace's 'empathetic' engagement with the phenomenal world is presented as a pathological tendency in which the human subject loses all sense of themselves and their ego boundaries through an overidentification with a non-human 'other'. The fact that this 'other' is experienced in spatial and kinaesthetic terms in the descriptions of Grace in the yard and Simon in the laundry room is illuminated by Vischer's theory. Simon's erotic consumption of the feminine space here and throughout the novel, nevertheless, also raises ethical concerns about this sort of bodily projection and – by implication – the reader's own immersive involvement in the spaces of the texts they read. As we will now see in my analysis of *Arthur & George*, Barnes's novel is marked by the *lack* of textual description of material places. Whereas Grace is 'too close' to what she sees, the character George in Barnes's text is 'too distant'. Further, this textual gap in *Arthur & George* also challenges the reader's desire to occupy the textual landscape(s) of their texts. By drawing upon the concept of *paratext* as a way of conceptualizing the reader–landscape dynamic in neo-Victorian fiction, I propose that the reader, instead, has to rely on their own paratextual knowledge to satisfy their desire to enter the world of the Victorians. I take my cue from Christian Lee's work on tourism and fan culture in arguing about how paratexts – specified as the invented traditions about the English, and the contemporary filmic or TV characterization of the Victorians and the Victorian landscape – have helped to inform the reader's 'reading strategies and expectations' (2014: 178).

Place, placelessness, identity

This section begins with a story about my own misrecollection. I started thinking about the human–landscape dynamic in Barnes's *Arthur & George* when I recalled that one of the protagonists, George, is presented as a habitual walker and regular train commuter. After a detailed re-reading of the text, I was surprised that I had failed to find any textual examples of the kind of human–landscape interaction I had expected. However, I had also noticed that the text seemed to draw the reader's attention to the fact that, although George is a habitual walker, he is not interested in the landscape, as evidenced by George's claim that although he walks every day, he 'never really pay[s] attention' to where he walks (2005: 102), and the omniscient narrator's remark that George is a character who 'ignores the landscape, which does not interest him' (66). Indeed, the textual foregrounding of George's *indifference* to the landscape may be seen as, in a seemingly paradoxical manner, an example of the writer Julian Barnes's *interest* in the significance of landscape. My personal reading experience of *Arthur & George* therefore suggests that the issue of landscape is played out in the text through its engagement with the reader's reading expectations or generic knowledge. In this regard, my own experience prompted me to reflect upon the process of my misrecollection, and the ways in which my reading expectation and strategy are informed.[10]

I therefore wish to propose that the filmic or TV representations of the Victorians and the Victorian landscape serve a crucial role in the reader's experience of neo-Victorian novels. Such paratexts 'fill in' gaps and absences in the texts themselves and, through the process of the readers' imaginary projections, vicariously satisfy their desire to enter the fully landscaped 'worlds' of Victorian fiction regardless of whether the text provides this sort of detail or not. Through a close examination of the 2015 TV adaptation of *Arthur & George*, we see that unlike the novel – where there is a marked lack of description of the landscape – the adaptation proactively involves the audience in the late-nineteenth- and early-twentieth-century landscape through processes involving the characters' corporeal movements and the spectator's 'virtual mobility', the latter a concept I take from Sarah Gibson (2004: 44). As Gibson argues in her engagement with the cinema and media critic Anne Friedberg, although 'the spectator is fixed in his/her immobility within the cinema (seat)', their 'cinematic gaze is virtually mobile' (63). Friedberg herself defines this 'mobile, virtual gaze' as

> a gaze that travels in an imaginary *flanerie* through an imaginary elsewhere and an imaginary elsewhen. This mobilized gaze has a history, which begins well before the cinema and is rooted in other cultural activities that involve walking and travel. The virtual gaze has a history rooted in all forms of visual

---

[10] While a good deal has now been written about the issue of national identity in *Arthur & George* in a neo-Victorian and postcolonial context, my focus on the landscape and the title characters' movements in it demonstrates new ways of reading and valuing the text. Elsa Cavalié argues that the story of *Arthur & George* is told in 'a "retro-Victorian" style' (2009: 89). Although she does not use the term 'neo-Victorian', her discussion of how *Arthur & George* explores 'Victorian values' such as 'gentlemanliness' and 'the code of conduct' engages with the core debate in the field of neo-Victorian studies – i.e. how the contemporary rewrites and reconstructs the Victorian(s) (ibid.). For Katherine Weese, although *Arthur & George* is 'not a post-colonial novel per se', it 'explores Western epistemologies against the background of British imperialism' (2015: 302). Taking up Weese's lead, Ed Dodson argues that 'the *partial* postcoloniality' of Barnes's novel is indicative of 'an unresolved yet productive tension between competing conceptions of Englishness and of the English novel' (2018: 114, original emphasis).

representation. [...] The cinema developed an apparatus that combined the 'mobile' with the 'virtual'. (1994: 60)

Friedberg's theorization of the cinematic gaze resembles Vischer's model of aesthetic empathy, since both highlight the importance of kinaesthesia in the perception process. Vischer's focus on the spectator's affective investment also adds another layer to Friedberg's model. Seen in this light, it is plausible that the analogy between the filmic character's corporeal movement and the spectator's virtual mobility facilitates an empathetic engagement between the film and the spectator. As I shall attempt to demonstrate, the TV adaptation of *Arthur & George* immerses the viewer in the material landscape affectively by adapting the character's/actor's journey to the audience's (virtual) journey. By doing so, it celebrates the perceived notion of the English landscape and its role in the construction of English identity, and simultaneously erases Barnes's critical interrogation of the myth of Englishness as it features in the novel.

Based on the famous Great Wyrley Outrages of the year 1903, the story of *Arthur & George* revolves around how Sir Arthur Conan Doyle, the creator of the famous literary character Sherlock Holmes, slips into the role of detective by trying to exonerate George Edalji, a half-Indian solicitor from Staffordshire, of the crime of horse mutilation. The fundamental difference between the novel and the TV adaptation lies in the mode of narration and narrative structure. The TV adaptation focuses on the process of detection and presents the audience with a fairly typical Holmesian drama. Like most Holmes stories in this genre, the drama proceeds from effect to cause; that is, it begins with the case of horse mutilations, and then moves to George's wrongful conviction and Doyle's intervention. This linear narrative structure encourages the audience to identify with the character Doyle, since their watching experience parallels Doyle's detective adventure. Following the character Doyle's movements in the drama, the contemporary audience is 'transported' back to the past. By following how Doyle travels around misty London and rural England by an iconic hansom cab and train, respectively, the filming fulfils the spectator's desire to occupy or, indeed, penetrate into the landscape of late-nineteenth- and early-twentieth-century England. In addition, the drama reinforces the established link between the landscape and English identity by choosing to focus on the movement of Doyle himself, who, of course, performs the role of the quintessential English gentleman. The intertextual references to other Sherlock Holmes adventures include the Sherlock-type costume of Doyle – the actor Martin Clunes is seen either in a black coat or a lumpy tweed suit – and the relationship between Doyle and his secretary, Woodie, which resembles the Sherlock/Watson double act in the original novels. The deliberate parallels to the Sherlock Holmes franchise may be seen as an example of how the TV adaptation celebrates the role of the Holmes stories in the construction of a particular version of cultural myth about the English. In his reading of the landscapes of the Sherlock Holmes tales Yi-Fu Tuan points out, the private detective is presented as the guardian of London – 'the heart of the imperial capital' – against 'seething unassimilated elements that might erupt in violence' (1985: 56). Also, Holmes's operations and movements take place across the world, which is indicative of the international scope of the British Empire and the Victorians' confidence in – and also subtle anxiety about – the management and comprehension of the increasingly large, turbulent and complex world (56–7). By structuring the whole story around Doyle's adventurous investigation of George's case, the TV adaptation celebrates this deliberate intertwining of the fictional detective and the landscape of late-nineteenth- and early-twentieth-century England. In this regard, it is not surprising to see that this adaptation has been viewed as another quasi-Sherlock Holmes drama (see Ramsey 2015; Wollaston 2015).

By contrast, the narrative structure of Barnes's original novel plays with the reader's generic expectations for the Holmes stories and prompts them to reflect upon the *constructed* nature of English identity and the formation of their reading expectations. The story is told in the form of intertwining third-person biographies of the title characters, ranging from their first memories to the death of Sir Arthur in the year of 1930. Barnes's own representation of the Great Wyrley Outrages challenges the mystery formula, which, as Ellen Burton Harrington explains, is about the procedure of 'using clues to expose secrets and solve the crime with a "rational solution"' (2007: 367). It also frustrates the reader's desire to identify with the heroic detective. Although the wrongful conviction of George is what links his life with Arthur's, Barnes spends two-thirds of the text chronicling the life events of Arthur and George in a parallel manner without making any direct connection between them, which arguably disorients the reader. As Marjorie Kehe remarks in her review of the novel,

Barnes seems to be 'indulging in a leisurely stroll through his characters' lives' (2006: n.p.). This sense of disorientation is reinforced by the fact that the parallel unfolding of Arthur's and George's lives only exists in Barnes's fictional universe. According to Olivia Frey's observation, Arthur was born eighteen years before George in 1859, and the narration actually shifts back and forward between the two historical periods (2009: 2). The historical gap that exists between the lives of Arthur and George is also emphasized by the use of tense in the first section of the text: the use of the past tense for Arthur and the present for George. Further, the typical Sherlock Holmes moment – which is usually in the form of the fictional detective being approached by some visitor with a mystery to investigate – only takes place in the third and final section of the text. By then, George has been paroled after serving three years of the seven-year sentence that he received. He is now hoping that Arthur may be able to help to clear his name, in order to enable him to continue his practice as an attorney. The most striking point is, the text offers no solution to the mystery of the Edalji case, making it clear that Barnes's *Arthur & George* is hardly a classical 'whodunit intended for mystery fans' (Kehe 2006: n.p.). The way the text plays with the reader's generic reading expectations thus helps to demonstrate the dynamic between order and uncertainty, which necessarily impacts upon the reader affectively as well as cognitively.

This seemingly disorientating reading experience thus undermines the identificatory reading pleasure afforded by the whodunit or mystery genre. It also introduces a different kind of text–reader relationship, one that is marked by an embodied communication between the human mind and the form of the text. Here I take my cue from the writings of Ann Daghistany and J. J. Johnson. In their study of narrative, Daghistany and Johnson point out that certain texts encourage the reader to identify 'not as a particular human being with particular characters but as a human mind experiencing a form, such as a square or labyrinth, created by the interaction of fictional beings with one another and with their environment' (1981: 53). Although Daghistany and Johnson limit their discussion to modernist texts such as James Joyce's *Ulysses* (1922), their presentation of the text–reader relationship speaks to my discussion of certain neo-Victorian metafictions such as Barnes's *Arthur & George*. As outlined before, the narrative structure of *Arthur & George* discourages any easy or superficial readerly empathy. By moving between different perspectives, the text prompts the reader to reflect upon their position in the textual world as a whole rather than a narrow focus on this or that character. In spatial terms, the act of reading can thus be seen as an example of how the reader's immersive 'virtual movements' help to map out and materialize the textual landscape.

By positioning the reader as the active participant in the construction of the textual world, Barnes's text creates a compelling immersive experience. This form of readerly participation is reinforced by the link the text makes between the past, the present and the future. The chapter titles *Arthur & George* adopts – 'Beginnings', 'Beginning with an Ending', 'Ending with a Beginning' and 'Endings' – clearly suggest a circular loop, one that resembles Coleridge's use of the symbolic image of a serpent in describing the poetic process of 'uniting and fusing opposites' in a letter to Joseph Cottle in March 1815 (Toor 2004: 84). By evoking a cyclical notion of time, Barnes makes it explicit that his dramatization of the Great Wyrley Outrages has important contemporary resonance and that the view of the past presented in the text is more or less informed or mediated by contemporary needs. In this regard, readers are no longer positioned as the distant and passive consumer of the past; rather, they are urged by the text to take responsibility for their desire to occupy that past.

The way the text reimagines the crime scene – the mutilation of animals in the field – is a good example in this respect. This section, entitled 'Arthur & George', establishes the link between the two characters for the first time to the reader. By granting them this additional information and the following graphic account of the potential crime site, the text may be seen as privileging the reader:

> It was a cold, clear February night, with half a moon and a heavenful of stars. In the distance the head gear of Wyrley Colliery stood out faintly against the sky. Close by was the farm belonging to Joseph Holmes: house, barn, outbuildings, with not a light showing in any of them. Humans were sleeping and the birds had not yet woken. (72)

Through the use of this 'camera-eye technique', Barnes presents the reader with a panorama of the field, which arguably places them in an omniscient position (Frey 2009: 4). This illusion of omniscience is, however, disrupted by the subsequent intrusion of an omniscient narrator, which, Christine Berberich observes, prevents the reader from getting involved in the scene in an affective way (2011: 122). Berberich draws this conclusion from her discussion of the use of illustrations in the text, noting the significance of the three images: one a reproduction of the title page of George Edalji's 1901 publication *Railway Law for the 'Man in the Train'* (67), the other of George's invitation to Sir Arthur Conan Doyle's wedding with Miss Jean Leckie (317), together with a sketch of the potential mutilation instrument (290). For Berberich, the inclusion of these images is marked by the '*ex*clusion of others', by which she means 'the setting and characters involved' (121, 122, original emphasis). Indeed, as Berberich remarks, Barnes could have chosen to use some visual aids to help his readers 'visualize' the story and get better involved but chooses not to (122). The absence of such cues in the original novel can therefore be considered as indicative of how self-consciously Barnes's text frustrates the reader's generic reading expectations. However, the reader's paratextual knowledge, such as his or her familiarity with period drama (i.e. the Merchant and Ivory films in the 1980s and 1990s, which are also well received in the international market) may help them 'fill-in' what is lacking in the text itself, hence satisfying their desire to empathize with the world of neo-Victorian fiction.[11]

Interestingly, this readerly expectation and desire are fully acknowledged by and reflected in the TV adaptation. As argued previously, the way the miniseries is structured – beginning the first episode with the crime scene – makes it clear that the adaptation is presented as a fairly typical crime drama. Through the use of chilling music and atmospheric lighting, episode 1 of ITV's *Arthur & George* presents the scenario of horse mutilation in a violent yet compelling manner. It also facilitates the spectator's vicarious experience of the material landscape through 'the visual plotting of space and movement' (Pidduck 1998: 6). The first episode begins with the silhouette of a village against the dark blue sky and moving clouds, providing the audience with a

---

[11] Although most Merchant and Ivory films are set in Edwardian England, it is arguable that their characterization of a particular version of Englishness influences the viewer's – international and otherwise – expectations of period drama. Indeed, as Simon Joyce argues in his engagement with Spencer Golub, these films 'reawake[n] a ghost-limb Englishness not only in England but in the world' (2007: 74). Quoting from Julianne Pidduck, Dianne F. Sadoff suggests that heritage films 'travel because they "deploy, rework and sometimes subvert foundational English cultural references and discourses"; culled from the English novel's "canonical traditions" or theater's bardic texts [...] these references form a "common postcolonial cultural legacy for English-speaking audiences"' (Sadoff 2010: xv). Also, Barnes's *Arthur & George* straddles the Victorian and Edwardian periods.

dramatic yet stereotypical view of the mysterious English countryside. This movement-image also helps the audience to get affectively immersed in the televisual world by creating a parallel between the form and movement of clouds and the spectator's virtual mobility. A similar device is used in the televisual presentation of the crime scene. The audience is guided by the camera to follow the physical trajectories of an unidentified character, who walks into the screen from the right corner and attacks a group of horses brutally with his/her back facing us. The filming of the movements of the supposed perpetrator creates a sort of three-dimensional space, which 'draws in' the viewers literally. The subsequent introduction to the information about when and where the police investigation takes place in the subtitle – 'Great Wyrley, Staffordshire, 12th September 1903' – further illustrates how the drama uses the audio-visual language to fulfil the audience's desire to 'travel' back to the Edwardian England.

By contrast, Barnes's text further challenges the readerly desire to possess the past by highlighting its unknowability and inaccessibility. In the case of horse mutilation, Barnes's fictive rewriting makes it clear that, although this clearly happened, the truth about who did it may never be resolved. As we see from the following account: 'He continued his gabble of nonsense, however, and continued looking straight towards the horse. Beneath his feet the ground was solid after nights of frost, and his boots left no print on the soil' (73). Under the guidance of the omniscient narrator, the reader's attention is directed to the movements and behaviours of a suspicious and unidentified man in the field. However, the fact that the potential suspect does not leave any footprint on the soil frustrates the reader's attempt to retrace his movements in a Holmesian manner. This is mirrored in the way in which Inspector Campbell interrogates George about his movements on one night of the horse and cattle maiming:

> 'Where did you walk?'
> 'Around. Around the lanes. I walk every day. I never really pay attention.'
> 'So you walked over towards the Colliery?' 'No, I don't think so.'
> 'Come on, George, you can do better than this. You said you walked in every direction but you didn't remember which. One of the directions from Wyrley is towards the Colliery. Why wouldn't you walk in that direction?'

'If you will give me a moment', George pressed his fingers to his forehead. 'I remember now. I walked along the road to Churchbridge. Then I turned right towards Watling Street Road, then to Walk Mill, then along the road as far as Green's farm.'

Campbell thought this very impressive for someone who didn't remember where he walked. (102)

As well as contributing to his character profile and the mystery at the heart of the plot, this dialogue also underlines the *disengagement* between George and the physical landscape, since he claims that he never pays any attention to his locations or surroundings when he walks around. From the perspective of Campbell, George's later recollection of his movements that night therefore sounds suspicious. Indeed, the text deliberately calls for the reader's attention to the peculiarity of George's relationship with the landscape by remarking more than once that although George is a habitual walker, he 'ignores the landscape, which does not interest him' (66). The text also reminds us repeatedly of George's indifference to the landscape by providing us with several examples of George's travelling experience. George is presented as someone who does not see 'what his fellow passages would see – a few intertwined bushes blown by the wind, home to some nesting birds – ' when he looks out of the window at a hedgerow during his train journey between Bloxwich and Birchills (64). The textual emphasis on the difference between George and his fellow passengers clearly emphasizes George's position as an outsider of the text's 'ideal' community, one that is presented as celebrating and championing the idyllic landscape – and by extension, one that is essentially English. As Nigel Thrift notes, 'a key tradition in English culture has been that of the countryside and nature in a suitably tamed and romanticized form' (1989: 25). In this regard, it is possible to propose that there is a politics to George's mobility, and in particular, the relationship between mobility, legitimacy and identity in George's case. Rather than the investigative question, 'Who did what to whom, where, when, how and why?' the readers are positioned to ask questions about George's 'queer' way of travelling about the English countryside through which he passes.[12] In this way, the text draws critical attention to the interrelationship

---

[12] George's peculiar relationship with his surroundings has different interpretive possibilities. He could be considered as someone suffering from Asperser Syndrome, a point that is supported

between the activity of walking, the idea of English countryside and the issue of English identity.

Having a Scottish mother and a Parsee father who moved to Wyrley, England from Bombay in the 1860s, George experiences a particular kind of identity crisis in the context of the British Empire, which, as Ian Baucom observes, dramatizes the tension between the 'localist ideology' and the 'racial' one in the construction of collective identity (1999: 17). As Baucom explains, 'localist discourse' identifies 'English place as the one thing that could [...] secure England's continuous national identity' (16). This localist discourse is challenged by England's imperialist expansion, since its 'vast imperial abroad' is the place 'onto which the island kingdom arrogantly displaces itself' and cultivates confusion about its narrative of identity (3). In response to the ambiguity attendant on the localist narrative of what it means to be English, Baucom suggests that these 'spatial and territorial ideologies' have been replaced by 'a racial "discourse of loyalty" and coidentity' (12) which privileges 'England's bloodlines' (17). The issue of collective identity thus becomes 'an affective condition', in the sense that legal pronouncements may never confer English identity (12). This is indeed the case in George's story. Although he is born and educated in England, George's status as an 'Englishman' has been constantly challenged. The dialogue between George and his two fellow clerks Greenway and Stentson is a good example in illustrating the tension between the localist discourse and the racial one in understanding identity:

> 'George, where do you come from?'
>
> 'Great Wyrley.'
>
> 'No, where do you *really* come from?'
>
> George ponders this. 'The Vicarage,' he replies, and the dogs laugh. (56, original emphasis)

George's inability to capture the racialist connotation of his colleagues' question makes it clear that for him, being born and educated in England makes him English. Nevertheless, as Katherine Weese points out, his

---

by the actor Arsher Ali. In a 2015 interview, Ali asserts that 'by today's standards, George would certainly be someone who would live on the autism spectrum' and admits that he 'felt very strongly about including this element in [his] performance' (n.p.).

insistence on his Englishness is against 'the dominant ideology of the Victorian and Edwardian periods', referring to what Stuart Hall calls 'that great unspoken British value – "whiteness"' (qtd in Weese 2015: 319). Indeed, the implicit emphasis George's colleagues place on his visual ethnic difference reveals the role race plays in their understanding of Englishness. This racial understanding of Englishness is also shared by the establishment in the text, as evidenced by Inspector Campbell's remark that 'if you shut your eyes, you'd think [George] an Englishman' (Barnes 2005: 90). Clearly Greenway and Stentson's question is not about where George came from. Rather, it is about who his parents were and where they came from. As Baucom argues, the idea of Englishness as a racial category challenges the aforementioned localist ideology which positions 'English "places"' as what 'preserv[es]', 'enchant[s]' and 'transform[s]' English identity (19). It also implies a 'repudiation of the aura of the English place' (21), since George's contact with the 'locations' of Englishness through birth, education, religion and profession does not make him sufficiently English.

The sense of racial prejudice is further illustrated by the similar – but also fundamentally different – life story of Arthur. Although Arthur is 'Irish by ancestry, Scottish by birth', he 'became English' through his education (23). As the omniscient narrator remarks, 'instructed in the faith of Rome by Dutch Jesuits, Arthur became English. English history inspired him; English freedoms made him proud; English cricket made him patriotic' (ibid.). Unlike George, Arthur's 'learnt' Englishness is recognized and acknowledged by Englishmen in the text, such as Captain Anson, the Chief Constable of Staffordshire. In his internal monologue Anson makes it clear that he positions Arthur as someone equal or at least similar to him: 'It could so easily have been a pleasant evening: two men of the world, each approaching fifty, one the son of an earl and the other a knight of the realm, both of them, as it happened, Deputy Lieutenants of their respective counties. They had far more in common than was setting them apart' (271–2). In comparison to George's 'Parsee origin', Arthur's 'Scottish and Irish blood' does not render him 'evil' to Anson, as exemplified by his rhetorical question 'What Englishman – what Scotsman – what half Scotsman – would take a blade to a horse, a cow, a sheep?' (275). The different recognition and treatment George and Arthur receive from their fellow countrymen reveals the hierarchy that exists between the citizens of the UK (i.e. people born in England, Scotland, Wales and Ireland) and those descended from (former) colonial subjects in late-nineteenth- and early-twentieth-century Britain (in the era before Irish independence). This hierarchy, Baucom explains, indicates that 'the territory of the United Kingdom' and that of 'the United Kingdom's overseas territories' are not 'interchangeable' regarding the issue of collective identity (13). It also, as argued before, brings to the fore the racial essence of Englishness and its 'slippery' as well as 'dangerous' nature (Tate 2011: 63).

As a habitual walker and a regular train commuter, George's mobilities, meanwhile, are indicative of how he is trapped in the irreconcilable clash between the markers of place and race in the discourse of English identity. The fact that George's train journeys are, themselves, characterized by the tension between mobility and immobility demonstrates George's desire for a sense of purpose and belonging:

> George finds something both serious and comforting in his daily transit into the city. There is a journey, there is a destination: this is how he has been taught to understand life. [...] The railway suggests how it ought to be, how it could be: a smooth ride to a terminus on evenly spaced rails and according to an agreed timetable, with passengers divided among first-, second- and third-class carriages. (50)

The description conjures up values such as order, class, reason and the sense of immobility and confinement, which arguably challenges the reader's typical perception of the railway. As a means of transit, the railway is often presented as expressive of mobility and freedom in Victorian novels, such as Elizabeth Gaskell's *Mary Barton* (1848) and Charles Dickens's *Dombey and Son* (1846–8) (see Mathieson 2015). For George, however, the railway seems to represent what Michel de Certeau calls 'the rational utopia', since its operation is underlined by ideas of regulation, order and stability (1984: 111). As Certeau explains, 'Only a rationalised cell travels. A bubble of panoptic and classifying power, a module of imprisonment that makes possible the production of an order, a closed and autonomous insularity – that is what can traverse space and make itself independent of local roots' (ibid.). Here Certeau identifies a set of paradoxes in the railway system. Although the railway represents mobility and the act of moving away, its operation is facilitated by 'the immobility of order' (ibid.).¹³ Also, the railway can be seen as a means of connecting with different places, although the train itself comprises an enclosed space. Certeau's incisive analysis of how the railway functions as a rational utopia helps the reader to see into George's subtle and latent sense of identity anxiety. His desire for 'the immobility of order' may be seen as expressive of his oppressed fear and frustration about not being able to position himself in a way that is acceptable to others. In this regard, George is arguably the psychological opposite of Grace (as in *Alias Grace*) who is 'too close' to the people and places she encounters, whose extreme 'empathy' has become a mark of her pathology. By contrast, George's relationship to the places through which he passes is profoundly disconnected and 'queer' (in Barnes's word). If Grace struggles to disentangle herself, and her 'feeling' from the phenomenal world, George suffers from an extreme inability to relate to it – even to 'see' it. As the example of George's travelling experience demonstrates, Barnes chooses not to present George's identity crisis through any actual descriptions of what he sees on his travels. Unlike other neo-Victorian fictions that I have examined in previous chapters, *Arthur & George* is marked by 'a more subdued approach of story-telling' (Cavalié 2009: 89), which, as argued before, is predicated upon the reader's paratextual information and their corresponding ability to make connections between various textual details.

Yet it is arguable that this sense of placelessness is potentially liberating for both the character George and the reader. As the following account illustrates, George's walking experience may be seen as indicative of 'the freedom of renunciation' – a term I borrow from Frédéric Gros and go on to discuss below:

> He still retains the habit, which has now grown into a necessity, of walking the lanes for an hour or so after he gets back from the office. It is one detail of his life in which he will not be ruled. He keeps a pair of old boots by the back door, and rain or shine, hail or snow, George takes his walk. He ignores the landscape, which does not interest him; nor do the bulky, bellowing animals

---

¹³ In their co-editorial for the inaugural issue of the journal *Mobilities*, Kevin Hannam et al. present a similar argument by suggesting that 'there is no linear increase in fluidity without extensive systems of immobility' (2006: 2). Using the example of airports, Hannam et al. point out that the operation of airports involves a number of what Sven Kesselring and Gerlinde Vogl call 'transfer points', referring to 'lounges, waiting rooms, cafés, amusement arcades, parks, hotels, stations, motels, harbours'. These 'places of in-between-ness' form 'an immobile network so that others can be on the move' (6).

it contains. As for the humans, he will occasionally think he recognizes someone from the village school in Mr Bostock's day, but he is never quite sure. [...] Some days George gives a kind of half-greeting, a sideways raising of the head, to everyone he meets; at other times he greets no one, even if he remembers having acknowledged them the day before. (Barnes 2005: 66)

The point that walking is one detail of George's life 'in which he will not be ruled' is telling. For George, walking is perceived as something that takes one outside the rules. Although Barnes does not elaborate what he means by 'rules' in a straightforward manner, his description of George's untypical walking is suggestive. As we see from the passage above, George is presented as a walker who is *not* interested in clothes, weather, landscape or animals, all of which are associated with the idyllic English lifestyle. Although he does 'occasionally' recognize people he would meet on his way, he is not bothered with the established social protocols. The use of negative words and phrases such as 'ignore' and 'not interested in' demonstrates the separation between George and the community; he is the 'queer' one who does not comply with the rules, conventions and expectations of country living.

In this regard, walking may be seen as an act of liberation and political resistance for George. The fact that George finds himself 'not [being] ruled' when walking arguably links the activity of walking with the idea of cognitive as well as embodied freedom. This sense of liberty, as my previous discussion of Barnes's choice of vocabulary makes clear, is marked by what Gros calls 'renunciation'. As Gros explains, 'You can hardly remember where you are going or why; that is as meaningless as your history, or what the time is. And you feel free, because whenever you remember the former signs of your commitments in hell – name, age, profession, CV – it all seems absolutely derisory, minuscule, insubstantial' (2014: 9). Following Gros, we may suggest that it is while walking that George feels like he can disconnect himself from the unsettling issues about the tension between the perceived notion of Englishness and his Parsee origin. Questions about what England is, what values and behaviours it sets upon its citizens, are irrelevant. It is liberating precisely because it represents a time and space in which he no longer has to think 'who' or 'what' he is; as Gros observes, he is temporarily free from 'the very idea of identity, the temptation to be someone, to have a name and a history' (6–7).

However, other episodes in the text make it clear that this sense of freedom is both temporary and illusory. In the context of traditional nationalist ideology, George's mobility is perceived as a threat to the core of Englishness. 'His right as a freeborn Englishman' to move freely in his homeland is violated when he is constantly 'spied upon' by the local police after the incident of the horse mutilations (91). Based on circumstantial evidence, virulent rumour and racial prejudice, the Chief Constable Anson quickly identifies George as the suspect responsible for the maiming of the animals. According to Anson's hypothesis, the motivation behind George's malicious behaviours involves some 'sacrificial principle', and the mysterious instrument they are looking for is 'a ritual knife of Indian origin' since the Parsee 'worship fire' (90). His decision to order more police force to follow George clearly reveals the tension between Englishness, racial and ethnic identities. During the confrontation between George and the constable who is assigned to follow him that day, George is questioned about why he is 'walking the lanes of Great Wyrley at this time of day' (91). For the police, it is clear that given his Parsee origin, George's activity of walking must have some suspicious purpose. Or, put differently, George's identity does not fit with the image of the English countryside walker, whose activities are often marked by narratives about 'the sublime and romantic figurations of self, travel, landscape and nature' (Wylie 2005: 235). Although George is born and has grown up in England, his Parsee origin renders him the abstract, symbolic and threatening other in the discourse of English identity, which also reminds us of the conflicted relationship between England and the British Empire at this time. As Baucom aptly articulates, the question is about whether the Empire was 'the domain of England's mastery of the globe or the territory of the loss of Englishness' (1999: 6). This is certainly one of the questions that is raised – but remains unanswered – by Barnes's *Arthur & George*.

Returning to the personal anecdote I began this section with, it seems that my misrecollection of the novel was largely the consequence of the construction of a particular cultural myth about the English countryside and the practice of walking in it. Unlike the drama that facilitates the contemporary audience's vicarious consumption of the Victorian and Edwardian England and celebrates the established link between the English landscape and English identity, the presentation of George as a habitual but 'unseeing' walker and a regular train commuter in Barnes's original novel challenges my paratextual expectations. In this manner, George's discomforting relationship with his surroundings sheds light on how the notion of English landscape is politically and ideologically charged. It also exemplifies Tim Edensor's observation that national identity is constituted primarily out of 'the everyday habits and routines' rather than 'spectacular, formal, invented ceremonies' (2004: 101).

Conclusion

With a focus on the dynamic that exists between space, place and empathy, this chapter has moved from a philosophical and psychological examination of how human subjects develop empathetic relationships with their surroundings to a consideration of how this is represented in literary texts and how this, in turn, impacts upon readers. By tracing the idea of empathy back to its aesthetic origins, this chapter has addressed the issues about the ways in which the representation of space and place in neo-Victorian literature and culture involves the reader/audience affectively, and the ways it plays with – and depends upon – their paratextual knowledge and expectations. In doing so, it has, I hope, further enriched the discussion of reading pleasure afforded by neo-Victorian literature and the study of narrative empathy.

The project of Thames Town in Shanghai that I introduced at the beginning of this chapter is an interesting example of how a constructed landscape facilitates a fairly straightforward empathetic engagement with its visitors. The immersive and embodied experience it affords can also be found in a great number of neo-Victorian products: the Dickens World theme park (see Heilmann and Llewellyn 2010: 213–20), and TV series, including ITV's *Victoria* (see Franchi 2016) and its 2015 adaptation of Barnes's novel *Arthur & George*. Unlike Victorianists such as Heilmann and Llewellyn, who in their study trace the contemporary interest in adaptation and appropriation back to the Victorians, in this chapter I chose to examine the dynamic that we see/experience between the landscape and the body in neo-Victorianism in relation to Robert Vischer's work on aesthetic empathy. Vischer's writing on embodied space offers us with a new perspective on Grace's psychological condition in Atwood's *Alias Grace*. Grace is presented as a character who 'over-identifies' with her surroundings; her idiosyncratic sensitivity to external stimulus is symptomatic of her troubled mentality. The transformative and affective body–space relationship advocated by Vischer, however, is not what we see in Barnes's novel. Barnes's portrayal of the 'subaltern' subject George's emotional detachment – specified as his 'queer' indifference to the natural world – challenges the reader's paratextual knowledge about the English countryside and the activity of walking on it. It is through this means that the text enables the reader to become aware of their complicity in the formation and continuation of an essentially racist model of English national identity.

In the context of Brexit, *Arthur & George* has particular contemporary resonance.[14] The politics of mobility that I have identified in my reading of George's story resembles the key issue of Brexit; that is, free movement. Although George's status as one of the 'unofficial Englishmen' (217) – being half-Indian and half-Scottish – is quite different from the type of immigrants that Brexit is primarily concerned with, the issue that his experience raises about the tension between two different models of identity construction – the localist and the racial one – still matters in many respects. The resurgence of English nationalism – as illustrated by the slogan used by the Leave Campaign, 'I want my country back', in the EU 2016 referendum – and the then prime minister Theresa May's political interpretation of the referendum result – 'Embracing the World' – indicate how a post-imperial Britain still struggles with the concept of English identity and who acts as the 'other' against which the notion of Englishness is constructed. This is arguably where 'paranoid' discussions of Barnes's *Arthur & George* continue to be needed in the sense that we, as readers, need to remain vigilant about the mystification of English identity. By implicating the reader in the construction of the textual world and encouraging them to adopt a more critical approach to the discursive nature of Englishness, *Arthur & George* also exemplifies the role 'paranoid' inquiry could play in a wider reparative project: reflections on the imperial legacy are essential for the present and the future sociopolitical landscape of Britain.

---

[14] On 23 June 2016, the British government held a referendum to decide whether the UK should remain in or leave the European Union. With more than thirty million people voting, the Leave campaign won by 51.9–48.1 per cent. For more details about Brexit, see Alex Hunt and Brian Wheeler's report for the BBC on 16 October 2018.

Conclusion

In her 2004 book *The Cultural Politics of Emotion*, Sara Ahmed stresses the transformative potential of what 'have often been described as negative or even destructive' emotions, suggesting that these emotions can 'also be enabling or creative, often in their very refusal of the promise of the social bond' (201). Ahmed's advocacy for the political significance of affective experiences that are disruptive to intimacy and connection is echoed by Clare Hemmings, who likewise proposes for a model of political transformation that is premised on 'the affective dissonance' rather than identification (2012: 147). Hemmings lists, in particular, anger, frustration and rage as important affects in imagining 'a politics that begins from experiences of discomfort'; in the meantime, she warns against 'generalising these as shared by all subjects or as the basis of transcendence of difference' (158). The past experience of pain, to both Ahmed and Hemmings, is powerful in prompting us to act.[1] Ahmed links emotion with knowledge by suggesting that these strong bodily sensations and feelings not only move us; the interpretation of them involves further examination of how such feelings are 'implicated in structural relations of power' (2004: 172). She calls for a reading of 'the relation between affect and structure' (174) in transforming the individual experience of pain into 'collectivity and resistance' (172). In line of Ahmed's work, Hemmings challenges the imagination of affect as 'a key of sorts to life lived beyond or beside the social regulation of our existence' (which, for her, is a limitation to the approach adopted by Eve Sedgwick and Brian Massumi), and considers, instead, affect as a useful resource

---

[1] Sianne Ngai's *Ugly Feelings* (2005), by contrast, focuses on the negative affects that are related to situations in which agency is obstructed and political action is suspended. She considers envy, anxiety, paranoia, irritation and 'stuplimity' – a term she coins in describing 'a strange amalgamation of shock and boredom' – as the affective states of late capitalism (2–3).

in understanding the dissonance between 'an embodied sense of self and the self we are expected to be in *social* terms' (Hemmings 2012: 148, 149, emphasis added). The foregrounding of affect as a means of political transformation in both writings of Ahmed and Hemmings refigures politics as 'that which moves us, rather than that which confirms us in what we already know', the latter referring to the established knowledge about identity politics (Hemmings 2012: 151). Focusing on the intersection between neo-Victorianism, empathy and reading, this book explores the ways in which feelings can mobilize socially situated knowledge and contribute to political transformation.

The turn to (negative) affect that we witness in the field of feminist criticism and cultural studies is also motivated by a reconsideration of critical enterprise per se. More specifically, the shift of critical interests to affect is relevant to the debate about 'the affective registers' of criticism (Felski 2011: 215). As early as the 1990s, Sedgwick lamented on the ways in which the habitual practices of criticism reduce our lives and experiences to predicable and binary power relations and used Paul Ricoeur's noton of a 'hermeneutics of suspicion' as her example. She deems such practice 'paranoid' since much critical energy is placed on 'the epistemologies of enmity' (Sedgwick 2003: 127). Sedgwick notes that paranoid readers approach the critical object in a rather vigilant and rigid manner since their reading practices are featured with anticipatory anxiety: they are on guard in anticipation of something unexpected or contingent happening in the future (see the introduction). Their aversion to 'bad' surprise – together with the fact that this model of reading has become the 'standard' practice in criticism – deprives suspicion of its original subversive power. As my discussion of Margaret Atwood's *Alias Grace* in Chapter 1 indicates, suspicion could also serve the 'narcissistic' needs of the analyst/reader. As such, Hemmings warns us, critique risks the danger of 'confirm[ing] us in what we already know' (2012: 151). Nikolas Kompridis further contends that 'the goal of critique shifts inexorably' from 'producing new insights' to 'the achievement of *tour de force* performances of unmasking' (2000: 37). It is in this context that Sedgwick turns to affect, which, to her, has 'greater freedom with respect to object' and is therefore full of reparative potentials: "Affects can be, and are, attached to things, people, ideas, sensations, relations, activities, ambitions, institutions, and any number of other things, including other affects. Thus, one can be excited by anger, disgusted by shame, or surprised by joy' (2003: 19). The malleability of affect renders it possible for Sedgwick to argue for a new political vision that is characterized by connection and attachment rather than negativity or opposition. Focusing on how individuals *experience* affects, Sedgwick proposes that alongside the paranoid inquiry of knowledge and structure, there exists a reparative discussion of subjectivity and intersubjectivity. To read reparatively, however, does not signal a (re)turn to literary aesthetics, which is arguably the difference between Sedgwick's formulation of reparative reading and Rita Felski's notion of 'postcritique' (see Felski 2008; Anker and Felski 2017).² Sedgwick's own writing on shame makes it clear that a reparative approach to shame 'opens a lot of new doors for thinking about identity politics' (2003: 62). In the words of Sara Callahan, 'being in favor of leaving behind the knee-jerk versions – or perversions – of critique does not mean that one is in favor of leaving behind all forms of critique' (2021: 58).

Although the dichotomy Sedgwick sets between these two different styles of reading remains tendentious (see Hemmings 2005; Kurnick 2020), paranoia and reparation are useful concepts in understanding the aesthetics, politics and ethics of neo-Victorianism. As a genre that is full of suspicious sentiments, in the sense that it offers 'a non-normative view of assumed notions regarding the Victorian frame of mind' (Tomaiuolo 2018: 5), neo-Victorian fiction, as my review of relevant criticism in the introduction has demonstrated, is critically acclaimed for its reparative potential. Through a 'deviant' or 'subversive' engagement with the Victorians, neo-Victorian fiction is seen to involve a desire to redress or rectify the imperial legacy in the fields of race, gender, class, sexuality and so on. (see, e.g. Heilmann and Llewellyn 2010; Kohlke and Gutleben 2010; Ho [2012] 2013; Tomaiuolo 2018). Taking up the lead of Ahmed and Hemmings, this book has explored the transformative powers of the neo-Victorian genre by focusing on, instead, the ways in which neo-Victorian fiction affectively positions the reader within its textual landscape, which is often characterized by a painful and unsettling version of the past.

---

² Felski's envisioning of postcritique is rather fuzzy. Although in various occasions she insists that postcritique is not a retreat to formalism or aestheticism, in the introduction to their co-edited book *Critique and Postcritique*, Felski and her co-author Anker call for critical approaches that take the 'formal qualities' of the literary work and 'the sensual dimensions of aesthetic experience' into consideration (2017: 16). Felski's 2008 book *Uses of Literature* also focuses on the aesthetic experience of reading.

It groups together a number of neo-Victorian texts that tell different kinds of 'disturbing' stories about the past: child prostitution and sexual harassment in Jane Harris's *The Observations* and Margaret Atwood's *Alias Grace*, respectively (Chapter 1); 'shameless' same-sex desire in Sarah Waters's *Tipping the Velvet* and *Affinity* (Chapter 2); existential crisis and violence against innocent others in Michael Cox's *The Meaning of Night* and Graeme Macrae Burnet's *His Bloody Project* (Chapter 3) and lack of emotional connection with the surroundings in Julian Barnes's *Arthur & George* (Chapter 4). Focusing on various experiences of 'reader discomfort', this book has challenged the widely received understanding of the success of the neo-Victorian genre; that is, the assumption that its reading pleasures come from textual immersion or transgressive and voyeuristic identifications. Through these means, I have also shifted the study of neo-Victorian literature from a 'self-confirming' discussion of the similarities and/or differences between the Victorians and the contemporary period, to a more profound exploration of the dynamic that exists between the past, the present and the future.

The overarching concern of the book, then, is how neo-Victorian narratives mobilize individual experiences of stigma, shame, violence and injustice to reparative ends. The issue about how literary works move the reader to act in the material world has attracted large numbers of responses. Feminist critics including Ahmed and Hemmings (as introduced before) believe in the importance of 'negative feelings' or 'experiences of discomfort'. Ahmed emphasizes, in particular, that feeling should not be taken as 'the ground for action'; it is 'an effect of the repetition of some actions rather than others' (2004: 196). In this way, Ahmed demonstrates the importance of feelings in prompting reflections on social norms (which is, admittedly, the preliminary yet essential step in political transformation). In thinking about the change of individual experience into collective resistance, Hemmings turns to empathy, which is a 'key for challenging the opposition between feeling and knowing, self and other' (2012: 151). As argued in the introduction, empathy has long been celebrated as a virtue that is essential for political justice and ethics. However, it has also been criticized for serving the interest of the empathizer. Lauren Berlant, for instance, expresses her concern that 'the ethical imperative toward social-transformation is replaced by a civic-minded but passive ideal of empathy' in her 1998 essay 'Poor Eliza' (641). Taking Toni Morrison's *Beloved*

(1987) as her example, Berlant asserts that literary works need to 'refuse [the reader] to take on the history of the Other' through empathetic identification in order to usher real changes in the material world (665).[3] In response to the possibility that 'positive' or 'morally rewarding' affective responses such as empathy and compassion could reinforce rather than challenge the dominant social order, Berlant recognizes the importance of *affective disruption* in waking the (privileged) subjects from any moral smugness they might enjoy from their immersive and vicarious experience of the other's suffering. This critical reflection on the perils of affective politics has particular resonance for neo-Victorianism, a literary and cultural movement that seems to be preoccupied with affective – if not 'sentimental' – narratives about the historically marginalized or 'deviant' other.

As I hope to have demonstrated in this book, neo-Victorian texts – be they literary or filmic – often explore and contest the possibilities and limits of empathy as well as its reparative potentials through its foregrounding of the 'perversity' of certain empathetic practice (Chapter 1), textual rejection of readerly empathy (Chapter 3) and use of narrative techniques that serve to undermine the reader's reading expectations and desires (Chapters 2 and 4). In every case, an unsettling empathetic engagement with the textual other pushes readers to critically reflect upon their reading expectations and strategies, as well as their wider ethical responsibilities. Here I concur with Kompridis that 'crisis' – in the form of hermeneutic uncertainty in Chapter 1, retrospective narrative and narratological intrusion in Chapter 2, textual refusal against readerly expectation in Chapter 3 and lack of emotional connection in Chapter 4 – 'is a form of experience that can also disclose new kinds of awareness and new possibilities' (2000: 40). The unsettling text–reader relationship afforded by neo-Victorian fiction, I would thereby suggest, ultimately encourages readers to envisage a potentially different future for both the text's characters and human behaviour in general. In this way, I approach empathy as not only a thematic concern of these literary works but also the dynamic that exists between the text and the reader.

---

[3] Berlant has expressed her unease about the sentimentalization of culture that she witnesses in America more systematically in her national sentimental trilogy – *The Anatomy of National Fantasy* (1991), *The Queen of America Goes to Washington City* (1997) and *The Female Complaint* (2008).

I want to finish by addressing how neo-Victorianism contributes to the study of narrative empathy and affective politics. One particular feature of the neo-Victorian genre, as I argued throughout the book, is its sense of temporality. All the chosen texts engage deeply with the past in order to help us better prepare for the future; and this 'double temporality' is played out at two levels: narratological and ethical. My engagement with Mark Currie's work on narrative temporality has made it clear that future orientation is a feature of even the most backward-looking literary text. This future-orientated model of thinking provides us with a different approach to neo-Victorian fiction and its preoccupation with retrospective accounts of the past (e.g. collections of volumes found in historical archives, journal entries, Bildungsroman and biographies). Currie's study of the dynamic between narrated time and the time of narration makes it clear that the 'present present' is 'actually structured in relation to the future present from which it is narrated' ([2007] 2012: 39). This narratological awareness of anticipation is further enriched by my discussion of the ethical imperative of neo-Victorian literature. With a focus on the use of literary devices such as the first-person narrator, diary entries and direct address to the intradiegetic narratees (all of these characterize what I term the 'dialogic' nature of the neo-Victorian genre), I examined the ways in which neo-Victorian fiction facilitates the contemporary reader's desire to empathize with the textual other, which is portrayed as either the 'victim' of difficult sociopolitical circumstances or the 'troubled soul' of some psychological or existential crisis. As we have seen, this empathetic engagement between the text and the reader arguably entails an ethical responsibility, which also involves a concern about the future, and in particular, a concern about what the readers can do in both the textual and the material worlds in order to avoid repeating the same traumatic stories (as those featured in the text) and to move towards a different – even if not necessarily better – future. By staging an alternative version of the past and affectively implicating the reader in the textual world, neo-Victorian fiction places the initiative to act for change in the hands of the reader: if the past could have happened otherwise, then the future could also be different.

Bibliography

Agosta, Lou (2014), *A Rumor of Empathy: Rewriting Empathy in the Context of Philosophy* (New York: Palgrave Macmillan).

Ahmed, Sara (2000), *Strange Encounters: Embodied Others in Post-Coloniality* (London: Routledge).

Ahmed, Sara (2004), *The Cultural Politics of Emotion* (Edinburgh: Edinburgh University Press).

Alden, Natasha (2013), '"Possibility, Pleasure and Peril": *The Night Watch* as a Very Literary History', in Kaye Mitchell, ed., *Sarah Waters: Contemporary Critical Perspectives* (London: Bloomsbury), 70–83.

Allesch, Christian G. (2017), '*Einfühlung* – a Key Concept of Psychological Aesthetics', in Vanessa Lux and Sigrid Weigel, eds, *Empathy: Epistemic Problems and Cultural-Historical Perspectives of a Cross-Disciplinary Concept* (London: Palgrave Macmillan), 223–43.

Amiel-Houser, Tammy, and Adia Mendelson-Maoz (2014), 'Against Empathy: Levinas and Ethical Criticism in the 21st Century', *Journal of Literary Theory*, 8/1, 199–218.

Amiel-Houser, Tammy (2019), 'The Neoliberal Mobilization of Empathy in the Era of the Financial Crisis: A Case-Study', *Law, Culture and the Humanities*, 4/22, 1–26.

Anderson, Amanda (2017), 'Therapeutic Criticism', *NOVEL: A Forum on Fiction*, 50/3, 321–8.

Anker Elizabeth S., and Rita Felski (2017), 'Introduction', in Elizabeth S. Anker and Rita Felski, eds, *Critique and Postcritique* (Durham, NC: Duke University Press), 1–28.

Arias, Rosaria, and Patricia Pulham (eds) (2009), *Haunting and Spectrality in Neo-Victorian Fiction: Possessing the Past* (Basingstoke: Palgrave Macmillan).

Armitt, Lucie (2007), 'Interview with Sarah Waters', *Feminist Review*, 85, 116–27.

Armitt, Lucie (2016), 'Teasing (Out) a New Generation: The Writing of Sarah Waters', in Adele Jones and Claire O'Callaghan, eds, *Sarah Waters and Contemporary Feminisms* (London: Palgrave Macmillan), 25–42.

Armitt, Lucie, and Sarah Gamble (2006), 'The Haunted Geometries of Sarah Waters' *Affinity*', *Textual Practice*, 20/1, 141–59.

Armstrong, John (2018), 'Pastoral Place and Violence in Contemporary British Fiction', *Concentric: Literary and Cultural Studies*, 44/2, 51–79.

Arthur & George (2015), [TV programme] ITV, 2–16 March.

Assmann, Aleida, and Ines Detmers (2016), 'Introduction', in Aleida Assmann and Ines Detmers, eds, *Empathy and Its Limits* (Basingstoke: Palgrave Macmillan), 1–17.

Atwood, Margaret (1996), *Alias Grace* (London: Bloomsbury).

Atwood, Margaret (1998), 'In Search of *Alias Grace*: On Writing Canadian Historical Fiction', *The American Historical Review*, 103/5, 1503–16.

Auden, W. H. ([1960] 2007), 'The More Loving One', in Edward Mendelson, ed., *Collected Poems* (New York: Random House), 237.

Bacal, Howard A. (1994), 'The Selfobject Relationship in Psychoanalytic Treatment', in Arnold Goldberg, ed., *Progress in Self-Psychology: V. 10: A Decade of Progress* (Hillsdale, NJ: Analytic Press), 21–30.

Bachelard, Gaston (1964), *The Psychoanalysis of Fire*, tr. Alan C. M. Ross (London: Routledge & Kegan Paul).

Bachelard, Gaston (1983), *Water and Dreams: An Essay on the Imagination of Matter*, tr. Edith R. Farrell (Dallas: The Pegasus Foundation).

Baker, A. Geoffrey (2016), *The Aesthetics of Clarity and Confusion: Literature and Engagement since Nietzsche and the Naturalists* (Cham: Palgrave Macmillan).

Barnes, Julian (1998), *England, England* (London: Jonathan Cape).

Barnes, Julian (2005), *Arthur & George* (London: Jonathan Cape).

Barthes, Roland ([1974] 2002), *S/Z*, tr. Richard Miller (Oxford: Blackwell).

Barthes, Roland ([1978] 2002), *A Lover's Discourse: Fragments*, tr. Richard Howard (London: Vintage Books).

Basch, Michael Franz (1976), 'The Concept of Affect: A Re-Examination', *Journal of the American Psychoanalytic Association*, 24, 759–78.

Basch, Michael Franz (1994), 'The Selfobject Concept: Clinical Implications', in Arnold Goldberg, ed., *A Decade of Progress: Progress in Self-Psychology Volume 10* (Hillsdale, NJ: Analytic Press), 1–8.

Bateman, Anthony, and Jeremy Holmes (1995), *Introduction to Psychoanalysis: Contemporary Theory and Practice* (London: Routledge).

Battersby, Doug (2021), 'Reading Ishiguro Today: Suspicion and Form', *MFS Modern Fiction Studies*, 67/1, 67–88.

Baucom, Ian (1999), *Out of Place: Englishness, Empire and the Locations of Identity* (Princeton, NJ: Princeton University Press).

Baucom, Ian (2000), 'Found Drowned: The Irish Atlantic', *Nineteenth Century Contexts*, 22/1, 103–38.

Baudrillard, Jean (1988), 'Simulacra and Simulations', in Mark Poster, ed., *Jean Baudrillard: Selected Writings* (Stanford: Stanford University Press), 166–84.

Bennett, Ashly (2010), 'Shameful Signification: Narrative and Feeling in *Jane Eyre*', *Narrative*, 18/3, 300–23.
Bentley, Nick (2007), 'Re-writing Englishness: Imagining the Nation in Julian Barnes's *England, England* and Zadie Smith's *White Teeth*', *Textual Practice*, 21/3, 483–504.
Berberich, Christine (2011), '"All Letters Quoted Are Authentic": The Past after Postmodern Fabulation in Julian Barnes's *Arthur & George*', in Sebastian Groes and Peter Childs, eds, *Julian Barnes: Contemporary Critical Perspectives* (London: Continuum), 117–28.
Bergson, Henri ([1913] 2001), *Time and Free Will: An Essay on the Immediate Data of Consciousness*, tr. F. L. Pogson (Mineola, NY: Dover Publications).
Berlant, Lauren (1998), 'Poor Eliza', *American Literature*, 70/3, 635–68.
Berlant, Lauren (1991), *The Anatomy of National Fantasy: Hawthorne, Utopia, and Everyday Life* (Chicago: The University of Chicago Press).
Berlant, Lauren (1997), *The Queen of America Goes to Washington City: Essays on Sex and Citizenship* (Durham, NC: Duke University Press).
Berlant, Lauren (2000), 'The Subject of True Feeling: Pain, Privacy and Politics', in Sara Ahmed et al., eds, *Transformations: Thinking Through Feminism* (London: Routledge), 33–47.
Berlant, Lauren (2004), 'Introduction: Compassion (and Withholding)', in Lauren Berlant, ed., *Compassion: The Culture and Politics of an Emotion* (New York: Routledge), 1–13.
Berlant, Lauren (2008), 'Thinking about Feeling Historical', *Emotion, Space and Society*, 1/1, 4–9.
Berlant, Lauren (2008), *The Female Complaint: The Unfinished Business of Sentimentality in American Culture* (Durham, NC: Duke University Press).
Berlant, Lauren (2011), *Cruel Optimism* (Durham, NC: Duke University Press).
Berleant, Arnold (1997), *Living in the Landscape: Towards an Aesthetics of Environment* (Lawrence: University Press of Kansas).
Bersani, Leo (1990), *The Culture of Redemption* (Cambridge, MA: Harvard University Press).
Bersani, Leo (1995), *Homos* (Cambridge, MA: Harvard University Press).
Best, Stephen, and Sharon Marcus (2009), 'Surface Reading: An Introduction', *Representations*, 108/1, 1–21.
Biddle, Jennifer (1997), 'Shame', *Australian Feminist Studies*, 12/26, 227–39.
Blake, Sarah (2000), *Grange House* (New York: Picador).
Blanc, Marie Thérèse (2006), 'Margaret Atwood's *Alias Grace* and the Construction of a Trial Narrative', *English Studies in Canada*, 32/4, 101–27.

Blanchot, Maurice ([1982] 1989), *The Space of Literature*, tr. Ann Smock (Lincoln: University of Nebraska Press).

Blaylock, James P. (1986), *Homunculus* (New York: Ace).

Bloom, Paul (2016), *Against Empathy: The Case for Rational Compassion* (London: Bodley Head).

Boehm-Schnitker, Nadine, and Susanne Gruss (2011), 'Introduction: Spectacles and Things – Visual and Material Culture and/in Neo-Victorianism', *Neo-Victorian Studies*, 4/2, 1–23.

Boehm-Schnitker, Nadine, and Susanne Gruss (2014), 'Introduction: Fashioning the Neo-Victorian – Neo-Victorian Fashions', in Nadine Boehm-Schnitker and Susanne Gruss, eds, *Neo-Victorian Literature and Culture: Immersions and Revisitations* (London: Routledge), 1–17.

Bouson, J. Brooks (1989), *The Empathic Reader: A Study of the Narcissistic Character and the Drama of the Self* (Amherst: The University of Massachusetts Press).

Breithaupt, Fritz (2017), *The Dark Sides of Empathy*, tr. Andrew B. B. Hamilton (Ithaca, NY: Cornell University Press).

Brindle, Kym (2013), *Epistolary Encounters in Neo-Victorian Fiction: Diaries and Letters* (Basingstoke: Palgrave Macmillan).

Brooks, Peter (1984), *Reading for the Plot: Designing and Intervention in Narrative* (Cambridge, MA: Harvard University Press).

Burdett, Carolyn (2011a), ' "The Subjective Inside Us Can Turn into the Objective Outside": Vernon Lee's Psychological Aesthetics', *19: Interdisciplinary Studies in the Long Nineteenth Century*, 12, https://19.bbk.ac.uk/article/id/1549/, accessed 30 August 2020.

Burdett, Carolyn (2011b), 'New Agenda: Is Empathy the End of Sentimentality', *Journal of Victorian Culture*, 16/2, 259–74.

Burnet, Graeme Macrae (2015), *His Bloody Project* (Glasgow: Contraband).

Byatt, A. S. (1990), *Possession: A Romance* (London: Chatto & Windus).

Byatt, A. S. (1991), *Passions of the Mind: Selected Writings* (London: Chatto & Windus).

Byatt, A. S. (1992), *Angels and Insects* (London: Chatto & Windus).

Bywater, William (1990), 'The Paranoia of Postmodernism', *Philosophy and Literature*, 1, 79–83.

Callahan, Sara (2021), 'Critique and Post-critique in Contemporary Art History: Excessive Attachment to Suspicion in Academic and Beyond', *Arts and Humanities in Higher Education*, 20/1, 42–65.

Campanella, Thomas J. (2008), *The Concrete Dragon: China's Urban Geography and What It Means for the World* (New York: Princeton Architectural Press).

Campbell, James, and John Fowles (1976), 'An Interview with John Fowles', *Contemporary Literature*, 17/4, 455–69.

Carroll, Rachel (2006), 'Rethinking Generational History: Queer Histories of Sexuality in Neo-Victorian Feminist Fiction', *Studies in the Literary Imagination*, 39/2, 135–47.

Carroll, Rachel (2012), '"Becoming My Own Ghost": Spinsterhood and the "Invisibility" of Heterosexuality in Sarah Waters' *Affinity*', in *Rereading Heterosexuality: Feminism, Queer Theory and Contemporary Fiction* (Edinburgh: Edinburgh University Press), 25–44.

Carroll, Samantha J. (2010), 'Putting the "Neo" Back into Neo-Victorian: The Neo-Victorian Novel as Postmodern Revisionist Fiction', *Neo-Victorian Studies*, 3/2, 172–205.

Cavalié, Elsa (2009), 'Constructions of Englishness in Julian Barnes's *Arthur & George*', *American, British and Canadian Studies*, 13, 88–100.

Certeau, Michel de (1984), *The Practice of Everyday Life*, tr. Steven F. Rendall (Berkeley: University of California Press).

Chambers-Letson, Joshua, Tavia Nyong'o, and Ann Pellegrini ([2009] 2019), 'Foreword: Before and After', in José Esteban Muñoz, *Cruising Utopia: The Then and There of Queer Futurity* (New York: New York University Press), ix–xvi.

Charmé, Stuart Zane (1991), *Vulgarity and Authenticity: Dimensions of Otherness in the World of Jean-Paul Sartre* (Amherst: University of Massachusetts Press).

Chase-Riboud, Barbara (2003), *Hottentot Venus* (New York: Anchor).

Churchill, Steven ([2013] 2014), 'Contingency and Ego, Intentionality and Nausea', in Steven Churchill and Jack Reynolds, eds, *Jean-Paul Sartre: Key Concepts* (London: Routledge), 44–65.

Clohesy, Anthony M. (2013), *Politics of Empathy: Ethics, Solidarity, Recognition* (London: Routledge).

Coplan, Amy (2004), 'Empathic Engagement with Narrative Fictions', *Journal of Aesthetics and Art Criticism*, 62/2, 141–52.

Coplan, Amy ([2011] 2014), 'Understanding Empathy: Its Features and Effects', in Amy Coplan and Peter Goldie, eds, *Empathy: Philosophical and Psychological Perspectives* (Oxford: Oxford University Press), 3–18.

Coplan, Amy, and Peter Goldie ([2011] 2014), 'Introduction', in Amy Coplan and Peter Goldie, eds, *Empathy: Philosophical and Psychological Perspectives* (Oxford: Oxford University Press), ix–xlvii.

Cox, Jessica (2019), *Neo-Victorianism and Sensation Fiction* (Cham: Palgrave Macmillan).

Cox, Michael (2006), *The Meaning of Night: A Confession* (London: John Murray).

Currie, Mark ([2007] 2012), *About Time: Narrative, Fiction and the Philosophy of Time* (Edinburgh: Edinburgh University Press).

Currie, Mark ([1998] 2011), *Postmodern Narrative Theory* (Basingstoke: Palgrave Macmillan).

Currie, Greg (2016), 'Does Fiction Make Us Less Empathetic?', *Teorema: Revista Internacional de Filosofía*, 35/3, 47–68.

Daghistany, Ann, and J. J. Johnson (1981), 'Romantic Irony, Spatial Form, and Joyce's *Ulysses*', in Jeffrey R. Smitten and Ann Daghistany, eds, *Spatial Form in Narrative* (Ithaca, NY: Cornell University Press), 48–60.

Davies, Helen (2012), *Gender and Ventriloquism in Victorian and Neo-Victorian Fiction: Passionate Puppets* (Basingstoke: Palgrave Macmillan).

Davies, Helen (2015), *Neo-Victorian Freakery: The Cultural Afterlife of the Victorian Freak Show* (Basingstoke: Palgrave Macmillan).

Decety, Jean, and Claus Lamm (2006), 'Human Empathy through the Lens of Social Neuroscience', *Scientific World Journal*, 6, 1146–63.

Denning, Penelope (1998), 'Inventing England', *Irish Times*, 8/9, http://www.irishtimes.com/culture/inventing-england-1.190953, accessed 13 February 2017.

Dennis, Abigail (2008), '"Ladies in Peril": Sarah Waters on Neo-Victorian Narrative Celebrations and Why She Stopped Writing about the Victorian Era', *Neo-Victorian Studies*, 1/1, 41–52.

Derrida, Jacques (1996), *Archive Fever: A Freudian Impression*, tr. Eric Prenwitz (Chicago: University of Chicago Press).

Dickens, Charles ([1846–8] 2002), *Dombey and Son*, Andrew Sanders, ed. (London: Penguin).

Dodson, Ed (2018), 'The Partial Postcoloniality of Julian Barnes's *Arthur & George*', *Journal of Modern Literature*, 41/2, 112–28.

Duncan, Ian (1998), 'Adam Smith, Samuel Johnson and the Institutions of English', in Robert Crawford, ed., *Scottish Invention of English Literature* (Cambridge: Cambridge University Press), 37–54.

Dvorak, Ken (2013), 'Foreword', in Cynthia J. Miler and Julie Anne Taddeo, eds, *Steaming into a Victorian Future: A Steampunk Anthology* (Lanham, MD: Rowman & Littlefield), ix–xi.

Eagleton, Terry ([1983] 1996), *Literary Theory* (Oxford: Blackwell).

Eagleton, Terry (2003), *Sweet Violence: The Idea of the Tragic* (Oxford: Blackwell).

Edensor, Tim (2001), 'Performing Tourism, Staging Tourism: (Re)producing Tourist Space and Practice', *Tourist Studies*, 1/1, 59–81.

Edensor, Tim (2004), 'Automobility and National Identity: Representation, Geography and Driving Practice', *Theory, Culture & Society*, 21/4–5, 101–20.

Escudero-Alías, Maite (2014), '"There's That Curtain Come Down": The Burden of Shame in Sarah Waters's *The Night Watch*', in Marita Nadal and Mónica Calvo, eds, *Trauma in Contemporary Literature: Narrative and Representation* (New York: Routledge), 223–36.

Eve, Martin Paul (2013), '"You Will See the Logic of the Design of This": From Historiography to Taxonomography in the Contemporary Metafiction of Sarah Waters's *Affinity*', *Neo-Victorian Studies*, 6/1, 105–25.

Faber, Michel (2002), *The Crimson Petal and the White* (Edinburgh: Canongate Books).

Fackenheim, Emil (1961), *Metaphysics and Historicity* (Milwaukee, WI: Marquette University Press).

Felski, Rita (2008), *Uses of Literature* (Malden, MA: Blackwell)

Felski, Rita (2011), 'Suspicious Minds', *Poetics Today*, 32/2, 215–34.

Felski, Rita (2015), *The Limits of Critique* (Chicago: University of Chicago).

Ferguson, Christine (2013), 'Neo-Victorian Presence: Tom Phillips and the Non-Hermeneutic Past', *Australasian Journal of Victorian Studies*, 18/3, 22–57.

Fish, Laura (2008), *Strange Music* (London: Jonathan Cape).

Fisher, Linda (1992), 'Hermeneutics of Suspicion and Postmodern Paranoia: Psychologies of Interpretation', *Philosophy and Literature*, 16, 106–14.

Foden, Giles (2006), 'Review: *The Meaning of Night* by Michael Cox', *The Guardian* (Saturday, 23 September), https://www.theguardian.com/books/2006/sep/23/featuresreviews.guardianreview15, accessed 5 February 2020.

Foster, Susan Leigh (2010), *Choreographing Empathy: Kinesthesia in Performance* (London: Routledge).

Foucault, Michel ([1977] 1991), *Discipline and Punish: The Birth of the Prison*, tr. Alan Sheridan (London: Penguin Books).

Fowles, John (1969), *The French Lieutenant's Woman* (London: Cape).

Fowles, John (1977), 'Notes on an Unfinished Novel', in Malcolm Bradbury, ed., *The Novel Today: Contemporary Writers on Modern Fiction* (Manchester: Manchester University Press), 135–50.

Franchi, Barbara (2016), 'Consuming Victoria: History as Neo-Victorian Fiction?', *Victorianist: BAVS Postgraduates* (19 September 2016), https://victorianist.wordpress.com/2016/09/19/consuming-victoria-history-as-neo-victorian-fiction/, accessed 9 February 2021.

Freeman, Elizabeth (2010), *Time Binds: Queer Temporalities, Queer Histories* (Durham, NC: Duke University Press).

Freud, Sigmund (1958), 'Psycho-Analytic Notes on an Autobiographical Account of a Case of Paranoia', *Standard Edition of the Complete Psychological Works of Sigmund Freud*, vol. XII, tr. James Straghey (London: Hogarth Press), 3–82.

Freud, Sigmund ([1955] 2010), *The Interpretation of Dreams*, tr. James Strachey (New York: Basic Books).

Frey, Olivia (2009), *Narrative Techniques in Julian Barnes's Arthur & George: Negotiating Truth and Fiction* (Munich: Grin Verlag).

Friedberg, Anne (1994), 'Cinema and the Postmodern Condition', in Linda Williams, ed., *Viewing Positions: Ways of Seeing Film* (New Brunswick, NJ: Rutgers University Press), 59–83.

Friedman, Richard A. (2017), 'What If Trump Is Actually a Master of Empathy?', *The Guardian* (30 September), https://www.theguardian.com/commentisfree/2017/sep/30/what-if-trump-is-actually-a-master-of-empathy, accessed 20 August 2020.

Fuss, Diana (2017), 'But What about Love?', *PMLA*, 132/2, 352–5.

Gallese, Vittorio M. D. (2009), 'Mirror Neurons, Embodied Simulation, and the Neural Basis of Social Identification', *Psychoanalytic Dialogues*, 19/5, 519–36.

Garber, Marjorie (2004), 'Compassion', in Lauren Berlant, ed., *Compassion: The Culture and Politics of an Emotion* (New York: Routledge), 15–27.

Gaskell, Elizabeth ([1848] 2006), *Mary Barton*, Shirley Foster, ed. (Oxford: Oxford University Press).

Ghosh, Amitav (2008), *Sea of Poppies* (London: John Murray).

Gilbert, Sandra M., and Susan Gubar (1979), *The Madwoman in the Attic: The Woman Writer and the Nineteenth-Century Literary Imagination* (New Haven, CT: Yale Nota Bene Press).

Gibson, Andrew (1999), *Postmodernity, Ethics and the Novel: From Leavis to Levinas* (London: Routledge).

Gibson, Sarah (2004), 'English Journeys: The Tourist, the Guidebook, and the Motorcar in *The Remains of the Day*', *Journeys*, 5/2, 43–71.

Gill, Merton M. (1994), 'Heinz Kohut's Self Psychology', in Arnold Goldberg, ed., *A Decade of Progress: Progress in Self-Psychology Volume 10* (Hillsdale, NJ: Analytic Press), 197–211.

Greiner, Rae (2009), 'Sympathy Time: Adam Smith, George Eliot, and the Realist Novel', *Narrative*, 17/3, 291–311.

Greiner, Rae (2011), 'Thinking of Me Thinking of You: Sympathy versus Empathy in the Realist Novel', *Victorian Studies*, 53/3, 417–26.

Greiner, Rae (2012), '1909: The Introduction of the Word "Empathy" into English', in Dino Franco Felluga, ed., *BRANCH: Britain, Representation and Nineteenth-Century History*, https://www.branchcollective.org/?ps_articles=rae-greiner-1909-theintroduction-of-the-word-empathy-into-english, accessed 20 July 2019.

Gros, Frédéric (2014), *A Philosophy of Walking*, tr. John Howe (London: Verso).

Gulli, Andrew (2015), 'Interview with *Arthur and George* Star Arsher Ali', *Strand Magazine* (19 September), https://strandmag.com/interview-with-arthur-and-george-star-arsher-ali/, accessed 3 February 2021.

Gutleben, Christian (2001), *Nostalgic Postmodernism: The Victorian Tradition and the Contemporary British Novel* (Amsterdam: Rodopi).

Gutleben, Christian (2015), 'Whither Postmodernism? Four Tentative Neo-Victorian Answers', *Études Anglaises*, 68/2, 224–36.

Hadley, Louisa (2010), *Neo-Victorian Fiction and Historical Narrative: The Victorians and Us* (Basingstoke: Palgrave Macmillan).

Hammond, Meghan Marie (2014), *Empathy and the Psychology of Literary Modernism* (Edinburgh: Edinburgh University Press).

Hammond, Meghan Marie, and Sue J. Kim (2014), 'Introduction', in Meghan Marie Hammond and Sue J. Kim, eds, *Rethinking Empathy through Literature* (New York: Routledge), 1–18.

Hannam, Kevin, Mimi Sheller and John Urry (2006), 'Editorial: Mobilities, Immobilities and Moorings', *Mobilities*, 1/1, 1–22.

Hanson, Ellis (2012), 'The Languorous Critic', *New Literary History*, 43/3, 547–64.

Harrington, Ellen Burton (2007), 'Nation, Identity and the Fascination with Forensic Science in *Sherlock Holmes* and *CSI*', *International Journal of Cultural Studies*, 10/3, 365–82.

Harris, Jane ([2006] 2007), *The Observations* (London: Faber & Faber).

Harrison, Paul (2007), '"How Shall I Say It …?" Relating the Nonrelational', *Environment and Planning*, 39, 590–608.

Heilmann, Ann (2009/10), 'Doing It with Mirrors: Neo-Victorian Metatextual Magic in *Affinity*, *The Prestige* and *The Illusionist*', *Neo-Victorian Studies*, 2/2, 18–42.

Heilmann, Ann, and Mark Llewellyn (2010), *Neo-Victorianism: The Victorians in the Twenty-First Century: 1999–2009* (Basingstoke: Palgrave Macmillan).

Hemmings, Clare (2005), 'Invoking Affect', *Cultural Studies*, 19/5, 548–67.

Hemmings, Clare (2012), 'Affective Solidarity: Feminist Reflexivity and Political Transformation', *Feminist Theory*, 13/2, 147–61.

Hickok, Gregory (2014), *The Myth of Mirror Neurons: The Real Neuroscience of Communication and Cognition* (New York: W. W. Norton).

Hinds, Hilary (2017), '"Let the More Loving One Be Me": The Paranoid and Reparative Dynamics of Editing Anna Trapnel's *Report and Plea* (1654)', *Journal of the Northern Renaissance*, 8, https://www.northernrenaissance.org/let-the-more-loving-one-be-me-the-paranoid-and-reparative-dynamics-of-editing-anna-trapnels-report-and-plea-1654/, accessed 30 August 2020.

Ho, Elizabeth (2011), '"I Think It's Really about Us": Review of Lisa See's *Snow Flower and the Secret Fan* & Wayne Wang's Film Adaptation', *Neo-Victorian Studies*, 4/2, 191–202.

Ho, Elizabeth ([2012] 2013), *Neo-Victorianism and the Memory of Empire* (London: Bloomsbury).

Ho, Elizabeth (2015), 'Adaptive Re-Use: Producing Neo-Victorian Space in Hong Kong', in Marie-Luise Kohlke and Christian Gutleben, eds, *Neo-Victorian Cities: Reassessing Urban Politics and Poetics* (Leiden: Brill Rodopi), 331–54.

Hoagland, Sarah (1991), 'Some Thoughts about "Caring"', in Claudia Card, ed., *Feminist Ethics* (Lawrence: University Press of Kansas), 246–63.

Hume, David (1978), *A Treatise of Human Nature*, L. A. Selbu-Bigge, ed. (Oxford: Clarendon Press).

Hunt, Alex, and Brian Wheeler (2018), 'Brexit: All You Need to Know about the UK Leaving the EU', *BBC* (16 October), https://www.bbc.com/news/uk-politics-32810887, accessed 29 October 2018.

Hutcheon, Linda ([1980] 1985), *Narcissistic Narrative: The Metafictional Paradox* (New York: Methuen).

Hutcheon, Linda (1988), *A Poetics of Postmodernism: History, Theory and Fiction* (London: Routledge).

Iacoboni, Marco (2008), *Mirroring People: The New Science of How We Connect to Others* (New York: Farrar, Straus, and Giroux).

Ingersoll, Earl G. (2001), 'Engendering Metafiction: Textuality and Closure in Margaret Atwood's *Alias Grace*', *American Review of Canadian Studies*, 31/3, 385–491.

'Interview with Arthur and George Star Arsher Ali', *The Strand Magazine* (19 September 2015), https://strandmag.com/interview-with-arthur-and-george-star-arsher-ali/, accessed 1 October 2021.

Iser, Wolfgang (1972), 'The Reading Process: A Phenomenological Approach', *New Literary History*, 3/2, 279–99.

Jacoby, Mario ([1990] 2006), *Individuation and Narcissism: The Psychology of Self in Jung and Kohut*, tr. Myron Gubitz and Francoise O'Kane (London: Routledge).

Jeremiah, Emily (2007), 'The "I" inside "Her": Queer Narrative in Sarah Waters's *Tipping the Velvet* and Wesley Stace's *Misfortune*', *Women: A Cultural Review*, 18/2, 131–44.

Jeter, K. W. ([1979] 2011), *Morlock Night* (Nottingham: Angry Robot), Kindle edition.

Jeter, K. W. ([1987] 2011), *Infernal Devices* (Nottingham: Angry Robot), Kindle edition.

Jones, Amelia (2012), 'Foreword', in Dee Reynolds and Matthew Reason, eds, *Kinesthetic Empathy in Creative and Cultural Practices* (Bristol: Intellect), 11–15.

Joshi, Priya (2011), 'Globalizing Victorian Studies', *Yearbook of English Studies*, 41/2, 20–40.

Joyce, James ([1922] 1986), *Ulysses* (New York: Vintage Books).

Joyce, Simon (2007), *The Victorians in the Rearview Mirror* (Athens: Ohio University Press).

Jurecic, Ann (2011), 'Empathy and the Critic', *College English*, 74/1, 10–27.

Kaplan, Cora (2007), *Victoriana: Histories, Fictions, Criticism* (Edinburgh: Edinburgh University Press).

Kaplan, Edward K. (1972), 'Gaston Bachelard's Philosophy of Imagination: An Introduction', *Philosophy and Phenomenological Research*, 33/1, 1–24.

Karnicky, Jeffrey (2007), *Contemporary Fiction and the Ethics of Modern Culture* (New York: Palgrave Macmillan).

Katz, Jack (1999), *How Emotions Work* (Chicago: University of Chicago Press).

Kaveney, Roz (2011), '*The Meaning of Night*, by Michael Cox: Double Visions of Victorian Vice', *The Independent* (Thursday, 20 October), https://www.independent.co.uk/arts-entertainment/books/reviews/the-meaning-of-night-by-michael-cox-415979.html, accessed 5 February 2020.

Keen, Suzanne ([2007] 2010), *Empathy and the Novel* (Oxford: Oxford University Press).

Keen, Suzanne (2013), 'Narrative Empathy', *Living Handbook of Narratology*, https://www.lhn.uni-hamburg.de/node/42.html, accessed 17 July 2017.

Kehe, Marjorie (2006), 'How Would Sherlock Holmes Fare in Real Life?', *Christian Science Monitor* (17 January), http://www.csmonitor.com/2006/0117/p13s01-bogn.html, accessed 5 January 2016.

Kelly, Frances (2017), 'The Time of the PhD: Doctoral Research in Neo-Victorian Fiction', *Neo-Victorian Studies*, 10/1, 42–63.

King, Jeanette (2005), *The Victorian Woman Question in Contemporary Feminist Fiction* (Basingstoke: Palgrave Macmillan).

Klass, David, and William Offenkrantz (1976), 'Sartre's Contribution to the Understanding of Narcissism', *International Journal of Psychoanalytic Psychotherapy*, 5, 547–65.

Kneale, Matthew (2000), *English Passengers* (London: Penguin).

Koehn, Daryl (1998), *Rethinking Feminist Ethics: Care, Trust and Empathy* (London: Routledge).

Kohlke, Marie-Luise (2008), 'Sexsation and the Neo-Victorian Novel: Orientalising the Nineteenth Century in Contemporary Fiction', in Marie Luise-Kohlke and Luisa Orza, eds, *Negotiating Sexual Idioms: Image, Text, Performance* (Amsterdam: Rodopi), 53–77.

Kohlke, Marie-Luise (2008/9), 'Editor's Note', *Neo-Victorian Studies*, 2/1, i–vii.

Kohlke, Marie-Luise (2014), 'Mining the Neo-Victorian Vein: Protesting for Gold, Buried Treasure and Uncertain Metal', in Nadien Boehm-Schintker and Susanne Gruss, eds, *Neo-Victorian Literature and Culture: Immersions and Revisitations* (New York: Routledge), 21–37.

Kohlke, Marie-Luise, and Christian Gutleben (2010), 'Introduction: Bearing After-Witness to the Nineteenth Century', in Kohlke Marie-Luise and Christian Gutleben, eds, *Neo-Victorian Tropes of Trauma: The Politics of Bearing After-Witness to Nineteenth-Century Trauma* (Amsterdam: Rodopi), 1–34.

Kohlke, Marie-Luise and Christian Gutleben (eds) (2010), *Neo-Victorian Tropes of Trauma: The Politics of Bearing After-Witness to Nineteenth-Century Trauma* (Amsterdam: Rodopi).

Kohlke, Marie-Luise, and Christian Gutleben (eds) (2011), *Neo-Victorian Families: Gender, Sexual and Cultural Politics* (Amsterdam: Rodopi).

Kohlke, Marie-Luise, and Christian Gutleben (2012), 'The (Mis)Shapes of Neo-Victorian Gothic: Continuations, Adaptations, Transformations', in Kohlke Marie-Luise and Christian Gutleben, eds, *Neo-Victorian Gothic: Horror, Violence and Degeneration in the Re-Imagined Nineteenth Century* (Amsterdam: Rodopi), 1–50.

Kohlke, Marie-Luise, and Christian Gutleben (2015), 'Troping the Neo-Victorian City: Strategies of Reconsidering the Metropolis', in Marie-Luise Kohlke and Christian Gutleben, eds, *Neo-Victorian Cities: Reassessing Urban Politics and Poetics* (Leiden: Brill Rodopi), 1–42.

Kohut, Heinz ([1971] 2009), *The Analysis of the Self: A Systematic Approach to the Psychoanalytic Treatment of Narcissistic Personality Disorders* (Chicago: University of Chicago Press).

Kohut, Heinz ([1984] 2013), *How Does Analysis Cure?*, Arnold Goldberg, ed. (Chicago: University of Chicago Press).

Kohut, Heinz ([1977] 2009), *The Restoration of the Self* (Chicago: University of Chicago Press).

Kompridis, Nikolas (2000), 'Reorienting Critique: From Ironist Theory to Transformative Practice', *Philosophy and Social Criticism*, 26/4, 23–47.

Kontou, Tatiana (2009), *Spiritualism and Women's Writing: From the Fin de Siècle to the Neo-Victorian* (Basingstoke: Palgrave Macmillan).

Koolen, Mandy (2010), 'Historical Fiction and the Revaluing of Historical Continuity in Sarah Waters's *Tipping the Velvet*', *Contemporary Literature*, 51/2, 371–97.

Koopman, Emy (2010), 'Reading the Suffering of Others: The Ethical Possibilities of "Empathic Unsettlement"', *Journal of Literary Theory*, 4/2, 235–52.

Koopman, Eva Maria, and Frank Hakemulder (2015), 'Effects of Literature on Empathy and Self-Reflection: A Theoretical-Empirical Framework', *Journal of Literary Theory*, 9/1, 79–111.

Koss, Juliet (2006), 'On the Limits of Empathy', *Art Bulletin*, 88/1, 139–57.

Kucich, John, and Dianne F. Sadoff (2000), 'Introduction: Histories of the Present', in John Kucich and Dianne F. Sadoff, eds, *Victorian Afterlife: Postmodern Culture Rewrites the Nineteenth Century* (Minneapolis: University of Minnesota Press), ix–xxx.

Kundera, Milan ([1984] 1999), *The Unbearable Lightness of Being*, tr. Michael Henry Heim (New York: Harper Perennial).

Kurnick, David (2020), 'A Few Lies: Queer Theory and Our Method Melodramas', *ELH*, 87/2, 349–74.

LaCapra, Dominick (1999), 'Trauma, Absence, Loss', *Critical Inquiry*, 25/4, 696–727.

Lanzoni, Susan (2018), *Empathy: A History* (New Haven, CT: Yale University Press).

Lee, Christian (2014), '"Welcome to London": Spectral Spaces in Sherlock Holmes's Metropolis', *Cultural Studies Review*, 20/2, 172–95.

Lee, Vernon (1913), *The Beautiful: An Introduction to Psychological Aesthetics* (Cambridge: Cambridge University Press).

Lee, Vernon, and Clementina Anstruther-Thomson (1897), 'Beauty and Ugliness', Part I, *Contemporary Review*, 72, 544–88.

Lee, Vernon, and Clementina Anstruther-Thomson (1897), 'Beauty and Ugliness', Part II, *Contemporary Review*, 72, 669–88

Lee, Vernon, and Clementina Anstruther-Thomson (1912), 'Anthropomorphic Aesthetics', in *Beauty and Ugliness and Other Studies in Psychological Aesthetics* (London: John Lane), 1–44.

Letissier, Georges (2004), 'Dickens and Post-Victorian Fiction', in Susana Onega and Christian Gutleben, eds, *Refracting the Canon in Contemporary British Literature and Film* (Amesterdam: Rodopi), 111–28.

Levy, Andrea (2010), *The Long Story* (New York: Farrar, Straus and Giroux).

Leys, Ruth (2011), 'The Turn to Affect: A Critique', *Critical Inquiry*, 37/3, 434–72.

Littau, Karin (2006), *Theories of Reading: Books, Bodies and Bibliomania* (Cambridge: Polity Press).

Llewellyn, Mark (2004), '"Queer? I Should Say It Is Criminal!": Sarah Waters' *Affinity* (1999)', *Journal of Gender Studies*, 13/3, 203–14.

Llewellyn, Mark (2008), 'What Is Neo-Victorian Studies?', *Neo-Victorian Studies*, 1/1, 164–85.

Llewellyn, Mark (2009), 'Neo-Victorianism: On the Ethics and Aesthetics of Appropriation', *Lit: Literature Interpretation Theory*, 20/1–2, 27–44.

Llewellyn, Mark, and Ann Heilmann (2013), 'The Victorians Now: Global Reflections on Neo-Victorianism', *Critical Quarterly*, 55/1, 24-42.

Love, Heather ([2007] 2009), *Feeling Backward: Loss and the Politics of Queer History* (Cambridge, MA: Harvard University Press).

Love, Heather (2010a), 'Truth and Consequences: On Paranoid Reading and Reparative Reading', *Criticism*, 52/2, 235–41.

Love, Heather (2010b), 'Close but Not Deep: Literary Ethics and the Descriptive Turn', *New Literary History*, 41/2, 371–91.

Lovelady, Jennifer (1999), 'I Am Telling This to No One but You: Private Voice, Passing, and the Private Sphere in Margaret Atwood's *Alias Grace*', *SCL/ÉLC*, 24/2, 35–63.

Lowe, Brigid (2007), *Victorian Fiction and the Insights of Sympathy: An Alternative to the Hermeneutics of Suspicion* (London: Anthem Press).

Lucas, John Randolph (1989), *The Future: An Essay on God, Temporality, and Truth* (Oxford: Basil Blackwell).

Macpherson, Heidi Slettedahl (2010), *The Cambridge Introduction to Margaret Atwood* (Cambridge: Cambridge University Press).

Maier, Sarah E., and Brenda Ayres (eds) (2020), *Neo-Victorian Madness: Rediagnosing Nineteenth-Century Mental Illness in Literature and Other Media* (Cham: Palgrave Macmillan).

Mallgrave, Harry Francis, and Eleftherios Ikonomou (1994), 'Introduction', in Harry Francis Mallgrave and Eleftherios Ikonomou, eds, *Empathy, Form, and Space: Problems in German Aesthetics, 1873–1893* (Santa Monica, CA: Getty Center for the History of Art and Humanities), 1–85.

Maltz, Daniel (1999), 'Engaging "Delicate Brains": From Working-Class Enculturation to Upper-Class Lesbian Liberation in Vernon Lee and Kit Anstruther-Thomson's Psychological Aesthetics', in Talia Schaffer and Kathy Alexis Psomiades, eds, *Women and British Aestheticism* (Charlottesville: University of Virginia Press), 211–29.

Marcus, Steven (1966), *The Other Victorians: A Study of Sexuality and Pornography in Mid-Nineteenth-Century England* (New York: Basic Books).

Martin, Kirsty (2013), *Modernism and the Rhythms of Sympathy: Vernon Lee, Virginia Woolf, D. H. Lawrence* (Oxford: Oxford University Press).

Massey, Irving (1990), 'Freud before Freud: K. A. Scherner (1825–1889)', *Centennial Review*, 34/4, 567–76.

Mathieson, Charlotte (2015), *Mobility in the Victorian Novel: Placing the Nation* (Basingstoke: Palgrave Macmillan).

Maxine Sheets-Johnstone (2009), *The Corporeal Turn: An Interdisciplinary Reader* (Exeter: Imprint Academic).

Mayers, William Federick (1906), 'The Treaty of Nanjing', in *Treaties between the Empire of China and Foreign Powers* (Shanghai: North-China Herald), 1–4.

McHale, Brian ([1987] 2001), *Postmodernist Fiction* (London: Routledge).

Menninghaus, Winfried (2003), *Disgust: The Theory and History of a Strong Sensation*, tr. Howard Eiland and Joel Golb (New York: State University of New York Press).

Michael, Magali Cornier (2001), 'Rethinking History as Patchwork: The Case of Atwood's *Alias Grace*', *MFS Modern Fiction Studies*, 47/2, 421–47.

Miler, Cynthia J., and Julie Anne Taddeo (2013), 'Introduction', in Cynthia J. Miler and Julie Anne Taddeo, eds, *Steaming into a Victorian Future: A Steampunk Anthology* (Lanham, MD: Rowman & Littlefield), xv–xxvi.

Miller, D. A. (1988), *The Novel and the Police* (Berkeley: University of California Press).

Miller, J. Hillis (1987), *The Ethics of Reading: Kant, Eliot, Trollope, James, and Benjamin* (New York: Columbia University Press).

Mitchell, Kate (2010), *History and Cultural Memory in Neo-Victorian Fiction* (Basingstoke: Palgrave Macmillan).

Mitchell, Kaye (2012), 'Cleaving to the Scene of Shame: Stigmatized Childhoods in the *End of Alice* and *Two Girls, Fat and Thin*', *Contemporary Women's Writing*, 7/3, 309–27.

Mitchell, Kaye (2013), '"I'd Love to Write an Anti-*Downton*!": An Interview with Sarah Waters', in Kaye Mitchell, ed., *Sarah Waters: Contemporary Critical Perspectives* (London: Bloomsbury), 129–41.

Mitchell, Kaye (2020), *Writing Shame: Contemporary Literature, Gender and Negative Affect* (Edinburgh: Edinburgh University Press).

Mitchell, Rebecca N. (2011), *Victorian Lessons in Empathy and Difference* (Columbus: Ohio State University Press).

Moi, Toril (2017), *Revolution of the Ordinary: Literary Studies after Wittgenstein, Austin and Cavell* (Chicago: University of Chicago Press).

Morgan, Benjamin (2012), 'Critical Empathy: Vernon Lee's Aesthetics and the Origins of Close Reading', *Victorian Studies*, 55/1, 31–56.

Morgan, Michael L. (2008), *On Shame* (New York: Routledge).

Morrison, Toni (1987), *Beloved* (New York: Penguin).

Morris, Ruth (2013), 'Why China Loves to Build Copycat Towns', *BBC* (1 July), http://www.bbc.co.uk/news/magazine-23067082, accessed 5 November 2016.

Munt, Sally R. (2000), 'Shame/Pride Dichotomies in *Queer as Folk*', *Textual Practice*, 14/3, 531–46.

Murray, Jennifer (2003), 'History as Poetic Indetermination: The Murder Scene in Margaret Atwood's *Alias Grace*', *Etudes Anglaises*, 56/3, 310–22.

Nairn, Thomas (1981), *The Break-Up of Britain: Crisis and Neo-Nationalism* (London: Verso).

Nathanson, Donald L. (1987), 'A Timetable for Shame', in Donald L. Nathanson, ed., *The Many Faces of Shame* (New York: The Guilford Press), 1–63.

Nathanson, Donald L. ([1992] 1994), *Shame and Pride: Affect, Sex, and the Birth of the Self* (New York: W. W. Norton).

Ngai, Sianne (2005), *Ugly Feelings* (Cambridge, MA: Harvard University Press).

Nicol, Bran (1999), 'Reading Paranoia: Paranoia, Epistemophilia and the Postmodern Crisis of Interpretation', *Literature and Psychology*, 45, 44–62.

Niederhoff, Burkhard (2006/7), 'The Return of the Dead in Margaret Atwood's *Surfacing* and *Alias Grace*', *Connotations: A Journal for Critical Debate*, 16, 60–91.

Noddings, Nel (1984), *Caring: A Feminine Approach to Ethics and Moral Education* (Berkeley: University of California Press).

Nussbaum, Martha ([2001] 2003), *Upheavals of Thought: The Intelligence of Emotions* (Cambridge: Cambridge University Press).

Nussbaum, Martha (2004), *Hiding from Humanity: Disgust, Shame and the Law* (Princeton, NJ: Princeton University Press).

Obama, Barack (2006), 'Northwestern University Commencement Address' [video], YouTube (recorded 16 June, uploaded 16 June), https://www.youtube.com/watch?v= 2MhMRYQ9Ez8, accessed 20 August 2020.

Obama, Michelle (2020), '2020 DNC Keynote Speech' [video], YouTube (uploaded 17 August), https://www.youtube.com/watch?v=uKy3iiWjhVI, accessed 20 August 2020.

O'Callaghan, Claire (2012), 'The Equivocal Symbolism of Pearls in the Novels of Sarah Waters', *Contemporary Women's Writing*, 6/1, 20–37.

O'Callaghan, Claire (2014), 'Sarah Waters's Victorian Domestic Spaces; Or, the Lesbians in the Attic', *Peer English*, 9, 122–38.

O'Callaghan, Claire (2015), ' "The Grossest Rakes of Fiction": Reassessing Gender, Sex, and Pornography in Sarah Waters's *Fingersmith*', *Critique: Studies in Contemporary Fiction*, 56/5, 560–75.

O'Callaghan, Claire (2017), *Sarah Waters: Gender and Sexual Politics* (London: Bloomsbury).

O'Neill, John (2013), 'Dying in a State of Grace: Memory, Duality, and Uncertainty in Margaret Atwood's *Alias Grace*', *Textual Practice*, 27/4, 651–70.

Osterhammel, Jürgen (1986), 'Semi-Colonialism and Informal Empire in Twentieth-Century China: Toward a Framework Analysis', in Wolfgang J. Mommsen and

Jürgen Osterhammel, eds, *Imperialism and After: Continuities and Discontinuities* (London: Allen & Unwin), 290–314.

Pan, Tianshu (2004), 'Uneven Development Among Shanghai's Three Urban Districts', in Laurence Ma and Fulong Wu, eds, *Restructuring the Chinese City: Changing Society, Economy and Space* (London: Routledge), 124–39.

Pater, Walter ([1873] 1980), *The Renaissance: Studies in Art and Poetry: The 1893 Text*, Donald L. Hill, ed. (Berkeley: University of California Press).

Pearce, Lynne (1997), *Feminism and the Politics of Reading* (London: Arnold).

Pearce, Lynne (2016), *Drivetime: Literary Excursions in Automotive Consciousness* (Edinburgh: Edinburgh University Press).

Pedwell, Carolyn (2012a), 'Affective (Self-)Transformations: Empathy, Neoliberalism and International Development', *Feminist Theory*, 13/2, 163–79.

Pedwell, Carolyn (2012b), 'Economics of Empathy: Obama, Neoliberalism, and Social Justice', *Environment and Planning D: Society and Space*, 30, 280–97.

Pedwell, Carolyn (2014), *Affective Relations: The Transnational Politics of Empathy* (Basingstoke: Palgrave Macmillan).

Phelan, James (2007), 'Estranging Unreliability, Bonding Unreliability, and the Ethics of "Lolita"', *Narrative*, 15/2, 222–38.

Pidduck, Julianne (1998), 'Of Windows and Country Walks: Frames of Space and Movement in 1990s Austen Adaptations', *Screen*, 39/4, 381–400.

Pigman, George W. (1995), 'Freud and the History of Empathy', *International Journal of Psychoanalysis*, 76, 237–56.

Pike, David (2010), 'Afterimages of the Victorian City', *Journal of Victorian Culture*, 15/2, 254–67.

Pinar, William F. (2003), 'Queer Theory in Education', *Journal of Homosexuality*, 45/2, 357–60.

Powers, Tim (1983), *The Anubis Gates* (New York: Ace).

Primorac, Antonija, and Monika Pietrzak-Franger (2015), 'Introduction: What Is Global Neo-Victorianism?' *Neo-Victorian Studies*, 8/1, 1–16.

Ramsey, Terry (2015), 'Arthur & George, ITV, Review: Hard to Care About', *Telegraph* (2 March), http://www.telegraph.co.uk/culture/tvandradio/tv-and-radio-reviews/11445 646/ArthurandGeorgeITV-episode-1-review.html, accessed 15 February 2017.

Relph, Edward (1976), *Place and Placelessness* (London: Pion).

Renk, Kathleen (2020), *Women Writing the Neo-Victorian Novel: Erotic 'Victorians'* (Cham: Palgrave Macmillan).

Rhys, Jean ([1966] 1968), *Wide Sargasso Sea* (Harmondsworth, UK: Penguin).

Ricoeur, Paul (1970), *Freud and Philosophy: An Essay on Interpretation*, tr. Denis Savage (New Haven, CT: Yale University Press).

Rimmon-Kenan, Shlomith ([1983] 2002), *Narrative Fiction: Contemporary Poetics* (New York: Routledge).

Rizzolatti, Giacomo, and Laila Craighero (2004), 'The Mirror-Neuron System', *Annu. Rev. Neurosci*, 27, 169–92.

Rizzolatti, Giacomo, and Maddalena Fabbri Destro (2008), 'Mirror Neurons', *Scholarpedia*, 3/1, http://www.scholarpedia.org/article/Mirror_neurons, accessed 28 August 2018.

Probyn, Elspeth (2005), *Blushes: Faces of Shame* (Minneapolis: University of Minnesota Press).

Prout, Matt (2020), 'Reading Others/Reading Texts: The Hermeneutics of Suspicion in *Brief Interviews with Hideous Men*', *Critique: Studies in Contemporary Fiction*, 61/5, 606–16.

Rita, Felski (2008), *Uses of Literature* (Malden, MA: Blackwell).

Rita, Felski (2015), *The Limits of Critique* (Chicago: University of Chicago Press).

Robinson, Bonnie J. (2011), 'The Other's Other: Neo-Victorian Depictions of Constance Lloyd Wilde Holland', *Neo-Victorian Studies*, 4/1, 22–43.

Rogerson, Margaret (1998), 'Reading the Patchworks in *Alias Grace*', *Journal of Commonwealth Literature*, 33/1, 5–22.

Rüggemeier, Anne, and Maren Scheurer (2019), 'Autobiography and/as Narcissism? Psychoanalysis and Self-Reflexive Life-Writing in Eve Kosofsky Sedgwick's *A Dialogue on Love* and Alison Bechdel's *Are You My Mother?*', *a/b: Auto/Biography Studies*, 34/2, 167–95.

Sadoff, Dianne F. (2010), *Victorian Vogue: British Novels on Screen* (Minneapolis: University of Minnesota Press).

Sartre, Jean-Paul (1948), *Existentialism and Humanism*, tr. Philip Mairet (London: Methuen).

Sartre, Jean-Paul ([1956] 1978), *Being and Nothingness: A Phenomenological Essay on Ontology*, tr. Hazel E. Barnes (New York: Pocket Books).

Sartre, Jean-Paul ([1963] 2000), *Nausea*, tr. Robert Baldick, with an introduction by James Wood (London: Penguin Books).

Scherner, Karl Albert (1861), *Das Leben des Traums* (Berlin: Verlag von Heinrich Schindler).

Sedgwick, Eve Kosofsky (1993), 'Queer Performativity: Henry James's *The Art of the Novel*', *QLG: A Journal of Lesbian and Gay Studies*, 1, 1–16.

Sedgwick, Eve Kosofsky (1996), 'Introduction: Queerer than Fiction', *Studies in the Novel*, 28/3, 277–80.

Sedgwick, Eve Kosofsky (1997), 'Paranoid Reading and Reparative Reading; or, You're So Paranoid, You Probably Think This Introduction Is about You', in Eve Kosofsky

Sedgwick, ed., *Novel Gazing: Queer Readings in Fiction* (Durham, NC: Duke University Press), 1–37.
Sedgwick, Eve Kosofsky (2003), *Touching Feeling: Affect, Pedagogy, Performativity* (Durham, NC: Duke University Press).
Sedgwick, Eve Kosofsky, and Adam Frank (1995), 'Shame in the Cybernetic Fold: Reading Silvan Tomkins', in Eve Kosofsky Sedgwick and Adam Frank, eds, *Shame and Its Sisters: A Silvan Tomkins Reader* (Durham, NC: Duke University Press).
Shead, Jackie (2015), *Margaret Atwood: Crime Fiction Writer: The Reworkings of a Popular Genre* (London: Routledge).
Shen, Jie, and Fulong Wu (2012), 'The Development of Master-Planned Communities in Chinese Suburbs: A Case Study of Shanghai's Thames Town', *Urban Geography*, 33/2, 183–203.
Shiller, Dana (1997), 'The Redemptive Past in the Neo-Victorian Novel', *Studies in the Novel*, 29/4, 538–60.
Showalter, Elaine (1985), 'Representing Ophelia: Women, Madness, and the Responsibilities of Feminist Criticism', in Patricia Parker and Geoffrey Hartman, eds, *Shakespeare and the Question of Theory* (New York: Routledge), 77–94.
Showalter, Elaine ([1985] 1987), *The Female Malady: Women, Madness and English Culture, 1830–1980* (London: Virago).
Shuman, Amy (2005), *Other People's Stories: Entitlement Claims and the Critique of Empathy* (Champaign: University of Illinois Press).
Shuman, Amy (2011), 'On the Verge: Phenomenology and Empathic Unsettlement', *Journal of American Folklore*, 124/493, 147–74.
Shuttleworth, Sally (1998), 'Natural History: The Retro-Victorian Novel', in Elinor S. Shaffer, ed., *The Third Culture: Literature and Science* (Berlin: Walter de Gruyter), 253–68.
Smith, Adam ([1976] 1982), *The Theory of Moral Sentiments*, D. D. Raphael and A. L. Macfie, eds (Indianapolis, IN: Liberty Fund).
Solomon, Robert C. (2006), *Dark Feelings, Grim Thoughts: Experience and Reflection in Camus and Sartre* (Oxford: Oxford University Press).
Sontag, Susan ([1966] 2009), *Against Interpretation and Other Essays* (London: Penguin).
Stacey, Jackie (2014), 'Wishing Away Ambivalence', *Feminist Theory*, 15/1, 39–49.
Staels, Hilde (2000), 'Intertexts of Atwood's *Alias Grace*', *Modern Fiction Studies*, 46/2, 427–50.
Starling, Belinda ([2006] 2007), *The Journal of Dora Damage* (London: Bloomsbury).
Steel, Mel (1998), 'Books: Fiction in Brief', *The Independent* (22 March), http://www.independent.co.uk/arts-entertainment/books-iction-inbrief1151853.html, accessed 30 September 2014.

Stein, Edith (1964), *On the Problem of Empathy*, tr. Waltraut Stein (The Hague: Martinus Nijhoff).

Sterne, Laurence ([1759] 1980), *Tristram Shandy*, Howard Anderson, ed. (New York: W. W. Norton).

Stoehr, Kevin L. (2011), 'Michael Haneke and the Consequences of Radical Freedom', in Jean-Pierre Boulé and Enda McCaffrey, eds, *Existentialism and Contemporary Cinema: A Sartrean Perspective* (New York: Berghahn Books), 33–45.

Stolorow, Robert D., and George E. Atwood (1994), 'The Myth of the Isolated Mind', in Arnold Goldberg, ed., *A Decade of Progress: Progress in Self-Psychology Volume 10* (Hillsdale, NJ: Analytic Press), 233–50.

Strauss, Darin (2000), *Chang and Eng: A Novel* (London: Allison & Busby).

Stueber, Karsten R. (2006), *Rediscovery Empathy: Agency, Folk Psychology, and the Human Sciences* (Cambridge, MA: MIT Press).

Swift, Graham (1992), *Ever After* (London: Pan Books).

Tate, Andrew (2011), '"An Ordinary Piece of Magic": Religion in the Work of Julian Barnes', in Sebastian Groes and Peter Childs, eds, *Julian Barnes: Contemporary Perspectives* (London: Continuum), 51–68.

The Samaritans, 'What We Do', https://www.samaritans.org/about-samaritans/our-organisation/what-we-do/, accessed 20 August 2020.

Thrift, Nigel (1989), 'Images of Social Change', in Chris Hamnett, Linda McDowell and Philip Sarre, eds, *Restructuring Britain: The Changing Social Structure* (London: Sage), 12–42.

Titchener, Edward Bradford (1895), 'A Psychological Vocabulary', *American Journal of Psychology*, 7/1, 78–85.

Titchener, Edward Bradford (1909), *Lectures on the Experimental Psychology of the Thought-Processes* (New York: Macmillan).

Tolan, Fiona (2007), *Margaret Atwood: Feminism and Fiction* (Amsterdam: Rodopi).

Tomaiuolo, Saverio (2018), *Deviance in Neo-Victorian Culture: Canon, Transgression, Innovation* (Cham: Palgrave Macmillan).

Tomalin, Claire ([1990] 1991), *The Invisible Woman: The Story of Nelly Ternan and Charles Dickens* (London: Penguin).

Tomkins, Silvan (1995), 'Shame-Humiliation and Contempt-Disgust', in Eve Kosofsky Sedgwick and Adam Frank, eds, *Shame and Its Sisters: A Silvan Tomkins Reader* (Durham, NC: Duke University Press), 133–78.

Tomkins, Silvan (2008), *Affect Imagery Consciousness: The Complete Edition* (New York: Springer).

Toor, Kiran (2004), 'Dream Weaver: Samuel Taylor Coleridge and the Prefiguring of Jungian Dream Theory', *Coleridge Bulletin*, 24, 83–90.

Tuan, Yi-Fu (1985), 'The Landscapes of Sherlock Holme!', *Journal of Geography*, 84/2, 56–60.
van Herk, Aritha (1998), 'Partners in Crime', *Canadian Literature: A Quarterly of Criticism and Review*, 156, 110–13.
Vevaina, Coomi S. and Coral Ann Howells (eds) (1997), *Margaret Atwood: The Shape-Shifter* (New Delhi: Creative Books).
Vincent, Timothy C. (2012), 'From Sympathy to Empathy: Baudelaire, Vischer and Early Modernism', *Mosaic: An Interdisciplinary Critical Journal*, 45/1, 1–15.
Vischer, Robert (1994), 'On the Optical Sense of Form: A Contribution to Aesthetics', in Harry Francis Mallgrave and Eleftherios Ikonomou, eds, *Empathy, Form and Space: Problems in German Aesthetics, 1873–1893* (Santa Monica, CA: Getty Center for the History of Art and Humanities), 89–124.
Voigts-Virchow, Eckart (2009), 'In-yer-Victorian-face: A Subcultural Hermeneutics of Neo-Victorianism', *Lit: Literature Interpretation Theory*, 20/1–2, 108–25.
Ward, Lewis (2012), 'A Simultaneous Gesture of Proximity and Distance: W. G. Sebald's Empathic Narrative Persona', *Journal of Modern Literature*, 36/1, 1–16.
Waters, Sarah (1998), *Tipping the Velvet* (London: Virago).
Waters, Sarah (1999), *Affinity* (London: Virago).
Waters, Sarah (2002), *Fingersmith* (London: Virago).
Waters, Sarah (2006), *The Night Watch* (London: Virago).
Waters, Sarah (2009), *The Little Stranger* (London: Virago).
Waters, Sarah (2014), *The Paying Guest* (London: Virago).
Watts, Jonathan (2004), 'Shanghai Surprise … A New Town in Ye Olde English Style', *The Guardian* (2 June), https://www.theguardian.com/world/2004/jun/02/arts.china1, accessed 5 November 2016.
Weese, Katherine (2015), 'Detection, Colonialism, Postcolonialism: The Sense of an Ending in Julian Barnes's *Arthur & George*', *Journal of Narrative Theory*, 45/2, 301–29.
Whitehead, Anne (2012), 'Reading with Empathy: Sindiwe Magona's *Mother to Mother*', *Feminist Theory*, 13/2, 181–95.
Whitehead, Anne (2017), *Medicine and Empathy in Contemporary British Fiction: An Invention in Medical Humanities* (Edinburgh: Edinburgh University Press).
Wiegman, Robyn (2014), 'The Times We're In: Queer Feminist Criticism and the Reparative "Turn"', *Feminist Theory*, 15/1, 4–25.
Williams, Bernard (1993), *Shame and Necessity* (Berkeley: University of California Press).
Williams, Raymond (1973), *The Country and the City* (New York: Oxford University Press).

Wilson, Cheryl A. (2006), 'From the Drawing Room to the Stage: Performing Sexuality in Sarah Waters's *Tipping the Velvet*', *Women's Studies*, 35/3, 285–305.

Wirth, Robert (2019), '*His Bloody* Deceptive *Project*: The Unjustified Confessions of Roderick Macrae', in Jean Berton and Bill Findlay, eds, *Le crime, le châtiment et les Écossais/Crime, Punishment and the Scots* (Besançon: Presses Universitaires de Franche-Comté), 175–95.

Wolfreys, Julian (2015), '"Part Barrier, Part Entrance to a Parallel Dimension": London and the Modernity of Urban Perception', in Marie-Luise Kohlke and Christian Gutleben, eds, *Neo-Victorian Cities: Reassessing Urban Politics and Poetics* (Leiden: Brill Rodopi), 127–50.

Wollaston, Sam (2015) '*Arthur & George* Review – The Mysterious Case of the Shadow of Sherlock Holmes', *The Guardian* (3 March), https://www.theguardian.com/tv-andradio/2015/mar/03/arthur-george-review-sherlock-holmes-julian-barnes, accessed 15 February 2017.

Wylie, John (2005), 'A Single Day's Walking: Narrating Self and Landscape on the South West Coast Path', *Transactions of the Institute of British Geographers*, 30/2, 234–47.

Yates, Louisa (2016), '"My Dress Is Not a Yes": Coalitions of Resistance in Slut Walk and the Fictions of Sarah Waters', in Adele Jones and Claire O'Callaghan, eds, *Sarah Waters and Contemporary Feminisms* (London: Palgrave Macmillan), 173–91.

Zahavi, Dan (2014), *Self and Other: Exploring Subjectivity, Empathy and Shame* (Oxford: Oxford University Press).

Index

Note: Endnotes are indicated by the page number followed by 'n' and the endnote number e.g., 20n1 refers to endnote 1 on page 20.

adaptation 2, 8, 11, 81, 145, 155, 157, 160, 169
aesthetics 2, 6, 7, 12, 25, 27n21, 39, 142, 144, 173
affect 4, 12, 16, 21n4, 69, 71–2, 73n2, 79–80, 85, 87, 103, 171–2, 173
  freedom 79
  negative 134, 171n1, 172
  theory 38, 73, 78, 79, 81–2
affective turn 79–82
agency 62, 95, 100, 106, 112, 120, 124, 126, 128, 130, 132, 136, 171n1
  personal 33
Agosta, Lou 83, 84
Ahmed, Sara 72, 76, 95, 171–2, 173, 174
Alden, Natasha 85
Allesch, Christian G. 26
alterity 24n17, 36, 84
Amiel-Houser, Tammy 58
Anderson, Amanda 21
Anker, Elizabeth S. 173
Anstruther-Thomson, Clementina 26n20
anticipation 5, 8, 12, 13–14, 114, 115, 172, 176
  of recollection 2
  of retrospection 2, 8, 120, 129
appropriation 2, 5, 8, 11, 18, 20, 169
archivization/'archive fever' 2, 13
Arias, Rosario 6
Armit, Lucie 71, 97, 102, 106, 108
Armstrong, John 8, 47, 133
Asperser Syndrome 162n12
Assmann, Aleida 26, 28
Atwood, George E. 115
Atwood, Margaret 43, 55, 55n3, 69

Alias Grace 10, 19–20, 37, 40, 43, 52, 53, 58, 72, 105, 107, 123, 125, 131, 140, 141, 147, 150, 151, 172, 174
Auden, W. H. 24
Austin, J. L. 82
Ayres, Brenda 47n2

Bacal, Howard A. 118
Bachelard, Gaston 61n4, 149n9
Baker, A. Geoffrey 112
Barnes, Julian 143, 154, 155, 158, 167, 170, 174
  Arthur & George 10, 19, 40, 140, 141, 150, 154, 155m10, 156, 158, 160n11, 168, 169
  England, England 143
  TV adaptation 39, 140, 141, 155, 157, 160
Barthes, Roland 4, 13, 53
Basch, Michael Franz 81, 116, 117
Bateman, Anthony 81n7
Battersby, Doug 55
Baucom, Ian 61n5, 163, 164, 165, 168
Baudrillard, Jean 8, 139
Bennett, Ashly 94
Bentham, Jeremy 98
Bentley, Nick 143
Berberich, Christine 159–60
Bergson, Henri 148–50, 153, 154
Berlant, Lauren 4, 12, 31, 174
  compassion 34, 175
  sentimental narrative and politics 34
Berleant, Arnold 89, 144
Bersani, Leo 18, 58, 94, 96, 101, 102
Best, Stephen 21n13, 54
Biddle, Jennifer 95
Bischof-Köhler, Doris 83

Blake, Sarah
  Grange House 72
Blanc, Marie Thérèse 61, 63
Blanchot, Maurice 20
Blaylock, James P.
  Homonculus 12n6
Bloom, Paul 31, 34–5
Boehm-Schnitker, Nadine 80, 89, 140n2
Booth, Wayne 24n17
Bouson, J. Brooks 3–4, 116n5, 117, 129
Breithaupt, Fritz 32
Brindle, Kym 7, 56, 97, 98, 151
British architectural styles 142
Brooks, Peter 3, 14, 120
Burdett, Carolyn 27
Burnet, Graeme Macrae 39
  His Bloody Project 39, 103, 109, 120, 130–5, 137, 174
Butler, Judith 106, 108
Byatt, A. S. 107, 108
  Angels and Insects 136n10
  Possession: A Romance 107
Bywater, William 16n8

Callahan, Sara 173
Campanella, Thomas J. 144
Carroll, Rachel 99
Carroll, Samantha J. 8, 44
Cavalié, Elsa 155n10, 166
Chambers-Letson, Joshua 22n15
characterization 40, 109, 123, 127, 129, 154, 160n11
Charmé, Stuart Zane 76
Chase-Riboud, Barbara
  Hottentot Venus 72
China 39, 140n3, 145n6
Churchill, Steven 110, 112, 142
Clayton, Jay 9
Clohesy, Anthony 32
contemporary
  fantasy 89, 109, 130
  literature 2, 7n3
contingency 38, 39, 103, 105, 107, 108, 109–15, 121–30, 131, 133, 136
Coplan, Amy 4, 11n5, 25, 29, 37, 45, 52, 63, 83
costume 91, 157
Cottle, Joseph 159
Cox, Jessica 121n6

Cox, Michael
  The Meaning of Night 10, 38, 44, 103, 107, 109, 120, 121, 122, 127, 129, 130, 136, 174
Craighero, Laila 28n22
Culler, Jonathan 4
Currie, Greg 11n5
Currie, Mark 2, 4, 5, 12, 13, 14, 31, 43–4, 107–8, 176

Daghistany, Ann 158
Davies, Helen 85, 87
de Certeau, Michel 165
Decety, Jean 28n22
Denning, Penelope 143
Dennis, Abigail 19, 80n6, 92
Derrida, Jacques 22
Destro, Maddalena Fabbri 28n22
detective fiction 6, 57, 156, 157, 158
Detmers, Ines 26, 28
dialogic encounters 5–12
Dickens, Charles 30, 44, 45–6, 169
  Dombey and Son 165
Dodson, Ed 155n10
double story 43, 44, 51, 130
Doyle, Arthur Conan, Sir 156, 157, 160, 164
Duncan, Ian 30, 85
Duncker, Patricia 108
Dvorak, Ken 12

Eagleton, Terry 15, 134
Edensor, Tim 143, 169
1881: Heritage project 141, 142, 145
Einfühlung 25, 26n19, n20, 27, 37, 39, 139
  and embodied simulation 146–50
Eliot, George 30, 40
embodiment 37, 66, 75, 152
  affective 139
empathetic engagement 4, 30, 31, 37, 39, 40, 44, 45, 51, 60, 65n8, 97, 98, 129, 137, 140, 150, 152, 153, 156, 169, 175, 176
  with fictional characters 39–40
  between text and reader 4
empathetic narrative 40
empathetic receptivity 65n8, 80–1

empathy 3n1, 4, 5, 12, 22, 28n22, n23, 32–6, 37–40, 45, 62, 64, 65n8, 67, 74n3, 94, 97–102, 116–21, 134, 136–7, 139–40, 144, 166, 172, 174–5
  abnormal 150–4
  in aesthetic 25, 26, 141, 146–7, 156, 169
  affective 38
  against 35, 130–5
  and care 65n8
  conceptualization of 4, 64
  deficit 32
  failure of 40
  genealogy of 24–31
  narcissism and 109
  narrative 30–1, 169, 176
  and novel reading 3
  in philosophy 25
  and pity 134
  political value of 33
  in psychology 25
  and reparation 22
  reparative 37
  readerly 11n5, 44, 51, 69, 103, 105, 109, 123, 127
  and shame 82–6
  and sympathy 30–1, 62n6
  in Western culture 31
Englishness 140n3, 143, 155n10, 156, 160n11, 164, 167, 168, 170
erotic voyeurism 37
Escudero-Alías, Maite 85, 92
essentialism and anti-essentialism 78
ethics 2, 25, 29, 34, 173, 174
  narrative 24n17
  of reading 31
  reader responsibility 15
Eve, Martin Paul 106
existentialism 38, 112, 122, 131, 135–6
exposure 21n13, 44, 46, 52, 58, 59, 63, 67, 68, 69

Faber, Michel
  The Crimson Petal and the White 19, 88, 107
Fackenheim, Emil L. 127
fate 106–8, 121–30, 132
Felski, Rita 18n11, 46, 53, 56, 57, 67, 71, 172, 173n2
Ferguson, Christine 19

First Opium War 144, 145n6
Fish, Laura
  Strange Music 72
Fish, Stanley 4
Fisher, Linda 16n8
Flanders, Sapphic Moll 108
Foden, Giles 126
Foster, Susan Leigh 148n8
Foucault, Michel 8, 98, 106, 108
  repressive hypothesis 73
Fowles, John 107, 135
  The French Lieutenant's Woman 3, 107, 135–6
Franchi, Barbara 169
Frank, Adam 72, 73, 78, 79n4, 80n5
  Shame and Its Sisters: A Silvan Tomkins Reader 73
freedom 20, 79, 106, 108, 111, 112, 118, 126–8, 130, 133, 134, 136n10, 152, 164, 168, 172
  embodied 167
Freeman, Elizabeth 21n13
Freud, Sigmund 16n8, 17n10, 23n16, 116, 147
  drive theory 73
  psychoanalysis 81n7, 116n5
Frey, Olivia 158, 159
Friedberg, Anne 155, 156
Friedman, Richard A. 32
Fuss, Diana 23
futurity
  already-thereness 15
  future-orientation 13, 45, 51, 109, 176

Gallese, Vittorio M. D. 28
Gamble, Sarah 97, 102
Garber, Marjorie 33
Gaskell, Elizabeth 30
  Mary Barton 165
gaze 46, 50, 51, 78, 90, 91, 92
  cinematic 155, 156
  panoptic 98
  mobilized 155–6
  virtual 155–6
gender 5, 6, 8, 16, 55n3, 71, 76, 86, 95, 102, 106, 135, 173
genre 1, 3, 4, 6, 8, 9, 10–11, 18, 21, 22, 23, 30, 40, 44, 67–9, 72, 105, 108, 109, 156, 158, 173, 174, 176

biography 6, 176
Bildungsroman 15, 112, 176
crime fiction 15
diaries and journals 123
epistolary narrative 68
detective fiction 6
Gerlinde, Vogl 166n13
Ghosh, Amitav
    Sea of Poppies 10
Gibson, Andrew 22, 24n17
Gibson, Sarah 155
Gilbert, Sandra M. 8, 47
Gill, Merton M. 118
Glyver, Edward 39, 109, 121, 123, 124
Goldie, Peter 65
Golub, Spencer 160n11
Greiner, Rae 26, 27–8, 29, 30, 35
Gros, Frédéric 166, 167
Gruss, Susanne 80, 89, 140n2
Gubar, Susan 8, 47
Gutleben, Christian 3, 6, 10, 68, 71, 113, 142, 145, 173

Hadley, Louisa 6
Hakemulder, Frank 11n5
Hammond, Meghan Marie 31, 34, 63, 97
Hannam, Kevin 166n13
Hanson, Ellis 22, 73
Harrington, Ellen Burton 157
Harris, Jane 44, 46–7, 48, 69, 174
    The Observations 19, 37, 44, 46–7, 68, 88
Harrison, Paul 33
Hawthorne, Nathaniel
    The Scarlet Letter 43
Heilmann, Ann 7, 18, 52, 99, 140n2, 143, 169, 173
Hemmings, Clare 21n14, 34, 79n4, 134, 171, 173, 174
hermeneutic uncertainty 36, 37, 175
hermeneutics of suspicion/suspicious hermeneutics 4, 16, 17, 18, 58, 65, 67, 172
Hickok, Gregory 28n22
Hinds, Hilary 24
historiographic metafiction 7, 14, 52
Ho, Elizabeth 8, 11, 19, 68, 142, 145, 173
Hoagland, Sarah 65n8
Holmes, Jeremy 81n7
Holmes, Sherlock 156, 157

Holocaust 36
Hong Kong 141, 142, 145n6
Houser, Tammy Amiel 32, 58
Howells, Coral Ann 55n3
Hume, David 25, 27, 28–9
Hunt, Alex 170n14
Husserl, Edmund 25, 26n19, 74, 83, 84
Hutcheon, Linda 7, 14, 52, 88, 106, 107, 108, 119, 122, 135

Iacoboni, Marco 28
identity 154–69
Ikonomou, Eleftherios 39, 146, 147, 148, 151
Ingersoll, Earl G. 55
interest 4, 7, 10, 11, 32, 43, 48, 57, 59, 62, 71, 73, 74n3, 79–80, 87, 91, 92, 103, 105, 135, 136, 143, 154, 162, 166, 169, 172, 174
intersubjectivity 24, 25, 38, 74, 81, 84–6, 173
Iser, Wolfgang 4, 15
Ivory, Merchant 2, 160n11

Jacoby, Mario 116
Jeremiah, Emily 65–6, 67, 86
Jeter, K. W.
    Infernal Devices 12n6
    Morlock Night 12n6
Johnson, J. J. 158
Jones, Amelia 149
Jordan, Simon 44, 66, 106, 150
Joshi, Priya 140n2
Joyce, James
    Ulysses 158
Joyce, Simon 1, 2, 22, 160n11
Jurecic, Ann 67

Kaplan, Cora 11
Kaplan, Edward K. 149
Karnicky, Jeffrey 23
Katherine Weese 163
Katz, Jack 78
Kaveney, Roz 125
Keen, Suzanne 3, 4, 30, 31, 53
Kehe, Marjorie 157–8
Kelly, Frances 108n2
Kim, Sue J. 31, 34, 63
King, Jeanette 58

Klass, David 114n4
Klein, Melanie 20, 77
Kneale, Matthew
  English Passengers 10
Koehn, Daryl 134
Kohlke, Marie-Luise 3, 6, 9–10, 52, 68, 72, 88, 112, 142, 145, 173
Kohut, Heinz 4, 25, 38, 108, 116
Kompridis, Nikolas 172, 175
Kontou, Tatiana 5
Koolen, Mandy 91
Koopman, Emy 36
Koopman, Eva Maria 11n5
Koss, Juliet 26
Kucich, John 8
Kundera, Milan 115
  The Unbearable Lightness of Being 115
Kurnick, David 21n14, 173

Lacan 16n8
LaCapra, Dominick 31, 36, 64
Lamm, Claus 28n22
Lanzoni Susan 25n18, 29
Leckie, Jean 160
Lee, Christian 154
Lee, Vernon 25, 26n20
Levy, Andrea
  The Long Song 72
Leys, Ruth 73, 79
Lipps, Theodor 25, 26n19, 27
Littau, Karin 48
Llewellyn, Mark 6, 7, 7n3, 8, 9, 18, 86, 122, 140n2, 143, 169, 173
Lodge, David 108
Love, Heather 18, 21n13, 67, 71
Lovelady, Jennifer 53
Lowe, Brigid 29
Lucas, John Randolph 15

Macpherson, Heidi Slettedahl 55
Maier, Sarah E. 47n2
Mallgrave, Harry Francis 39, 146, 147, 148, 151
Mallon, Thomas 97
Maltz, Daniel 27n21
Marcus, Sharon 54, 71
Marcus, Steven 19, 21n13
Martin, Kirsty 30n24

Marx 16, 17n9
Massey, Irving 151
Massumi, Brian 21n14, 171
Mathieson, Charlotte 165
Maxine, Sheets-Johnstone 141
Mayers, William Federick 144
McHale, Brian 106–7
memory 10, 13–14, 44, 93, 115, 142
Mendelson-Maoz, Adia 58
Menninghaus, Winfried 110, 112
Michael, Magali Cornier 53
Miler, Cynthia J. 12n6
Miller, D. A. 18
Miller, J. Hillis 20
mirroring 28–9, 74, 81, 84, 97, 101, 121, 122
mirror neurons 28n22, n23
  and emotional contagion 84
Mitchell, Kate 102
Mitchell, Kaye 71, 86
Mitchell, Rebecca N. 24n17
mobility 146, 148, 162, 168, 170
  and immobility 165
  virtual 155, 156, 161
Moi, Toril 17
morality 25, 27, 28, 30, 103, 125, 135
Moretti, Franco 21
Morgan, Benjamin 26n20
Morgan, Michael L. 100
Morris, Ruth 143, 144
Morrison, Toni
  Beloved 174–5
Muldoon, Paul 61n5
Munt, Sally 95
murder 44, 52, 55, 57, 59, 63, 105, 121, 125, 126, 128, 130, 133n9
murderess 20, 39, 53, 60
Murray, Jennifer 53

Nairn, Thomas 140n3
narcissism 37, 38, 106, 108, 109, 115, 116–21
  and empathy 109
  primary 81n7, 116
  readerly 106
  and shame 77
narcissistic personality disorder 114n4, 116

narrative 2, 3, 4–5, 17n10, 34, 35, 44, 47, 52, 53, 55, 56, 58, 61, 63, 71, 81, 86, 87, 90, 92, 97, 98, 99, 100, 102, 103, 108, 112, 114, 115, 121, 123, 126, 131, 156, 157, 158, 163, 168, 174, 175
   anachronism 107
   empathy 3, 30, 31, 169, 176
   ethics 24n17
   extradiegetic 45n1
   intradiegetic 45n1, 141, 150, 153, 176
   retrospective 8, 107, 109, 123, 126, 132, 175
   temporality 5, 11, 12–15
narratorial intrusion 38, 91
Nathanson, Donald L. 79, 80
nausea/disgust 39, 103, 109–15
   existential 105, 113, 119, 131
neo-Victorian literature 2, 3, 4, 5, 6, 7, 8, 9, 11, 12, 15, 18, 19, 23, 36–7, 40, 44, 45, 68, 74, 106, 108, 113, 125, 137, 140, 141, 146, 169, 174, 176
   and culture 4, 10, 39, 72, 146
   definition of 10
   dialogic relationship 7
   ethical approach 38
   historical approach 9
   text–reader relationship in 122
Ngai, Sianne 171n1
Nicol, Bran 16n8
Niederhoff, Burkhard 60
Nietzsche, Friedrich 16, 17, 129, 135
Noddings, Nel 65n8
Nussbaum, Martha 24n17, 62n6, 74, 76, 78, 81
Nyong'o, Tavia 22n15

O'Callaghan, Claire 85n9, 87n10, 89n11, 91, 101
O'Neill, John 57
Obama, Barack 32
Obama, Michelle 31–2, 33
object-relations theory 23, 76, 78, 81, 117
Offenkrantz, William 114n4
orientalism 142
Osterhammel, Jürgen 140n3

Pan, Tianshu 145
paranoia 52, 77, 173

Pater, Walter 26n20
Pearce, Lynne 4, 48, 89, 149n9
Pedwell, Carolyn 28n23, 33, 34, 35, 80, 83
Pellegrini, Ann 22n15
performativity 10, 86–97, 99
perspective-taking 29, 30, 36
   other-orientated 37, 45, 63, 64, 69, 83
   self-orientated 37, 45, 63, 64, 83
Phelan, James 51
phenomenology 25, 33n26, 74n3
Phillips, Tom
   A Humunent 19n12
phrenology and ethnography 50
Pidduck, Julianne 160n11
Pietrzak-Franger, Monika 140n2
Pigman, George W. 26
Pike, David 19
Pinar, William F. 94, 96
place 13, 15, 29, 36, 39, 40, 59, 82, 85, 98, 110, 124, 137, 139, 141, 143, 150, 152, 154–69
placelessness 61, 154–69
postmodernism 2–3, 7, 8, 16n8, 71, 107n1
Powers, Tim
   The Anubis Gates 12n6
Primorac, Antonija 140n2
Probyn, Elspeth 72, 73, 79n4
Prout, Matt 21
psychoanalysis 10, 25, 116
psychology 5, 11, 23, 24, 25, 26, 30, 153
Pulham, Patricia 6

queer 16, 20, 38, 86–97, 101, 102, 103, 162, 163, 167, 170
   desire 97, 99
   lesbianism 86, 92
   subjectivity 86

Ramsey, Terry 157
reader 2, 7, 9, 11n5, 17, 18, 20–1, 31, 36, 38, 40, 46–50, 51–2, 53, 54, 58, 60, 61, 65, 66, 69, 71, 78, 80n6, 83, 86, 87–8, 90, 91, 92, 96–7, 99, 101, 103, 105, 106, 107, 108, 109, 112, 114, 116, 118–19, 122–3, 125, 126, 129, 130, 133n9, 134–5, 136n10, 140, 147, 152–3, 155, 157, 159–60, 162, 166, 169, 170, 172, 173, 174, 175, 176

empathic 3–4
extradiegetic 45n1, 59, 66
and intradiegetic addressees 48
readerly expectation 68, 69, 160, 175
reading 3, 4, 5, 6, 7, 8, 9, 11, 14, 16n8, 17, 18, 31, 43, 44, 45, 46, 48, 65, 71, 84, 88, 90, 92, 103, 106, 108, 109, 110, 113, 114n4, 118–19, 120, 122, 123, 126, 129, 131, 132, 142, 153, 155, 157, 158, 169, 170, 171, 172, 173, 174, 175
  descriptive 21
  and empathy 3, 82–6, 97–102
  future-orientated model 45
  guilty pleasures 45–52
  hermeneutic pleasures 46
  paranoid 16n7, 18, 37, 57
  pleasure 6, 48, 68, 93, 158, 174
  and queerness 86–97
  reparative 11, 16, 20, 21n13, 22, 24, 173
  surface 21
  without suspicion 16–24
  suspicious 19n12, 22, 29, 37, 43, 44, 52–60
  symptomatic 38
  voyeurism 46
Relph, Edward 139n1
Renk, Kathleen 61n4
reparation 11, 22–3, 52, 60–7, 77, 121, 173
responsibility 15, 46, 60, 66, 106, 108, 120, 122, 123, 128, 130, 134, 136, 159, 176
retrospection 2, 8, 13, 14, 120, 129
Rhys, Jean 3
  Wide Sargasso Sea 3
Ricoeur, Paul 14, 16, 17, 172
Rimmon-Kenan, Shlomith 45n1
Rita, Felski 46, 56, 71, 172, 173n2
Rizzolatti, Giacomo 28n22
Robinson, Bonnie J. 68
Rogerson, Margaret 55n3
Rüggemeier, Anne 81n7

Sadoff, Dianne F. 8, 160n11
Samaritans, The 33–4
Sartre, Jean-Paul 4, 38, 74, 75, 93, 110, 135, 136

Nausea 107, 109, 112, 113, 119, 123, 129, 136
Scheler, Max 74n3, 76, 83, 84
Scherner, Karl Albert 147, 150–1
Scheurer, Maren 81n7
Schreber 17n10, 23n16
Sedgwick, Eve Kosofsky 4, 5, 8, 11, 16n7, n8, 17n10, 19, 21n13, n14, 35, 44, 45, 52, 55, 58, 60, 71, 72, 78, 80n5, 82, 85, 86, 94, 106, 171, 172
self-concept 83, 93, 94
self-consciousness 7, 26, 36, 79, 119
self-psychology 116–21, 136
  'self-object' 109, 115, 133
sentimental narrative 34
sexual science 8
shame 38, 50, 61, 69, 72, 75–6, 38, 80, 86, 93, 94, 95, 97–102, 119, 173, 174
  and empathy 82–6
  and identity 81
  original fall 74–8
  reading 71
shame-proneness 80, 83
Shead, Jackie 52
Sheets-Johnstone, Maxine 141
Sheller, Mimi 166n13
Shen, Jie 139, 142
Shiller, Dana 2, 3, 6
Showalter, Elaine 8, 47, 61n4
Shuman, Amy 36, 134
Shuttleworth, Sally 135, 136
Sinclair, Ian 145
Smith, Adam 25, 27, 29
solipsism 38, 84, 113–14, 147n7
Solomon, Robert C. 110, 113
Songjiang 141n4
Sontag, Susan 17n9, 18
space 10, 89, 137, 139, 167
  countryside 160–1
  domestic 153
  gendered 153
spectrality 86n6
  ghost 6, 99
  haunting 6
spiritualism
  spiritualist medium 5
Stacey, Jackie 77
Staels, Hilde 152
Starling, Belinda

The Journal of Dora Damage 68, 72
steampunk 12n6
Steel, Mel 108
Stein, Edith 25, 74, 83
Sterne, Laurence
   Tristram Shandy 107n1
Stoehr, Kevin L. 128, 133
Stolorow, Robert D. 115
storytelling 13–14, 40
Strauss, Darin
   Chang and Eng: A Novel 10, 72
Stuart Hall 164
Stueber, Karsten R. 64n7
subjectivity 24, 25, 38, 74, 81, 82, 84–6, 93, 94, 101, 102, 103, 112, 113, 148, 151, 152, 173
suspicion 16–24, 51, 52–60, 65, 67–9, 125, 172
Swift, Graham
   Ever After 136
sympathy 3n1, 24, 26–7, 29, 30–1, 62n6, 63, 129, 134
   conception of 29
   Humean 27
   imagination-based model of 29
   model of 30, 63

Taddeo, Julie Anne 12n6
Tate, Andrew 165
text–reader relationship 3, 17, 21, 40, 44, 103, 105, 122, 136
Thames town in Shanghai 141–6, 169
theory fiction 108
Thrift, Nigel 162
time 1, 2, 3, 5, 15, 21n13, 22, 13, 35, 44, 66, 74, 84, 88, 96, 98, 100, 123, 124, 131, 159, 167, 168
   double 1, 3, 12, 14, 15, 43
   narrated 176
   of narration 176
Titchener, Edward Bradford 25
Todorov, Tzvetan 43–4
Tolan, Fiona 53
Tomaiuolo, Saverio 144n5, 173
Tomalin, Claire 44, 46
   The Invisible Woman 44, 56
Tomkins, Silvan 4, 54, 72, 73, 80
Toor, Kiran 159
transformative criticism 5, 67

transformative promises 31–6
trauma 10, 49, 60, 68, 72n1, 86n9
Trump, Donald 31–2, 32n25
Tuan, Yi-Fu 157

Urry, John 166n13

van Herk, Aritha 60
ventriloquism 5
Vevaina, Coomi S.
Victorian 1, 2, 3, 5, 7, 9, 11, 30, 44, 46, 68, 69, 71, 72, 135, 140n2, 154, 157, 164, 165, 169, 173, 174
   and contemporary periods 6
   fiction 46
   modernists approach 2
   social-problem novelists 30
   twentieth-century adaptations and appropriations of 2
Vincent, Timothy C. 147n7
Vischer, Robert 4, 25, 26n19, 39, 141, 146, 147, 149, 151, 153, 154, 156, 169
Voigts-Virchow, Eckart 18–19
voyeurism 37, 46, 59, 74, 78, 80, 83, 87, 92, 97, 174

walking 155, 163, 166–8, 170
Ward, Lewis 36
Waters, Sarah 71, 87, 90n12, 103, 106, 108
   Affinity 10, 19, 38, 44, 69, 72, 74, 80n6, 97, 106, 174
   Fingersmith 10, 19, 72, 85n9
   The Little Stranger 85n9
   The Night Watch 85n9
   The Paying Guest 85n9
   Tipping the Velvet 19, 38, 44, 69, 72, 74, 80n6, 89, 92, 94, 108, 174
Watts, Jonathan 141–2
Weese, Katherine 155n10, 163
Wheeler, Brian 170n14
Whitehead, Anne 69, 134–5
Wiegman, Robyn 16, 21, 21n13, 22, 141
Wilden, Anthony 79
Williams, Bernard 74, 75
Williams, Raymond 1, 23
Wilson, Cheryl A. 86
Winterson, Jeanette 108
Wirth, Robert 130
Wolfreys, Julian 145

Wollaston, Sam 157
Woods, James 115
Wu, Fulong 139, 142
Wylie, John 168
Wyrley, Great 156, 157, 159, 161, 168

Yates, Louisa 95

Zahavi, Dan 4, 25, 26n19, 74n3, 83, 84, 93

www.ingramcontent.com/pod-product-compliance
Lightning Source LLC
Chambersburg PA
CBHW061827300426
44115CB00013B/2276